The Arizona of
Joseph Pratt Allyn

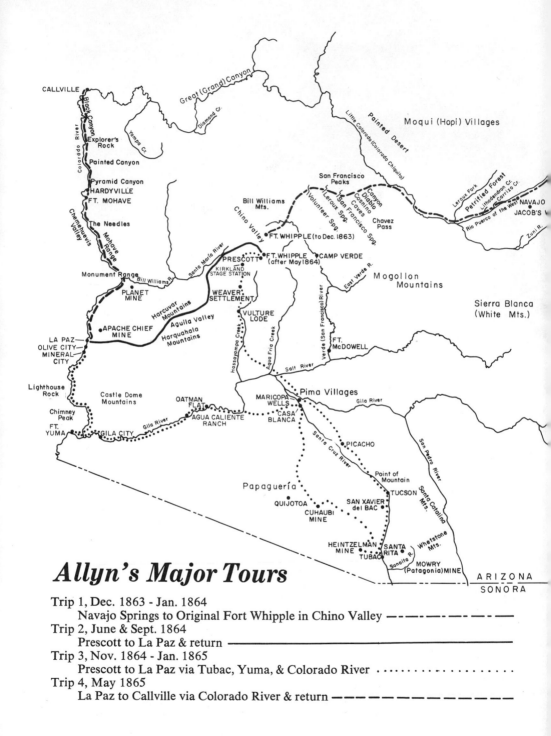

Allyn's Major Tours

The Arizona of
JOSEPH PRATT ALLYN

Letters From a Pioneer Judge:
Observations and Travels, 1863–1866

JOHN NICOLSON

editor

THE UNIVERSITY OF ARIZONA PRESS
TUCSON · ARIZONA

About the Editor . . .

JOHN ALLAN NICOLSON's studies of the American West have centered on its intellectual history, focusing on such diverse areas as the cultural impact of Chinese immigrants and motion pictures on American life. A holder of a Ph.D. from Claremont Graduate School, he has taught on various California campuses, at Prescott College in Arizona, and at Northern Arizona University. He also has made contributions to scholarly journals.

THE UNIVERSITY OF ARIZONA PRESS

ISBN-0-8165-0386-9
L. C. No. 73-94117

To my parents
COLL NICOLSON
and
REBECCA MCLENNAN NICOLSON

Acknowledgments

I am indebted to Professor John Niven of the Claremont Graduate School, author of *Connecticut for the Union,* for first introducing me to that circle of Connecticut leadership from which Judge Allyn came. The National Archives, the Library of Congress, and the Connecticut State Library provided important documentary material, including copies of the Allyn newspaper letters. The Connecticut Historical Society in Hartford gave helpful leads on the Allyn family background, and I am indebted to Mrs. Ruth R. Harlow, librarian, for copies of relevant geneologies.

My good friend James D. Hart, director of the Bancroft Library of the University of California, Berkeley, kindly searched that collection's Arizona files for Allyn material and supplied a copy of the judge's 1864 Fourth of July address at La Paz. Joseph Miller, Marguerite B. Cooley, and Blaise M. Gagliano, all of the Arizona State Library and Archives, were most helpful in securing territorial material. Dora Heap, director of the Sharlot Hall Museum, and Lorine Garrett located early Prescott sources in that collection.

I wish also to acknowledge the gracious and efficient assistance of Margaret J. Sparks and Loretta Davisson of the library staff at the Arizona Historical Society; John Thayer and Joseph F. Park of the University of Arizona Library; and Kathryn Arnhold, F. Earlene Sousa, and Diane T. Rose at the Arizona Historical Foundation in the Hayden Library of Arizona State University. The generous assistance and expertise of Sue Abbey in the Hayden Library's Arizona Room was extremely helpful. I appreciate the efforts of Ezra Fitch, Harlan R. Johnson, Charles L. Stahl, Jane A. Julien, and others of the staff of the library of Northern Arizona University in obtaining various materials. The warmest appreciation goes to Peggy Cheever Brown for indefatigable typing and other assistances.

James M. Murphy, in his book *Laws, Courts, and Lawyers: Through the Years in Arizona,* provided valuable clues as to the whereabouts of old court records in Prescott and Yuma. Helpful efforts toward locating these sources were offered by Sharon F. Urban of the Arizona State Museum at the University of Arizona; Stephen Bahre of the map collection at the University of Arizona Library; Grace Owen of the Arizona State Library and Archives; Mary Gonzales and the staff of the Yuma County Courthouse; and the staff of the Yavapai County Courthouse.

I am indeed grateful to Donald Mackenzie Brown of the University of California, Santa Barbara, who gave generously of his time in providing research materials from his Arizoniana files and elsewhere. Harwood P. Hinton and Emil W. Haury of the University of Arizona gave critical advice on Arizona territorial history and on certain archaeological problems. I am greatly indebted to my good friend Andrew Wallace of Northern Arizona University for his invaluable counsel as to sources and interpretation.

I wish to thank the staff of the University of Arizona Press and in particular Marshall Townsend and Karen Thure for grand efficiency, consideration, and many kindnesses. To my gentle wife and our children, heartfelt thanks.

J. N.

Contents

III. EPILOGUE

SUPPLEMENTARY INFORMATION

ILLUSTRATIONS

MAPS

Foreword

Judge Joseph Pratt Allyn, the young Connecticut Yankee whom Abraham Lincoln appointed to the first Supreme Court of Arizona Territory, came West to improve his health and to launch a political career. He failed to achieve either goal, but during the two years in which he served as judge of the district court at La Paz he sent a remarkable set of twenty-four letters to his friend, Charles Dudley Warner, editor of the *Hartford Evening Press*. Sensitive and articulate, and full of valuable historical information, these letters (published under the pseudonym "Putnam") establish Allyn as one of the most talented chroniclers of frontier life in American Arizona. His excellent descriptions, punctuated by shrewd insights, place him on a par with J. Ross Browne and Martha Summerhayes. Indeed, they provide ample evidence that he was, in the words of a contemporary, "the most able man in the territory."

Some years ago John Nicolson began to collect Allyn's letters and track down information about the judge's varied career. The successful results of his painstaking researches appear in this volume. Now we can follow in detail the semitragic career of Allyn, who early contracted tuberculosis and traveled to Europe and many parts of the United States in a vain search for good health. Those travels developed in him a trained reporter's eye for description as well as a cosmopolitan outlook. His association with a distinguished "circle of leadership" in Hartford added to his sophistication.

Allyn's letters are the more valuable not only because they cover the first two years of Arizona Territory's existence, but also because they treat such a wide range of topics, places, and people. Allyn was "historian" for the first party of federal officials who journeyed across the plains and the mountains to inaugurate the first territorial government. Unattached and restless, the young judge then traveled over much of the territory himself, and his reports include information about most of the major settlements and outposts. His comparisons were sometimes arresting: Prescott, he wrote, was a typical provincial American town similar to those found in the Mississippi Valley, while La Paz was "cosmopolitan." His record of life in the steaming town of La Paz is certainly one of the fullest we shall ever have.

Allyn's letters are further enhanced by a quiet humor, a talent for recording significant detail, and thoughtful generalizations. A humorless man would not have named his horse "Swindle," nor have recorded being lost with the understatement: "With the glass we tried to find Fort Whipple, but did not succeed. We did not know exactly where to look for it." The details of the frenzied and dangerous life he encountered on King Woolsey's frontier ranch epitomize the frontier condition and the unending Indian threat in Arizona. As did most Arizona pioneers, Allyn hated the warring Apache and praised the coming of civilization. "The single quartz and saw mill now on the Colorado River," he wrote, "will do more to destroy the Apache than all the bands King Woolsey leads, or the columns General Carleton hurls against them."

Allyn met and described with a few accurate phrases most of the now-famous Arizona pioneers whose names we associate with the dangerous 1860s. Unlike some of his contemporaries, however, he also tried to understand the different cultures he encountered. He studied the different Indian tribes, and he showed a rare appreciation of the Mexican character. "The perseverance of the Mexican race under the manifold difficulties of traveling in this country is almost as marked as their uniform good temper. Somehow they always get through.'"

Perhaps most important of all, Allyn reflected the go-ahead faith of his fellow pioneers in Arizona's future as a great mining and ranching state. As an advance agent of the rule of law he saw himself as forwarding the great enterprise of making Arizona civilized and productive. In these twenty-four letters the slight young judge, frustrated by ill health and an unsuccessful political career, nevertheless managed to catch the optimistic go-ahead spirit which characterized the American penetration of the desert Southwest. Allyn's letters, superbly annotated and supplemented by Professor Nicolson's useful Background section and Epilogue, seem destined to become a classic source for Arizona history.

HOWARD R. LAMAR

Editor's Preface

Editing Joseph Pratt Allyn's colorful and perceptive correspondence proved a major challenge. As they originally appeared in the *Hartford Evening Press*,[1] the letters contained many idiosyncratic spellings and usages, making them somewhat difficult to read. Rather than preserve these impediments to enjoyment, the publisher and I felt that best service to the reader would come from converting many of the words to their present standard spellings. In doing so, however, I tried to keep the original flavor of the judge's writing by retaining those phonetic spellings not subject to misinterpretation. Thus I changed *Trehacho* to *Pichacho* but left Allyn's *pinoly* and *cayote*.

Those who wish to read the letters exactly as they originally appeared may turn to the collections in the office of the *Hartford Courier* (Connecticut), the American Antiquarian Society (Worcester, Massachusetts), or the Arizona Historical Foundation (Arizona State University, Tempe). However, it seems likely that most readers will prefer a sprinkling of "Allynisms" to the whole box of salt.

---

[1] The *Hartford Evening Press* printed its first issue on February 27, 1856. In January 1868 it united with the *Hartford Daily Post* to continue as the *Hartford Evening Post* until it ceased publication on October 6, 1920. (Winifred Gregory, *American Newspapers, 1821–1936*, p. 76.)

Perhaps due to the style demands of the *Hartford Evening Press,* some of Allyn's paragraphs were excessively long. These have been broken down for ease in reading. At major changes of subject, space breaks have been added. The letters here carry Allyn's original headlines, under which they appeared in the newspaper.

Allyn's letters to the *Hartford Evening Press* cover his experiences from the time of his departure from Washington, D.C., in 1863 to his arrival in Salt Lake City in 1866. All letters written in and concerning Arizona, covering the period from December 29, 1863, through May 20, 1865, are presented in full in this book. Correspondence written previous to the judge's arrival in Arizona is summarized in the Background section, while that written after Allyn left the territory for California and returned to New England is discussed and quoted from in the Epilogue.

The Arizona letters were published in twenty-seven installments in the *Hartford Evening Press.* Some of these installments were excerpted from longer letters.[2] Excerpts which contained reasonably complete subject matter have been retained as "separate" letters in this book. Three which seemed incomplete have been combined with other installments. Each letter reproduced here carries both Allyn's dateline and a note as to the date it was published in the *Hartford Evening Press.* Some of the letters appeared out of their chronological sequence due to delay in the mail and, in the case of the letter of December 23, 1864, due to loss to Apaches.

Although these letters constitute important testimony regarding the first years of territorial Arizona, they have never before been edited and brought together for publication. The collection has remained buried in newspaper files, and only occasional snatches have appeared in Arizona historical works.[3]

---

[2] The following letters were written as units by Allyn and broken into installments by the *Press:* 6 and 7 (April 5, 1864); 8 and 9 (April 20, 1864); 17 and 18 (January 3, 1865); 20 and 21 (February 1, 1865); and 22, 23, and 24 (May 20, 1865).

[3] Some of the letters dealing with Allyn's trip from Fort Leavenworth to Arizona have been digested in Eva Favour's "Journey of Arizona's Territorial Party" in *Echoes of the Past: Tales of Old Yavapai,* edited by Robert C. Stevens. Pauline Henson, in her fine account *Founding a Wilderness Capital: Prescott, A.T., 1864,* has quoted from some of the early letters. In Benjamin Sacks' *Be It Enacted: The Creation of the Territory of Arizona,* as well as in other studies, Allyn and his correspondence have been referred to.

I first came across the letters when I was doing research on the role of Connecticut's Joseph R. Hawley in the Civil War. Hawley was editor and publisher of the *Hartford Evening Press,* and during his command of the Seventh Connecticut in the Atlantic coastal campaigns, his friend and partner Charles Dudley Warner continued to edit the newspaper. A series of letters to Warner published in the *Press* from an Arizona correspondent named "Putnam" led me to investigate the identity of Joseph Allyn, the man behind the pen name.[4]

Allyn's Hartford friends and neighbors, Warner, Hawley, Henry Ward Beecher, William Faxon, and Secretary of the Navy Gideon Welles, were leaders in the public life of Civil War Connecticut. Judge Allyn's perceptive letters reveal a man of culture and learning not unworthy of such company.

The historical scenes which the Arizona letters portray are preludes to those later events pictured in such accounts as Martha Summerhayes' *Vanished Arizona* and *John Spring's Arizona,* edited by A. M. Gustafson. Allyn's accounts give us vivid pictures of the river town of La Paz, of the creation of the city of Prescott, of communities raided by Apaches, with their burned and deserted cabins and fields. He provides us with original sketches of such pioneer figures as King Woolsey, Captain Joseph Reddeford Walker, and Bishop John Lamy.[5] Allyn observes and describes the archaeological remains of earlier civilizations, the appearance and character and behavior of Indians, Mexicans, and Anglos. He mentions such oddities as the weed which, when chewed, is such a perfect native antidote to rattlesnake bite that "it is an easy matter to get an Indian to allow himself to be bitten by a rattlesnake for a quarter of a dollar."[6]

---

[4] His later correspondence, including the Arizona letters, also were published under this signature. Allyn seems to have taken this pen name in memory of Israel Putnam (1718–90), the American Revolutionary general who was engaged in the skirmish at Bunker Hill. The young judge's will provided funds for a statue of the general, which was erected in Bushnell Park, Hartford.

[5] These figures and others, such as Henry Wickenburg, are identified as encountered in the letters.

[6] See Allyn's Letter 12 of August 12, 1864, for this quotation and identification of the weed.

Some comments are made straight-faced with New England tongue-in-cheek, and occasionally Allyn is taken in by some local superstition. But the accounts as a whole are a remarkably accurate, penetrating, and revealing panorama of Arizona during the Civil War period by one who was at the same time something of an amateur historian, anthropologist, geologist, naturalist, geographer, and economist. Readers of his letters will sense his enthusiasm and participate in the vivid life he pictures in pioneer Arizona.

JOHN NICOLSON

I. Background

YOUNG MAN FROM CONNECTICUT

His father was mayor of Hartford. A wealthy dry goods whole-saler, manufacturer, and merchant, Timothy Mather Allyn had married Susan Ann Pratt in 1831.

The Allyns were descended from Matthew Allyn, who migrated from Devon, England, to Massachusetts in 1632 and became the largest landholder in Cambridge. He lodged with Roger Williams and was a member of Thomas Hooker's Congregational church. But he seems to have been excommunicated for some sort of theological dissent, after which he moved to Connecticut, where he became very active politically and held various offices. But there, too, he had doctrinal troubles and was placed under ban by the Hartford church. For all that, he was highly esteemed in Connecticut and was consid-ered "a just, high-minded man, and one of the props of the infant colony."[1] Matthew Allyn's interest in public affairs and his outspoken manner would appear to have filtered down through two centuries of Hartford descendants to the oldest son of Susan and Timothy Allyn, who was himself to become one of the props of the infant Arizona colony and to speak his mind with frankness and eloquence.

Pre-Arizona Days

Joseph Pratt Allyn was born in Hartford, March 9, 1833. Unlike his younger brother Thomas, who graduated from Yale and the Harvard Medical School, he had little formal education.

---

[1] Henry R. Stiles, *History and Genealogies of Ancient Windsor, Connecti-cut*, pp. 27–28. See also Charles B. Whittelsey, *The Ancestry and the Descen-dants of John Pratt of Hartford, Connecticut*, pp. 77–78. Timothy Allyn was mayor of Hartford from April 12, 1858, through April 8, 1860. (Allyn file, Ben Sacks Collection, Arizona Historical Foundation, Arizona State Univer-sity; hereafter referred to as Sacks Collection.) See Timothy Allyn's biog-raphy in *Representative Citizens of Connecticut: A Biographical Memorial*, edited by Samuel Hart.

At the age of thirteen he had become so chronically ill with what proved to be tuberculosis that his father removed him from school and permitted him to work as a clerk in his wholesale business, performing outdoor tasks to restore his health. But the raw Connecticut weather was too severe for one in his condition and by the time he was nineteen, it was thought best to send him to a milder climate. He spent one winter in New Orleans and the next in Florida. Then in 1854 he accepted a partnership in a Hartford commission merchant house, performing his duties so conscientiously that he again impaired his health.[2]

Once more he was persuaded to travel to warmer climes. We have no account of all his European wanderings, but from various references, it is evident that they were extensive. We do know that he had a "long residence abroad" beginning in 1856 and that he became "conversant with the French and Spanish literatures" and that he had "considerable experience in art."[3] In his speeches and writings, he mentions his acquaintance with Turkey's Sea of Marmara, Switzerland's Lake Lucerne, and Rome's Sistine Chapel.[4] Sometime before he was twenty-six he returned home to Hartford, his health apparently well restored. For a period he seems to have studied law intensively (although there is no evidence of a formal college education) in preparation for his future career and then to have accepted an appointment as assistant clerk in the House of Representatives in Washington.[5]

Allyn resided in the capital for some years after 1859, during the Thirty-sixth and Thirty-seventh Congresses. In those critical early months of the election year of 1860, he studied carefully the

---

[2]*Connecticut Courant,* May 29, 1869. Biographical sources not otherwise identified have been found in this issue of the *Courant.*

[3]*Connecticut Courant,* June 26, 1869; Sacks Collection; Allyn's diary, and notes in Sacks Collection.

[4]See his letters to the *Hartford Evening Press,* May 25, 1866, and October 5, 1866. See also his Fourth of July address, La Paz, Arizona.

[5]*Hartford Evening Press,* February 15, 1860. He took no law degree, but his thorough familiarity with Blackstone and other legal texts is obvious. (See Joseph Pratt Allyn, *Charge of the Hon. Joseph P. Allyn, Associate Justice of the U.S. Court, to the U.S. and Territorial Grand Juries, September Term, A.D. 1864 of the District Court of the Third Judicial District of Arizona.*) Allyn refers in Letter 5 (March 16, 1864) to his New England Maine law education. He also probably tutored at home, for Dr. Sacks searched many contemporary college catalogues in which Allyn's name does not appear. (Sacks Collection.)

issues and events about him and, under the pseudonym Putnam,[6] corresponded frequently with the *Hartford Evening Press,*[7] edited by Joseph Hawley[8] and his close friend, Charles Dudley Warner.[9]

In March the clerk-correspondent returned to Hartford to campaign for Abraham Lincoln. Allyn's speeches, according to the *Press,* received the "closest attention," were impressive for depth and fact, and were altogether "interesting and instructive." Following the election victory, the president-elect was a guest at Allyn's father's famous hostelry, Allyn House, and was regaled by a torch-light parade of the "Wide-Awakes," which included young Allyn himself.[10]

Following such excitement, a rather restless Allyn returned to the humdrum pursuits of clerking at the Hartford Carpet Company. Then came the war and eleven days before Bull Run, Allyn applied for a commission in a volunteer line regiment but was turned down because the posts were filled.[11]

---

[6] See note 2, Editor's Preface, for information regarding Allyn's use of the name of this famous Revolutionary War general.

[7] See note 1, Editor's Preface, for capsule history of the *Hartford Evening Press.* Prior to the Arizona Putnam letters, Allyn's correspondence appeared under this pseudonym in the March 19, April 12, April 18, and April 23, 1860, issues of the newspaper.

[8] Joseph Roswell Hawley (1826–1905) was a graduate of Hamilton College in Clinton, New York. He turned briefly to the law before assuming the editorship of the *Hartford Evening Press* in 1856. Hawley was one of the founders of the Connecticut Republican party. At the outbreak of hostilities in 1861, the young editor was the first in his state to enlist. During the war he rose to the rank of brigadier general. In the postwar years he was governor of Connecticut, congressman, and U.S. senator. (John Nicolson, "New England Idealism in the Civil War: The Military Career of Joseph Roswell Hawley.")

[9] Charles Dudley Warner (1829–1900) is best remembered as the co-author, with Mark Twain, of *The Gilded Age: A Tale of Today.* Born in Massachusetts, Warner attended Hamilton College, where he met his good friend Joseph R. Hawley. Early in his career Warner was a railroad surveyor in Missouri (see *The Gilded Age*), a Philadelphia businessman, and a lawyer. In 1860 he joined Hawley on the editorial staff of the *Hartford Evening Press.* During the Civil War he became editor when Hawley entered the Union army. Though not an outstanding novelist, Warner excelled as an essayist. He was a prolific writer, his collected works comprising some fifteen volumes. Active in national and local affairs, Warner was esteemed for his wit, charm, and acute intelligence. (*Dictionary of American Biography,* 19: 462–63.)

[10] J. Allyn to Gideon Welles, March 10, 1861, Welles Collection, New York Public Library. *Hartford Evening Press,* Oct. 11, Oct. 26, Oct. 30, Nov. 15, 1861. Timothy Allyn's hotel was the most famous and the best hotel in Hartford of the day. His son Joseph apparently had a bachelor's apartment there. (Sacks Collection.)

[11] Sacks Collection; J. Allyn to Governor William A. Buckingham, July 15, 1861, in Sacks Collection.

Ill health apparently returned to plague Allyn in later months although he continued to be listed as a clerk. He was sufficiently recovered by April 1862 to enlist the support of a family friend, Gideon Welles, for a government position.[12] Allyn's efforts were duly rewarded, when on March 11, 1863, separate territorial status was established for Arizona, and President Lincoln appointed Allyn as associate justice of the supreme court of the new territory.[13]

Allyn had been in Washington earlier as correspondent for the *Press,* but returned to Hartford for the oath-taking. In the flush of the excitement and pride, Allyn confided in Welles as to the qualities of the new territorial leaders, himself included. Brushing aside misgivings about his own health, Judge Allyn felt he was the intellectual "superior" of Governor John A. Gurley and Chief Justice John N. Goodwin. Indeed, he thought that although Gurley was astute, he (Gurley) would very likely "lean" on him heavily. Prophetically, Allyn affirmed that he would denounce wrong-doing "even among party friends."

Also portentous was Allyn's appraisal of Goodwin as clever, limited, and lazy. Gurley apparently had picked Goodwin for the bench because he thought he would give it a good appearance. All in all, Allyn expected to be the "brains" of the new government.

The new judge was also ambitious for his new territory. In addition to the performance of his duties, Allyn looked forward to the founding of new communities, even to the extension of Arizona's territory down to the port of Guaymas.[14]

On August 19th, the new governor, John A. Gurley died. Two days later, Secretary of the Navy Gideon Welles took Allyn to meet Lincoln with the apparent purpose of urging the appointment of the young man from Connecticut to the now-vacant governorship. Welles' diary for August 21 reads, "Made an early call on the President with Joseph P. Allyn, one of the Judges for the Territory of Arizona, on the subject of Governor of that Territory. At a cabinet meeting, subsequently, the President concluded to appoint Goodwin,

---

[12] Sacks Collection; J. Allyn to G. Welles, April 5, 1862, in Sacks Collection.

[13] Allyn was appointed March 11, 1863, on the recommendation of Gideon Welles. See biographical typescript on Allyn in Connecticut State Library files. See also United States Senate, *Executive Journal* 13: 224, 282 and Abraham Lincoln to U.S. Senate, n.d., in Sacks Collection.

[14] J. Allyn to G. Welles, March 21, 1863, in Sacks Collection.

Governor, and Turner, Chief Justice."[15] The new federal court was therefore to consist of Associate Justices William T. Howell[16] and Joseph P. Allyn, with Chief Justice William F. Turner.[17]

The Trip West

Governor Goodwin[18] now made immediate plans for the organization and transportation of his official territorial party across the continent. On February 24, 1863, President Lincoln had signed the bill officially creating the United States Territory of Arizona, separated from New Mexico along the present boundary line.[19] Tucson was the most important community in the new territory, and the

[15] Gideon Welles, *Diary of Gideon Welles* 1:409.

[16] William T. Howell (1811–70) was appointed to the first judicial district, which covered Arizona south of the Gila and east of the 114th meridian. It was in Tucson that Howell first began work on a preliminary law code for use in his deliberations. He had been a noted Michigan legislator and lawyer and brought considerable expertise to the work. Coles Bashford and he adapted the codes of California, New York, and other states in constructing the code. This "Howell Code" was composed in three months and, after considerable debate and some amendments, was accepted by the First Territorial Legislature. (John S. Goff, "William T. Howell and the Howell Code of Arizona," pp. 221–33; Arizona Historical Society Biographical File.)

[17] William F. Turner, a native of Iowa, was assigned to the third judicial district at Prescott from 1864 to 1870. When he went back to Washington in the spring of 1864, Allyn had to assume his duties. Upon his return to Prescott, Turner held court in "Fort Misery," which still survives near the Sharlot Hall Museum, Prescott. Turner became a political foe of McCormick when the latter was appointed governor by President Johnson in 1866. McCormick was accused of using his newspaper, the *Arizona Miner*, to establish a machine to inflate his own political reputation and of using "the bottle" to win votes by catering to a "depraved class of saloon patrons for selfish ends." (Jay J. Wagoner, *Arizona Territory, 1863–1912*, p. 66; Arizona Historical Society Biographical File; Pauline Henson, *Founding a Wilderness Capital: Prescott A. T. 1864*, pp. 80, 222.)

[18] John Noble Goodwin (1824–87) was a native of Maine and a graduate of Dartmouth College. In 1860 he was elected as a Republican to Congress, but was defeated for reelection in 1862. As governor, Goodwin worked closely with Secretary of State McCormick in dealing with the legislature, and the resulting rapport expedited the necessary legislation. The most significant of these enactments included the division of the territory into districts, the passage of a code of laws (the Howell Code), and the location of a permanent capital at Prescott. Between September 1865 and April 1866, Goodwin served as both governor and delegate to Congress. He did not run for reelection in 1866 and instead of returning to Arizona took up the practice of law in New York. (Eugene E. Williams, "The Territorial Governors of Arizona: John Noble Goodwin," pp. 59–73; Arizona Historical Society Biographical File. See also, George H. Kelley, *Legislative History of Arizona 1864–1912*.)

[19] Wagoner, *Arizona Territory*, p. 28.

official party was now to proceed there and establish the government authorized by Congress.[20]

Allyn left Washington in late August by train to New York and from thence proceeded westward with the Goodwin party to Cincinnati on the Ohio River.[21] There he and Secretary of State Richard C. McCormick[22] and Governor Goodwin embarked on a steamer down the Ohio River and then up the Mississippi to Hannibal. From there they crossed Missouri by train to Iatan and from

---

[20] However, Senator Benjamin F. Wade of Ohio had voted for the bill only on condition that Tucson not be made the capital.

[21] The trip to Cincinnati and on to Leavenworth is described by Allyn in his letters published in the *Hartford Evening Press* for September 21 and September 29, 1863. The Goodwin party included McCormick and Henry Waring Fleury (*Hartford Evening Press*, September 1, 1863).

[22] Richard Cunningham McCormick (1832–1901) began his career as a newspaperman, following in his father's journalistic footsteps. He was a correspondent for several New York papers during the Crimean War, then edited a men's magazine and published two books. In 1860 he worked with William Cullen Bryant, editor of the *New York Post,* and the following year he reported on the Battle of Bull Run.

McCormick's appointment as secretary of Arizona Territory was possibly due to his friendship with Lincoln and Seward. He brought with him to the frontier a select historical library, a design for the territorial seal, and a newspaper press, on which he was to print the *Arizona Miner* (see n. 109, this section). Although he sold the *Miner* in 1867, three years later the journalist politician resumed his newspaper activity as one of the founders of the *Arizona Citizen* in Tucson.

When Allyn knew him, McCormick was a popular figure, polished, cultivated, a careful dresser, but above all a man of "drive and ambition." (Sidney B. Brinckerhoff, introduction to Richard Cunningham McCormick's *Arizona: Its Resources and Prospects. A Letter to the Editor of the New York Tribune,* p. i.) McCormick worked closely with Goodwin, with whom he shared a home, and when Goodwin was sent as delegate to Congress in 1865, McCormick took over as acting governor. Goodwin declined to serve an additional term, and McCormick was appointed governor by President Johnson, April 10, 1866.

Arizona's second governor was characterized by some contemporaries as a carpetbagger and a rapacious eastern opportunist. (R. C. McCormick, "There is no Humbug about the Gold," p. 62.) However, during the three years he served as governor (1866–69) he proved a vigorous and effective administrator, stabilizing the government, dealing successfully with the Apache problem, developing the postal service, and codifying the mining laws.

McCormick was elected to Congress in 1868, and he served there until 1875. Subsequently he was a frequent delegate to Republican national conventions, served as Centennial exposition commissioner, and acted as first assistant to the secretary of the U.S. Treasury. He served in Congress representing New York between 1895 and 1897. (Eugene Williams, "The Territorial Governors of Arizona," pp. 50–60; Brinckerhoff, Introduction to McCormick's *Arizona,* pp. i-xi. For the best summary of McCormick's political career, see Howard Roberts Lamar, *The Far Southwest, 1846–1912, a Territorial History* [New York, W. W. Norton and Company, 1970], especially pp. 443ff.)

Arizona's first territorial governor, John Noble Goodwin, initiated the exploring trip to the mining districts around Fort Whipple and the longer "Moqui expedition," which Allyn describes in detail in letters 4–9.

thence traveled by riverboat to Fort Leavenworth, where they met Attorney General Almon P. Gage,[23] Surveyor General Levi Bashford,[24] and Associate Justice William T. Howell. From Leavenworth they were to take the Santa Fe Trail westward. Other officials proceeded on a route different from that of the Governor's party. Charles D. Poston,[25] the superintendent of Indian Affairs, went by

[23] Almon P. Gage (1817–95), a Universalist minister of New York, was appointed United States attorney for Arizona Territory in 1863, replacing John Titus of Pennsylvania, the original appointee. He journeyed with the governor's party from Leavenworth to Fort Whipple. He was elected secretary of the First Territorial Legislative Council in 1864. Like many of his colleagues, he became a sometime gold-miner. Strongly anti-Southern, among his first acts was the filing of suits in Tucson against the property of six Confederate supporters. (Arizona Historical Society Biographical File; John S. Goff, "The Civil War Confiscation Cases in Arizona Territory," pp. 351–53.)

[24] Levi was the brother of Coles Bashford, who became the president of the council of Arizona's First Territorial Legislature. (Henson, *Wilderness Capital*, pp. 77, 125.)

[25] Charles Debrille Poston (1825–1902) was a native of Kentucky who went to San Francisco in 1850 to serve at the customshouse there. Fired by the potential prospects of the Gadsden Purchase, Poston agreed to head a

stagecoach via Kansas City and Sacramento to San Francisco, and
thence to Yuma and Tucson. Milton B. Duffield,[26] the United States
marshal, went by sea from New York, via the Isthmus of Panama,
to San Francisco. By arrangement with Charles Dudley Warner,
Allyn was to describe the journey of the territorial party in a series
of letters to be published in the *Hartford Evening Press*. Most of the
record which follows is based on these accounts.

Fort Leavenworth on the Missouri was not only of military
importance but was the major federal supply depot for the entire
West.[27] The nearby city of Leavenworth was also the center of Kansas
politics and culture, and it impressed the governor's party with its

---

French firm's expedition to search for silver. He arrived in Arizona following
shipwreck and a dangerous march through Mexico. Poston found evidence
of rich deposits and met and made future plans with Major Samuel P. Heintzelman, the commander of Fort Yuma. The Sonora Exploring and Mining
Company was organized in 1856, with Heintzelman as president and Poston
general manager. Poston was replaced as manager and left Arizona in 1861.
He returned to Washington and joined Heintzelman, now a general, and Sylvester Mowry in promoting a territorial government. Their major concern
was federal protection for their Arizona interests. The Organic Act (February 24, 1863) founding Arizona Territory, was aided by Poston's efforts and
gained him the title "Father of Arizona," though Heintzelman and Ohio con-
gressmen had been more important influences. (Sacks, B., "Charles Debrille
Poston: Prince of the Arizona Pioneers," *The Smoke Signal* 3, no. 7 (Spring
1963): 5; Wagoner, *Arizona Territory*, pp. 48–49, 61, 352–55; Lawrence
Poston, ed., "Poston vs. Goodwin: Document on the Congressional Election
of 1865," pp. 351–54; Charles D. Poston, *Building a State in Apache Land.)*
   [26] Milton B. Duffield (1810–74), a native of West Virginia, went to California as a 49-er. He was appointed the first United States Marshal in Arizona
Territory on March 10, 1863. Duffield seems to have taken his duties seriously
and traveled energetically in and beyond the territory. He resigned as marshal
effective April 1, 1866. (U.S. War Records Office, *War of the Rebellion*,
series I, vol. 50, part 2: pp. 669, 671, 685, 689, 740; Benjamin Sacks, "Arizona's Angry Man, U.S. Marshal Milton B. Duffield," pp. 1–29, 91–119.)
Henson (*Wilderness Capital*, p. 80) cites Charles D. Poston in the *Overland
Monthly* for October 1894 as saying that he and Duffield took a coach from
Kansas City to Sacramento. Sacks says that Governor Goodwin wanted Duffield to petition the Army Department of the Pacific at San Francisco for
military protection in Arizona and that Duffield took sea passage to California. Sacks' detailed data are convincing. (Sacks, "Arizona's Angry Man:
United States Marshal Milton B. Duffield," p. 16.)
   [27] The fort was named after Henry Leavenworth (1783–1834), born in
New Haven, Connecticut. He became a brigadier general in 1824 and by
1834 was commander of the whole Southwest frontier. In 1827 he established
the post later to be named for him by the war department. Leavenworth was
critical of provocative military actions against the Indians and died in 1834
on a peace mission to the warring tribes. (*Dictionary of American Biography*
11: 80; Francis Paul Prucha, *A Guide to the Military Posts of the United
States, 1789–1895*, p. 85.)

theaters, churches, and four newspapers. Although the Pacific Railroad had been graded westward a few miles beyond, the wagon train for Arizona was organized near the fort.

Allyn witnessed the pandemonium: "confusion reigned supreme; tents were struck; teams all harnessed; about half the soldiers feeling *good. . . .*"[28] Their cavalry escort of three companies of Missouri troops[29] was grotesque with "every conceivable sort of uniform and equipments; all sorts of weapons, from the Sharps' to the long Springfield rifle, slung in all sorts of ways; horses of all colors; the only uniform thing being good horsemanship." The thirty-odd white-topped wagons comprising the train finally stretched out in a line at four in the afternoon. The cavalry moved ahead across the rolling prairie, making an enormous cloud of dust. The ambulances followed, each pulled by four mules, then came the wagons of the territorial party, with the escort supply wagons in the van. The cavalcade was spread out for more than a mile. It was marked by the glint of burnished rifles and sabers, and by the alternating dark and light of wagon covers and mule backs.

Within an hour the mighty expedition was lost, mired in ravines and bedeviled by fences, to the amusement or exasperation of local farmers. Making camp that night, the exhausted party had covered all of four miles on the first day. The next morning brought much-needed reorganization and sharpened discipline under the barking orders of Major James A. Philips, the commanding military officer. Lost baggage was rediscovered, including Allyn's writing desk and the all-important ink.

By the third day, with everything repacked and in military order, the trek across the prairie was under way. The bugle sounded before sunrise, and the train moved promptly at six o'clock. Following breakfast, eaten "with ravenous appetites and chattering teeth," Allyn galloped ahead on his horse "Swindle"[30] to warm up and to look for dinner quail or prairie chickens. Governor Goodwin also

---

[28] *Hartford Evening Press,* October 8, 1863. Other quotations and descriptions in this and the following paragraph are from this same source.

[29] These troops consisted of Companies A and H of the Eleventh Missouri Volunteer Cavalry and Company I of the Fourth Militia Cavalry. (*Arizona Miner,* March 9, 1864.)

[30] *Hartford Evening Press,* October 14, 1863. "Swindle" was so named because the Leavenworth quartermaster had tried to prevent Allyn's taking him. (*Hartford Evening Press,* February 11, 1864.)

went hunting on his own, to the frustration of the troopers who were supposed to protect him. Among other perils was the real possibility of a visit from Quantrill's Raiders,[31] who had been active in the area.

The three escort companies of volunteer Missouri cavalry were a "gay set of birds," with a penchant for "jayhawking," or appropriating anything not nailed down, including even horses with a U.S. brand.[32] On the road to Fort Riley the prairies of Kansas provided few diversions except exploration wide from the slow-moving wagon train.[33] One such advance sortie was enlivened when Allyn reached a cabin where he found none other than the adjutant of the column "flirting with a buxom girl of perhaps sixteen." The officer was left to his devices after Allyn had been urged on with a quick lunch of bread and water from the hostess, who, it was observed, was "not averse to the attentions of our dashing friend."[34]

Arrival at the junction of the Kansas and the Big Blue rivers brought the expedition within a day's ride of Fort Riley.[35] At the fort they refitted and took on provisions for the drive across the western plains. Then following up the Smoky Hill River they passed through a series of the embryo towns which were a distinctive feature of early Kansas. At one of these, called Junction City (a metropolis of one hundred houses), Allyn was surprised to meet a fellow New Englander. The young judge had found that most settlers along the way were from "western" states such as Iowa, Illinois, and Indiana, and that very few came from east of Ohio. He commented, "The New Englander is not a pioneer: he follows the frontiersman just about the time the church and the school house catch up. By that time it becomes too crowded for the genuine pioneer and he sells out and again starts for the setting sun."[36]

---

[31] *Hartford Evening Press,* October 8 and October 14, 1863. William Clarke Quantrill (1837–65) headed an irregular force of guerillas, raiding in Kansas and Missouri in 1861–62. After joining the Confederate army, he defeated a force of Union cavalry in 1863 and was himself killed in 1865 in Kentucky.

[32] *Hartford Evening Press,* October 14, 1863.

[33] The wagon train made about twenty to thirty miles a day on level ground. This was slow compared to the railroad train Allyn had taken to New York, which sped along at twenty miles per hour.

[34] *Hartford Evening Press,* October 14, 1863.

[35] Fort Riley was founded in 1853 near Junction City, and because it was close to the geographical center of the United States it was originally known as Camp Center. It later became the largest cavalry station in the country. (Prucha, *Military Posts,* p. 102.)

[36] *Hartford Evening Press,* October 26, 1863.

Primitive as were these towns, the grog shops of civilization had already reached Junction City, and the troopers were soon gloriously drunk. As a result, Governor Goodwin and Judge Allyn had their wall-tent poles stolen and had to be content with a less stately dwelling. Allyn was a frequent witness to another of the hazards to western settlement and travel, namely the prairie fire. One was set off by the pipe ashes of a drunken or careless soldier and destroyed a settler's haystacks, winter corn stores, buildings, and farmhouse. The embarrassed column collected a purse for the unfortunate family and pushed on.

Still following the Smoky Hill River, the party sighted their first bison early one clear morning. "One's blood went quick," wrote Allyn, describing the exhilaration as he galloped off in pursuit of a huge bull.[37] He carried a seven-shot repeating Spencer carbine. Since Swindle was gun-shy, he dismounted after a fusillade of pistol shots from the troopers had halted the bison. He fired four shots. At first they had no obvious effect on the old bull. Then, as Allyn recounted, "the blood started from his nostrils in streams, his knees began to tremble, he fell on them, and slowly settled down dead."[38] Choice pieces were cut out by the chaplain of the expedition and the rest left to rot. When it was discovered that bulls required such a large expenditure of ammunition, the party's hunters then switched to shooting the buffalo cows and heifers, which were more easily killed.[39]

Crossing the watershed between the Smoky Hill and Arkansas rivers, the caravan entered upon the Great Plains. Allyn wrote, "This morning the view was novel and beautiful. From the bluff just beyond our camp a perfectly level, treeless plain, stretched out for fifteen miles across. . . . There is not the air of desolation about the plains I had imagined. . . ." The young man from Connecticut saw, in the presence of countless millions of bison, clear evidence that the region was hardly a barren wilderness but one of enormous agricultural potential.

----

[37] *Hartford Evening Press,* October 29, 1863.

[38] *Hartford Evening Press,* October 29, 1863. This may be the first record of the killing of bison by the Spencer. These rifles, the first really successful repeaters, were manufactured in Allyn's hometown of Hartford and were just coming into use in the Civil War. (Robert Easton, "Guns of the American West," pp. 387, 388, 394.)

[39] *Hartford Evening Press,* October 29, 1863. The meat, Allyn observed, "resembles leather more than any other substance I know." Quotations and descriptions in the following two paragraphs are from this same source.

Fort Larned[40] on the Pawnee fork of the Arkansas was commanded by Colonel Jesse Leavenworth,[41] son of the founder of the Kansas fort. Born on the Canadian frontier, the young Leavenworth had lived his life in remote frontier military posts. His father had been killed in an Indian battle just a hundred miles from Larned. This was now a most strategic outpost in the midst of Indian country; ten thousand Indians had camped nearby only recently. A group of the destitute Caddos tribe were present when the expedition arrived.[42] In Texas they had had their own farms and herds, but they were driven out, having refused to support the Confederacy. Their treatment farther north was not apparently much better, since they were rudely handled by the soldiers at Larned. Nevertheless, Allyn found these Indians gentle and intelligent.

Fort Lyon,[43] the next post, was 240 miles and two weeks travel ahead through hostile Indian country. While the soldiers prepared for this arduous next stage, the territorial party took advantage of the easy camp life at Larned. Allyn slept late, brushed his teeth several times a day, wrote letters, smoked his pipe, and read from the good library they had brought.[44] He observed the Indians there and was particularly intrigued by a Comanche chief whose wife sat silently at his feet. Allyn noticed that her face was never shown but that she "had a hand and foot that would have made her fortune."

---

[40] Fort Larned was constructed in 1859 at the junction of the Arkansas River and Pawnee Creek, near the present city of Larned, to protect overland travelers on the Santa Fe Trail from Indian attack. The adobe buildings of 1860 were replaced by stone ones in 1864 and 1868. The fort was a supply center and the agency headquarters for the Cheyenne and Arapaho tribes. It was abandoned in 1878. (Henry G. Alsberg, *The American Guide: A Source Book and Complete Travel Guide for the United States,* p. 662; Prucha, *Military Posts,* pp. 84–85.)

[41] This was Jesse Henry Leavenworth (1807–85), son of General Henry Leavenworth by his first wife. (*Dictionary of American Biography* 11:80.)

[42] The Caddoan Indians lived principally along the Red River in Arkansas, Texas, and Louisiana. For an illustrated and distribution map of these tribes see Alvin M. Josephy, ed., *The American Heritage Book of Indians,* pp. 252, 254, 406.

[43] Near modern Holly, Colorado, Fort Lyon was the place of Kit Carson's death in 1868. Lyon was 250 miles up the Arkansas beyond Fort Larned and was a principal post for military operations against the Cheyennes and Arapahos. In 1862 Colonel John Chivington had passed through Lyon on the way to Sand Creek and his bloody massacre of the Southern Cheyenne. (Alsberg, *American Guide,* p. 1059; Prucha, *Military Posts,* pp. 86–87.)

[44] *Hartford Evening Press,* November 5, 1863. Other quotations and descriptions in this and the following paragraph are from the same source.

The expedition was following the Santa Fe Trail, which paralleled the sandy Arkansas. The route provided few features outside of crumbling stage stations and Indian villages in various states of decay. On one occasion Allyn, riding ahead alone as he often did, entered one of these villages. Surrounded by hostiles who coveted his horse and equipment, he was rescued from the predicament by his threat of a loaded pistol and the opportune arrival of members of his party.

Pushing further across the plains, with November approaching, the column began to experience disagreeable weather and sharper temperatures. Camp life was somewhat less romantic than it had been and, of course, the eastern delicacies had long since been used up. It was therefore an unexpected pleasure when Allyn and Governor Goodwin, in advance of the main party, met a well-loaded oxtrain.[45] The chills and miseries of the travelers were soon succored with Baltimore oysters, Missouri Catawba, café noir, and fine Havanas. As temperatures dropped to ten above zero, Allyn's beard became at times a mass of ice; coffee for breakfast was cold before it reached his lips. But he marveled at the clear, sunny days which became comfortably warm by early afternoon.

Shortly before reaching Fort Lyon, some two or three thousand Arapahos passed the column peacefully on both sides for miles along the trail. They were returning from the annual distribution of presents at the post. Near Big Timbers, Allyn met a singularly interesting woman in Indian dress with a "white" child in her arms. She spoke, he noted, perfect English and had quite refined manners. Her father had been a Kentucky frontiersman, and at his death she had returned to the tribe of her mother. She was reunited with her Arapaho husband, who had accompanied the party to this place. Allyn wrote that these Arapahos warned the expedition about a planned uprising of the Sioux, which this tribe had refused to join. The revolt was to attempt the annihilation of all whites west of the Mississippi.[46]

When they arrived at Fort Lyon they found an ample and well-built post largely garrisoned with Colorado men, some of whom had participated in the battles which had thwarted Confederate penetra-

---

[45] *Hartford Evening Press,* November 20, 1863. The ox train belonged to James William Denver, who, as governor of Kansas Territory, had freed the area of lawless elements by 1858. Earlier he had been an important figure in California and national politics. The city of Denver was named after him. (*Dictionary of American Biography* 5: 242–43.)

[46] *Hartford Evening Press,* November 20, 1863.

tion of the Southwest.[47] After riding thirty to forty miles a day on the
plains, the relaxed immobility of life at Fort Lyon was extremely
appealing to the young judge. Soldiers of the escort busied themselves
restocking provisions, including ammunition for hunting and for
possible defense against Indians. These preparations were completed
all too soon and when the last stirrup cup[48] had been drunk, the
cavalcade again pressed along the Arkansas toward the Purgatoire,
Raton Pass, and northeast New Mexico.

At the junction of the Purgatoire and the Arkansas, Allyn
visited the fort of the renowned Colonel Bent.[49] This new Bent's Fort
was constructed around a square courtyard, with solid outside walls
for defense and interior court windows for light. The cottonwood
log walls were caulked with mud, topped with a dirt-sod roof. Bent's
good relationship with the surrounding, often hostile Indians, was
demonstrated by the ease with which Allyn had approached and
entered the unguarded establishment. Bent was now over fifty, having
settled on the Arkansas some thirty-five years before, when the massive herds of bison were relatively untouched. The young overland
traveler found this frontier aristocrat a fine-looking man, "grand and
refined in his manners."[50] The colonel sorrowed at the disappearance
of the old frontier and the rapid decline of the Indians. Inspired by
Bent's reminiscences, Allyn longed to explore the wild grandeur of
the Rockies. He had to be content, however, with a view of majestic
fourteen-thousand-foot Pike's Peak "clearly visible" two hundred
miles to the northwest.[51]

Beyond Colonel Bent's it was hard-going for the wagon train,
on what was perhaps the most rugged section of the trip. They made
their way along toward Raton Pass, paralleling, but not following
the Purgatoire, owing to its precipitous canyons. November snows
were upon them, and the water provided was a blessing because only

---

[47] These battles took place at Apache Canyon and Glorieta Pass east of
Santa Fe, from March 26–28, 1862. (U.S. War Records Office, *War of the
Rebellion,* series I, vol. 9: 530–45.)

[48] *Hartford Evening Press,* December 9, 1863. Webster defines "stirrup
cup" as "a cup of wine or the like taken by a rider about to depart; hence, a
farewell cup, a parting glass."

[49] *Hartford Evening Press,* December 9, 1863. This was William Bent
(1809–69). He and his brother, Charles (1799–1847) built the original Bent's
Fort near La Junta in 1828, which was operated as a trading post until 1832.
(David Lavender, *Bent's Fort,* pp. 132–33, 385–86, 323–24, 417.)

[50] *Hartford Evening Press,* December 9, 1863.

[51] Ibid.

four watering places were known along this hundred-mile stretch into New Mexico. Raton Pass itself offered magnificent vistas of the rugged mountain chain of the Sangre de Cristos. Allyn exulted, "It was an American scene, no other part of the globe I have seen can produce its rival . . . Six hundred-mile stretch of mountains . . . all within a glance of the eye."[52]

The expedition camped at the Canadian River[53] headwaters along the trail to Santa Fe. The fabulous Lucien B. Maxwell, who owned the largest ranch in the Southwest, provided the column with a "hospitality as rude and as lavish as that of the old Saxon thane."[54] Courteous but reserved, Maxwell abruptly rode away when quizzed by some of the ill-mannered visitors. Possibly he was touchy concerning his dealings with the Utes, who were said to have stolen horses for his vast holdings. Indeed, Allyn discovered that captive Navajo slave girls worked in the house and other Indians wandered in and out with ease and familiarity.

General James H. Carleton[55] came out from Fort Union[56] to greet the governor and his party and personally guide it into Santa Fe. Carleton's command was the principal military force for Arizona

[52] *Hartford Evening Press,* December 14, 1863.

[53] The Canadian River rises in the Raton Pass area of northeastern New Mexico and flows south through the Maxwell Grant.

[54] *Hartford Evening Press,* December 18, 1863. Lucien Bonaparte Maxwell inherited, through his wife's Spanish family, a grant of 1,700,000 acres near Cimarron. He is said never to have set table for less than two dozen guests. According to Bancroft, the Ute Indians considered the Maxwell land to be their own. (*History of Arizona and New Mexico 1530–1888,* p. 738.) For more on Maxwell see Hank and Toni Chapman, "Midas of New Mexico: the Lucien Bonaparte Maxwell Story," pp. 4–9, 62–63.

[55] James Henry Carleton (1814–73), a native of Maine, joined Stephen Watts Kearny's 1846 western expedition and explored and scouted extensively in the West before 1861. As Colonel Carleton, he organized the California Column and commanded it in Arizona. Promoted to brigadier general in 1862, he succeeded General Edward R. S. Canby as head of the Ninth Military District of the U.S. (New Mexico-Arizona). Operating from his headquarters in Santa Fe, Carleton defeated Confederate forces in the Southwest. His Indian policies were disastrous failures. The attempt to exterminate the Apaches resulted in their bloody defiance and years of warfare. Carleton was heavily criticized for his actions during these years and was relieved of the command of the department in 1866. His interest in a Walker District mining claim very likely influenced his support of Prescott as territorial capital. (Hubert Howe Bancroft, *History of Arizona and New Mexico* p. 655; Ezra J. Warner, *Generals in Blue: Lives of the Union Commanders,* pp. 68–69; Aurora Hunt, *Major James Henry Carleton, 1814–1873: Western Frontier Dragoon.*)

[56] Fort Union was originally constructed in 1851 to remove army garrisons from the Rio Grande towns and place them where they could operate

Territory and the only real government there, pending the arrival of Goodwin. At a council meeting twenty miles from the fort, it was decided by the officials and the general that the expedition would proceed not to Tucson but, instead, to a new fort to be built at Whipple in northern Arizona. This location was already reputed to have hordes of miners working the placers in the nearby hills.[57] Tucson was considered by some to be too Confederate and Mexican in sentiment and influence — factors which might prove hazardous for the fledgling Union government.

Two of the three companies of Missouri escort cavalry[58] were now detached from the rest of the train, and they regretfully headed back to their base at Fort Leavenworth in the dead of winter. The remainder of the party, with General Carleton guiding, proceeded to Santa Fe, passing the battlefield of Pigeon's Ranch[59] where Confederate Texans had recently gone down in defeat.

---

more effectively against hostile Indians and protect the all-important Santa Fe Trail. In 1861 a second and more rugged fort was built to use as a base for the defense of New Mexico against Confederate forces coming up from El Paso under the fort's pre-war commander, General Henry H. Sibley. After the defeat of the Southerners, a third fort was constructed, beginning in 1863 under orders of the new Union commander, General James H. Carleton. Most of the adobe ruins at the site are those of this third fort, under construction when Allyn passed through. (National Park Service, U.S. Department of the Interior, *Fort Union National Monument, New Mexico;* Ray C. Colton, *The Civil War in the Western Territories.*)

[57] *Hartford Evening Press,* December 21, 1863. For the mining situation around Prescott at this time see Harwood A. Hinton, "Frontier Speculation: A Study of the Walker Mining Districts."

[58] The Fort Union post returns for November 1863 state that 124 men of Companies A and H of the Eleventh Missouri Volunteer Cavalry under Major James A. Philips, arrived on November 9 and left for Leavenworth the following day. (*Returns from U.S. Military Posts 1800–1916.*) No mention is made in the Fort Union records of a third company. However, it is clear that a company of Missouri cavalry remained as part of the Allyn party's escort. The Fort Whipple post returns for January 1864 mention Company H of the Eleventh Missouri Volunteer Cavalry as having arrived with Governor Goodwin. (*Returns from U.S. Military Posts 1800–1916.*) The *Miner* (March 9, 1864) states that Company H of the Eleventh Missouri Volunteer Cavalry continued on to Prescott and that Company I of the Fourth Militia Cavalry and Company A of the Eleventh Volunteer Cavalry had returned to Leavenworth under Major Philips. This disagrees with the Fort Union post records but is probably correct.

[59] *Hartford Evening Press,* December 21, 1863. A battle between Union and Confederate forces took place at Pigeon's or Pidgin's Ranch March 28, 1862. After the destruction of their supply base, the Southerners were forced to retreat to Santa Fe. (Joseph Miller, Henry G. Alsberg, eds., *New Mexico, A Guide to a Colorful State,* pp. 76, 140–41; Martin Hardwick Hall, *Sibley's New Mexico Campaign,* pp. 141–60.)

Santa Fe was, initially, a disappointment to the New Englander used to the smooth, simple symmetry of Connecticut clapboard and brick. To Allyn the soft, tawny adobes were rather rude, shapeless, and undistinguished as architecture. The town square, unlike its eastern counterpart was adorned, he wryly noted, with a rickety fence and some half-dead trees. To top it all, the expedition was rather coolly received. There was no immediate official parade or reception, which is not surprising, considering Mexican reserve and the fact that the annexation was scarcely a score of years distant. Moreover, the Confederates had but recently ruled the city. Social relations with the women of the Mexican aristocracy were infrequent for Americans. The daughters of the great families were usually to be seen only at mass, since they rarely left the seclusion of their adobes. With its population of five thousand, including two hundred Anglos, Santa Fe was a strangely silent, peaceful place. In fact, the only sound heard as Allyn walked about the streets was the "crack of billiards."[60]

But one local institution helped to ameliorate the social disappointments of the expedition members: after months of plain and mountain, the female society provided by the local *baile* or fandango was distinctly appealing. These entertainments took place in narrow *salas* lined with benches. Two or three musicians performed at one end of the room, but the most interesting feature of all was the coterie of ladies known as the "Santa Fe Sixteen." Their number included a handsome Mormon woman who, it was said, had been an original member of the "famous hegira" to Utah.[61] She had later run away with an army detachment on its way to Santa Fe. Allyn was charmed, and observed that she dressed in style, was a brilliant dancer and conversationalist, and was obviously the belle of this "demimonde." The female entertainers danced and sang without vulgar word or gesture. They did not flirt with the guests, and Allyn was told that the reason for such discretion was the fear of reprisal by their lovers.

Reluctantly leaving the "unequaled" climate of Santa Fe and its lavish farewell entertainments, the train headed south and west, enjoying additional Mexican hospitality in ranchos and villages along the way. Allyn and the Americans particularly savored the entertainment given by the families of Albuquerque on the Rio Grande,

---

[60] *Hartford Evening Press*, December 24, 1863. Quotations and descriptions in the following two paragraphs are from this same source.

[61] The "famous hegira" to Utah took place from 1846 to 1851.

but the wagon train lost a week of good weather, which was sorely regretted later. The territorial party was joined in its final stages by Lieutenant Colonel José Francisco Chaves,[62] stepson of Governor Connolly[63] of New Mexico and a member of the famed Kit Carson regiment. Chaves was a veteran of the 1860–61 Navajo campaigns, and his intimate knowledge of the territorial terrain was to expedite the column's passage through the wilds of northern Arizona. Chaves now commanded, in addition to the one remaining company of Missouri cavalry, a detachment of the First New Mexico Volunteer Cavalry and a few soldiers of the First California Infantry Volunteers.[64] The officials of the party were assigned three army ambulances to ride, while the official baggage and provisions and animal fodder were carried in a train of sixty-six mule-drawn wagons.[65]

The expedition was to follow the westward route from Albuquerque which had been pioneered in 1853 by Amiel W. Whipple.[66] It would take Allyn west to Fort Wingate, south to Zuni, and thence

[62] Lieutenant Colonel José Francisco Chaves (Chávez) was born in 1833. A native of New Mexico, he was a member of a noted family which had produced many leaders in the territory. As an officer of the First New Mexico Cavalry, he commanded the joint Missouri and New Mexican units which accompanied the governor's party from Santa Fe to Whipple. Leaving July 6, 1864, he pioneered the military and wagon road through the pass, which was later named for him. This route saved some eighty miles over the Whipple route. It began at modern Camp Verde, paralleled West Clear Creek to Long Valley, and from thence traveled northeast through Chavez Pass near Soldier Lakes and on to the Little Colorado beyond Winslow. (Arizona Historical Society Biographical File; *Arizona Miner*, July 6, 1864.)

[63] Henry C. Conolly (Connelly) was an intermediary between Manuel Armijo, the Mexican governor of New Mexico, and General Stephen Watts Kearney during the Mexican War. He was later elected governor of New Mexico in 1850 and was again governor at the time of the Confederate invasion in 1862. He died in office. (Bancroft, *Arizona and New Mexico*, pp. 413–16, 448, 633, 690, 705.)

[64] James H. McClintock, *Arizona: Prehistoric, Aboriginal, Pioneer, Modern* 2:315; Thomas Farish, *History of Arizona* 3:68. McClintock says that Chávez had ten men of Troop E of the New Mexico Volunteer Cavalry, Farish says thirty men. McClintock says possibly two companies of the First California Infantry had preceded the governor's party west. Farish says that nine California soldiers wanted to go to Fort Whipple and so joined the party at Wingate.

[65] McClintock, *Arizona* 2:315.

[66] Grant Foreman, ed., *A Pathfinder in the Southwest: The Itinerary of Lieutenant A. W. Whipple During his Explorations for a Railway Route from Fort Smith to Los Angeles in the Years 1853 & 1854*, pp. 112–97. Amiel Weeks Whipple was a graduate of West Point assigned to the topographical engineers. He participated as chief astronomer in the Mexican-U.S. boundary survey in 1851. From 1853 to 1856 he was employed in locating the railroad route to the Pacific, which he graphically described in his *Explorations and*

west again across the Arizona line to Navajo Springs and the Little Colorado. Following this river westerly to the vicinity of the San Francisco Peaks near present-day Flagstaff, Allyn's party was to swing around the northern slope of Bill Williams Mountain and south across Hell's Canyon to the headwaters of the Verde River, where Fort Whipple had been established and garrisoned by troops of the California Column.[67]

Danger from possible Navajo attack and scarcity of water urged the wagons along at a steady clip. The marching day often began at 2:00 A.M. instead of the usual 6:00, the trek broken only by monotonous dinners of sardines, buffalo tongue, and water. On one occasion a colorful Indian funeral dance was observed, following which the deceased was buried in a grave packed with bread. Sandy and stony trails slowed the caravan's pace toward Fort Wingate.[68] At the Mexican village of Cubero[69] they danced their last fandango. Closing the festivities, the Americans sang "When this Cruel War is Over."

Wingate was the final outpost of civilization until Whipple. Here the territorial party came face to face with the Navajo tragedy. Allyn had already noted that along the party's route the former pastures of the tribe were now empty of stock. Numbers of Navajo captives, utterly destitute and forlorn, were being readied for transfer to a reservation established by General Carleton near Fort Sumner in eastern New Mexico.[70] After leaving Fort Wingate, the official party crossed the 109th meridian and entered the new territory of Arizona.

Allyn began his Arizona correspondence with a letter mailed

Surveys for a Railroad Route from the Mississippi River to the Pacific Ocean. He became a brigadier general in 1862 and was mortally wounded in 1863 at Chancellorsville. (Ibid. pp. 7–9.)

[67] The place names and locations mentioned in this paragraph are identified as encountered in Allyn's letters.

[68] Fort Wingate was established in October 1862 about twenty miles southwest of Mount Taylor, New Mexico. In July 1868 it was moved to a location just east of Gallup. (Prucha, *Guide to Military Posts,* p. 177.)

[69] *Hartford Evening Press,* February 12, 1864. Cubero lies some fifty miles west of Albuquerque.

[70] *Hartford Evening Press,* February 12, 1864. Fort Sumner was established by Colonel Kit Carson at Bosque Redondo on the Pecos River in eastern New Mexico. Some 7000 to 9000 Navajos were held there from 1863 for five years before being permitted to return to their old reservation. (Lynn R. Bailey, *Bosque Redondo: An American Concentration Camp,* pp. 4, 5, 31, 75–76, 141.)

from Navajo Springs, Arizona, under the date of December 29, 1863. There is a strange omission at this point. He makes no mention of what was, historically, the most important and dramatic event of the trip: the establishment of the first territorial government for Arizona on that same December 29. A possible explanation is that Allyn disliked Secretary of State McCormick, who was later to become his political enemy. McCormick dominated the show, and Allyn may have had little desire to publicize his activities.[71] The ceremony which Allyn's letters, for whatever reason, ignored was recorded by the secretary of state himself.[72] At four in the afternoon, in a chilling snowstorm,[73] Richard C. McCormick inaugurated the proceedings with a speech announcing that the new government was taking "possession of the Territory without resort to military force" despite its being "claimed by those now in hostility to the federal arms."[74] He administered the oath of office to Allyn and other officials and raised the United States flag. McCormick then read Governor Goodwin's proclamation declaring a temporary government for the territory with its seat "at or near Fort Whipple."[75]

Arizona Territory in 1864

The Arizona to which Allyn had come was indeed primitive.[76] Although the 1853 Gadsden Purchase had added the area south of the Gila to that part of New Mexico Territory acquired in the Treaty

---

[71] It is also possible that Allyn was merely pressed for time before the military express left. There is an editorial in the *New Mexican* for December 29, 1863, entitled "Government in Arizona," indicating the receipt of letters from Allyn and McCormick. Allyn also sent copies of the oaths of office to Attorney General Edward Bates. (Attorneys General Papers, 1790–1870, Record Group 60, National Archives.)

[72] Jonathan Richmond, a young Michigan court clerk, who had joined the party to serve as clerk to Justice William T. Howell, wrote many letters home to his parents, but he failed to do more than comment that "the Governor has issued his proclamation." (Farish, *History of Arizona* 3:65.) Farish published the Richmond letters in his third volume, pp. 47–70. McCormick, in the first edition of his newspaper, the *Arizona Miner,* issued at Fort Whipple, March 9, 1864, gave an account of the ceremonies. (See Eva Favour, "Journey of Arizona's Territorial Party," p. 57.)

[73] *Arizona Miner,* March 9, 1864. Rufus Kay Wyllys (*Arizona: The History of a Frontier State,* p. 167) mentions the snowstorm, but McCormick described the weather as "clear and frosty." Arizona had been a part of New Mexico Territory since 1850.

[74] *Arizona Miner,* March 9, 1864.

[75] Ibid.

[76] Unless otherwise noted, this account of Arizona in 1864 is drawn mainly from McClintock's *Arizona* and Wagoner's *Arizona Territory.*

of Guadalupe Hidalgo, it was some time before effective political organization could be established there. Tucson was not evacuated by the Mexican garrison until March 1856. Arizona's population at that time was chiefly in the Tucson area and in the Santa Cruz valley to the south. It was estimated that Tucson then had a population of approximately thirty Anglos and four hundred Mexicans.

Following the Treaty of Guadalupe Hidalgo and until the beginning of the Civil War much of American activity was along the Gold Rush route, which coursed westward through Tucson and along the Gila River to California. Surveys of a northern railroad route and explorations of the Colorado River were being conducted by the federal government. Mining activity was increasingly prevalent south of Tucson, along the Colorado River, and in the Bradshaw Mountains of central Arizona. There was little of civil rule.

A convention in August 1856 at Tucson had decided to press the United States Congress to make Arizona a territory separate from New Mexico. In the following year a bill was introduced in the United States Senate providing for a territory of Arizona, but it included only the area south of the Gila River eastward through New Mexico to Texas. This bill failed, as did similar efforts later. The New Mexico legislature in February 1860 established the county of Arizona, consisting of the Gadsden Purchase, with Tubac as the county seat. In 1862 the seat was moved to Tucson.

With the coming of the Civil War, Arizona became a political issue. Both Confederate and Union governments saw its value in relation to control of California and the West. On February 14, 1862, a bill was signed by President Jefferson Davis making southern Arizona a Confederate territory. Two weeks later a detachment of Rebel cavalry took over Tucson, a majority of whose citizens gave an enthusiastic welcome.[77] Aside from sympathy for the Southern cause, much of the enthusiasm was due to the need for protection. Union troops had abandoned Arizona in July 1861 in response to Confederate military activity along the Rio Grande to the east. Miners, traders, and ranchers were left helpless against roving bands of Apaches, and the raising of the Rebel flag over Tucson was a symbol of needed authority. Confederate rule was short-lived, how-

----

[77] See Boyd Finch, "Sherod Hunter and the Confederates in Arizona," pp. 169–74.

ever, as troops of the California Column[78] ordered to Arizona by
Colonel James H. Carleton reoccupied Tucson on May 20, 1862.
The town had been evacuated by Hunter on May 4.

When Carleton arrived in Tucson in June he set about immediately to establish martial law, with himself as military governor.
Much of the atmosphere of hostility among Confederate sympathizers during Allyn's visit stemmed from Carleton's punitive attitudes
and methods. Adults were required to take oaths of loyalty, anti-
Union acts or statements were forbidden, and Confederate supporters were arrested.

Lockwood remarks, "Civilization marched into Arizona with
the California Volunteers."[79] However much this statement may
overlook the Hispanic achievements in southern Arizona it is true
enough of the United States occupation. The California Column
reestablished some degree of order in the Southwest.[80] This meant,
primarily, the subjugation of the Apache, and that campaign began
in earnest in March 1863 and continued long after Allyn had left
the territory. Since Carleton had found practically all of Arizona,
with the exception of the southern Pima Indian area, "occupied" by
the Apaches, this involved strenuous campaigning. "Apacheria"
could not be settled by Americans without a constant military presence. Forts and posts were manned by the Californians at strategic
points along the principal rivers, settlements, and routes of travel.

In a land without civilian courts to enforce justice, Carleton's
military administration was indispensable in controlling crime in
an area of which it was said, "There is no law west of the Pecos."
Shortly after his arrival in Tucson, Carleton rounded up and imprisoned a group of the town's bad men, against whom citizens went
about constantly armed.

At the time of Allyn's arrival, Arizona's population was largely
concentrated in three areas, corresponding (with the exception of
Tucson's Mexican population) to the degree of mining activity. The
1864 United States census showed a total population of 2,377 in the
Tucson area to the south of the Gila River; a total of 1,157 in the

---

[78] For the activities of the California Column, see Aurora Hunt, *The
Army of the Pacific*, pp. 77–153.
[79] Frank C. Lockwood, *Pioneer Days in Arizona, from the Spanish Occupation to Statehood*, p. 87.
[80] For details of Carleton's problems and achievements see Hunt, *Major
James Henry Carleton*.

La Paz and Colorado River area; and a total of 1,039 in the Prescott area, including the remainder of the state. The grand total of the 1864 census, excluding Indians, was 4,573.[81]

These citizens lived under the most primitive conditions. Railroad and telegraph were nonexistent. By contrast, the neighboring Pacific Coast was enjoying a remarkable boom. San Francisco was humming with financial and industrial activity; San Jose, Los Angeles, and other garden cities were burgeoning with new immigrants. A large and well-organized public school system was in operation in California, while Arizona had none. With the exception of the Mexican and Indian populations, the territory was virtually without family life. Arizona was a man's world.

Judicial Activities

After entering Arizona, Allyn rode westward to Fort Whipple,[82] recently established in the Chino valley to provide protection to the miners against hostile Indians. He arrived January 17, 1864, on precisely the same day that Poston and his party reached Tucson by the California route. After a couple of weeks' rest at the fort, Allyn made exploratory trips to the mines in the Hassayampa Creek area, to the Verde valley, and then to the Pima villages along the Gila River.[83] In May 1864, Fort Whipple was moved southward to Granite Creek, and Allyn went along to the newly established town of Prescott, which was soon to become the territorial capital.[84]

---

[81] *The 1864 Census of the Territory of Arizona,* pp. i-vi.

[82] Fort Whipple was established on December 23, 1863, when it was garrisoned by two companies of California Volunteers under Major Edward B. Willis. It was located at what is now Del Rio Springs in the Chino valley some twenty miles north of present-day Prescott. The fort was moved to Granite Creek on May 18, 1864, and the old Del Rio site was renamed Camp Clark. (Granger, *Arizona Place Names,* pp. 362–63; Henson, *Wilderness Capital,* pp. 127, 153–55.

[83] *Arizona Miner,* May 11, 1864. Allyn condemned Major Willis for starting the Indian war with a "wanton and unprovoked murder of two Indians. . . ." (Allyn to G. Welles, January 27, 1864, in Welles Papers.) According to Colonel Poston, at a camp near the Pima villages Allyn narrowly avoided a shootout with a lieutenant. It seems that the two disagreed over a question of "military incompetency." Allyn supported his arguments with two pistols; the insulted lieutenant backed his with the bayonet. A duel was averted when the governor "seized" the officer, and Poston "embraced" the judge. Later apologies were exchanged amidst libations of whiskey, and the matter healed. (Charles D. Poston to J. Ross Browne, March 20, 1864, Sacks Collection.)

[84] See Henson, *Wilderness Capital,* pp. 148–69.

Three judicial districts had by then been formed for Arizona. The first included an area south of the Gila River with headquarters in Tucson; the second covered the area west of the 114th meridian with headquarters in La Paz; the third, centered in Prescott, included the remainder of the territory.[85] Allyn was assigned to the second district, the poorest of the three from the standpoint of climate and social life. It was not economically poor, however, since La Paz[86] and other towns had important mining operations nearby; and the Colorado River was a main artery of transportation from San Francisco and Wilmington on the Pacific coast. Judge Allyn was directed to hold court twice yearly at La Paz, in June and November for periods of two weeks each.

After Prescott had become established as the territorial capital, Allyn left Fort Whipple on June 9, 1864, and rode to La Paz for the first session of the second district court. He spent the hot summer there beside the Colorado. And what a headquarters was this raw and lawless desert camp for the refined New England judge! After the discovery of rich placer nuggets in 1862, an estimated five million dollars in gold was taken from just two gulches in the area.[87] La Paz became the haunt of swarms of miners, gamblers, traders, and toughs, "the worst mixture of Indians, Mexicans, Pikes, and white men from all parts of the earth."[88] Brawls in street and saloon were frequent. In its first year, the town had established two stores and twelve saloons.

---

[85] Proclamation of Governor Goodwin, April 9, 1864. *Journal of the First Legislative Assembly,* p. 5. See also *Arizona Miner,* May 25, July 20, 1864.

[86] In 1862 a group of prospectors with Powell (or Pauline) Weaver discovered gold in the Arroyo de la Tenaja. The town which developed near there on Goodman's Slough, a quarter mile from the Colorado River, acquired the name La Paz presumably because the strike was made on January 12, the Feast Day of Peace. La Paz grew rapidly, reaching a boom population of 5,000, but in 1869 the river shifted and isolated the landing. In 1870 it lost its status as the Yuma County seat and was thereafter abandoned by inhabitants and commerce. Ruins remained on the site north of Ehrenberg. (Granger, *Arizona Place Names,* p. 378; H. P. Wood, "Gold Fields of La Paz, Arizona," p. 22; LeRoy R. Hafen, *The Mountain Men and the Fur Trade of the Far West* 9: pp. 235, 238.)

[87] Except where noted, this description of La Paz is taken from Nell Murbarger, *Ghosts of the Adobe Walls,* pp. 19–23.

[88] *Alta California,* October 14, 1863. Webster defines *Pike* as "a term of contempt, especially and originally applied to emigrants from the Southern states, from the belief that the first came from Pike County, Missouri."

"Few men brought their families with them. Mojave squaws, comely and vigorous women, did the housework and . . . met the domestic needs of the camp."[89] An early resident and storekeeper, Michael Goldwater, wrote that flour cost from thirty to forty dollars per hundred pounds, and there was little to eat besides river fish and mesquite beans. And to add to Unionist Allyn's discomfiture, the camp was famed as a "hotbed of secession." Nevertheless, the judge from Connecticut seems to have taken it all in stride, commenting in his letters on the climate, the architecture, and the mining — and lecturing the inhabitants in scholarly voice on the virtues of the law, patriotism, and the Union cause.[90]

Under federal law, as district court judge Allyn was to serve four years at an annual salary of $2,500.[91] His powers were, in theory, extensive. His district court had the same jurisdiction in cases involving the federal constitution and laws as that of circuit and district courts in the various states of the Union. The first six days at least of each territorial district court term were reserved for the hearing of such federal cases. Beyond this, the territorial legislature gave the district courts extensive original jurisdiction in various kinds of civil and criminal cases as well as authority to hear appeals of cases from justices of the peace and the probate courts.[92] Within his legal jurisdiction thus defined, Allyn in adjudicating suits had impressive powers of investigation and action. He could determine the winner of contested elections, remove from office members of boards of supervisors, order the summoning of trial and grand juries, order confined in jail witnesses and those charged with crime.[93]

But aside from adjudicating one famous mining case while substituting for Chief Justice Turner at the third district court, Allyn seems to have had only moderate tasks as district court judge. He opened his first session at La Paz at the house of G. M. Holaday on June 28, 1864. After attorneys Charles Leib, William J. Berry,

[89] Arizona WPA Writers' Project, *Arizona: A State Guide*, p. 363.

[90] See Allyn, *Address: The Fourth of July 1864 at La Paz*. Allyn believed that the secessionists were in "a very decided majority . . ." in the Territory. (J. Allyn to G. Welles, January 27, 1864, in Welles Papers.) One Arizona wit named his two dogs Abe Davis and Jeff Lincoln. (Allyn to Mrs. G. Welles, April 4, 1864, in Welles Papers.)

[91] John S. Goff, "The Appointment, Tenure and Removal of Territorial Judges: Arizona — A Case Study," p. 213.

[92] *Howell Code*, p. 289.

[93] Norman E. Tutorow, *Records of the Arizona Territorial Court*, pp. 6–7.

Charles G. Johnson, C. A. Philips, and John Howard were admitted to practice, the session ended with no additional business.[94]

The next regularly scheduled session of the second district court was for a two-week period commencing the last Tuesday of November 1864. Whether this session was ever held is not clear, but in light of the lack of court business at La Paz, it seems likely that it was postponed until February.[95]

Thus Allyn was free to return to Prescott to participate in the formalities for the convening of the First Territorial Legislature and to open the third district court in the absence of Chief Justice Turner.[96] It was here that Allyn heard the noted mining case *Murray v. Wickenburg,* involving Henry Wickenburg, discoverer of the great Vulture gold mine located near the present town bearing his name. A Tucson resident, William R. Murray, sued Wickenburg for damages and requested an injunction to stop the latter's activities at the gold mine. Murray alleged that under Spanish-Mexican mining law, he held a one-third interest in the mine. Judge Allyn, in his decision, made an elaborately documented analysis of these laws and held that Murray had forfeited any rights by failure to register his claim. The injunction was denied.[97] In his letter of October 12, 1864 (Letter 13), Allyn, signing himself "Putnam," soberly reported the trial, without ever informing his readers that he himself was the judge.

Allyn's next experience on the bench was at his own second

---

[94] "Old Minute Book of the District Court of the Second Judicial District, June 28, 1864–October 28, 1872," p. 8. Hereinafter referred to as "Old Minute Book."

The original of this document is in the Yuma County Courthouse, Clerk's Office, Yuma. Copies of it and other scattered territorial records are available in the Arizona State Library, Capitol Building, Phoenix, the main repository of Arizona's territorial material.

[95] Since p. 10 of the "Old Minute Book," which may have contained this information, is missing, we must resort to conjecture. Governor Goodwin's original proclamation specified only the June and November regular district court sessions, but a regular February session was added in 1865. (Norman E. Tutorow, *Records of the Arizona Territorial Court,* p. 39; "Old Minute Book," p. 7.)

[96] His letter of October 12th merely says, "I left La Paz in September to attend the assemblage of the legislature and the opening of the District Court. . . ." To keep his identity secret, Allyn makes no mention in his newspaper correspondence of his serving as judge in Prescott or later of his having run for delegate to Congress.

[97] The full text of this decision is given in the *Miner* for October 26, 1864. Though Allyn regarded the territorial officials as "honest men," he had fears for their future amidst the rich temptations of gold and silver. (Allyn to G. Welles, January 27, 1864, in Welles Papers.)

district court at La Paz. This session, which convened from February 6 through 27, 1865, if not filled with the excitement of the Wickenburg trial, at least had a number of cases before it. The court met daily for more than two weeks, however, before the first suit was presented on February 23. This was *John Coin* v. *The Cosette Copper and Silver Mining Company,* in which the plaintiff demanded payment from the mine for fulfillment of contract. The defendant moved that the case be dismissed on the grounds that he had not been a resident of the territory when the complaint was first issued and that charges had not been adequately published in the *Arizona Miner.* Judge Allyn denied the dismissal and awarded a judgment to John Coin of $412.14 in damages.[98]

This case was rather typical of the seventeen which Allyn considered during his second meeting of the district court.[99] The majority of decisions concerned breach of contract, fraudulent deeds, and the nonpayment of debts connected with various mining claims. The plaintiffs were frequently Mexicans or Mexican-Americans making charges against Anglo defendants.[100]

This second meeting of Allyn's district court appears to have been his most active. He presided on the bench for two additional meetings, one in November 1865 and one in April 1866.[101] Of the

---

[98] "Old Minute Book," p. 15.

[99] An eighteenth case was heard by Allyn, but judgment was deferred until the regular court session of September 17, 1866. This case was *José María Figuera* vs. *Eulogio del Castillo.* ("Old Minute Book," pp. 27, 28, 30.)

[100] Although somewhat neglected in histories of Arizona's territorial period, the influence of the Mexican and his contribution to the development of settlement, law, and justice was considerable.

[101] There is no evidence in the surviving district court records of a spring 1865 session. At the end of the February court is the notation that the court will adjourn "until the next Regular Term." ("Old Minute Book," p. 20.) On the following page, a three-day district court session convening on November 13, 1865, is reported. The next regular term began on April 2, 1866, ending the next day. As far as can be determined, this was Allyn's last court session. At the next regular session on September 17, 1866, the judge was not present, and the court adjourned that same day. Allyn also was not present at the regular session of April 1, 1867. In September 1867, Judge H. H. Cartter presided. ("Old Minute Book," pp. 21–33.)

Note that the spring session date originally set for June in Governor Goodwin's 1864 proclamation was not strictly adhered to; meeting dates varied from April to June. The National Archives records specifying regular May sessions from 1865 onward are in error. (Tutorow, *Records of the Arizona Territorial Court,* p. 39.) Undoubtedly the sessions were arranged in April, November, and February as a means of avoiding the heat of late spring and summer.

latter session the *Miner* reported that there was "no charge, no jury, and but two unimportant cases before the court.[102]

But if Allyn's duties as a district court judge were minimal, his activities on the territorial supreme court were more so. The supreme court met only once during the young judge's time in Arizona, and for unknown reasons he was not present for this session. First scheduled for early December 1865, then postponed to December 26 because two of the judges were not available, the first meeting of the territorial supreme court was presided over by Chief Justice William F. Turner and Justice Henry T. Backus without Allyn. Whether Allyn finally participated in the decision on *Davis* v. *Simmons* is unknown, for it was signed "By the Court," and not by individual judges.[103]

In point of fact, Allyn's whereabouts is conjectural during the time between the November 1865 district court session and February 28, 1866, when the *Miner* reported that he had gone to San Francisco. Deeply involved in furthering his political ambitions at this time, he could have been traveling about, rallying friends' support.

Political Involvements

Allyn's Arizona political embroilments had begun back in 1864 when he had addressed the territorial grand jury.[104] In a carefully worded charge he had warned of the dangers of murder and other crimes among a population accustomed to wearing guns at all times.[105] But a more sensational and controversial charge was also given. Allyn referred to a crime, more serious than murder, which "takes first rank in enormity in the codes of all nations." This latter

---

[102] *Arizona Miner,* April 25, 1866.
[103] "Supreme Court Calendar, Territory of Arizona, 1866–1884," pp. 1–3. Original mss. in State Library, Capitol Building, Phoenix.
[104] Allyn, "Charge to the U.S. and Territorial Grand Juries." The charge was published in 1864 by the office of the *Miner*. A copy is contained in the Connecticut State Library, Hartford. All quotes appearing in this paragraph are from this source.
[105] The *Arizona Miner* of October 13, 1866, contemptuously accused Allyn of using fractured and unintelligible English in this address to the grand jury. However, a careful reading of the speech shows a very high quality of persuasive English prose, although one passage seems to have been garbled in printing. Allyn's remarks about murder may have been partly due to personal fears; earlier he had written Welles that he was afraid that his enemies were trying to destroy him. (Allyn to G. Welles, May 4, 1864, Welles Papers.)

offense strikes a blow "at government itself, at social order, by under-mining the confidence of the community in the honesty of disbursing officers, and of executive action, and in the purity of the judi-ciary. . . ." The judge then referred to the "universal talk of fraud and corruption that fills the air" of Prescott. He spoke of rumors of the sale of votes, of forgery of ballots, and bribery in the recent terri-torial election. He urged the jury to use its power of investigation to examine the rumors and, if warranted, to bring "to condign punish-ment the guilty parties." Allyn also charged the United States grand jury, which had powers in relation to federal crimes paralleling those powers of the grand jury impaneled to investigate territorial crime. He urged that the strongest vigilance be maintained to root out trea-son during the critical period of the Civil War through which the country was passing.

But it was the charge asking for an investigation of the recent July election[106] that aroused opposition and catapulted Allyn into a web of political controversy that clung to him for the rest of his stay in Arizona. If the frauds hinted at by the judge had basis, then his far-reaching powers of legal action would certainly have given offenders some anxious thoughts. It is also possible that the mere fact of his being a federal appointee from the East made Arizonans resentful of any criticism he might offer, for the call for "home rule" with elected territorial officials was already being heard.

Whatever the reason, McCormick, a fellow Easterner, was quick to publicly challenge Allyn. Animosity between these two appointees had been smoldering for some time, possibly originally due to differences in temperament and character. Allyn with his wealth, aristocratic sophistication, and New England morality and reserve might well have exasperated the volatile, aggressive, urbanely intelligent McCormick. The two undoubtedly considered each other political rivals, and McCormick had the advantage of a public mouthpiece in his newspaper, the *Miner*.[107]

---

[106]On May 26, 1864, Governor Goodwin had issued an official proclama-tion calling for the first Arizona territorial election to choose the member of the First Legislative Assembly and a delegate to Congress. (Wagoner, *Arizona Territory*, pp. 41–44.)

[107]As well as functioning as territorial secretary, Richard C. McCormick, a former journalist (see note 22, this section), brought a printing press over-land with the Goodwin party and became owner-editor of the *Arizona Miner*. First published at Fort Whipple beginning March 9, 1864, the semi-monthly

Volatile, aggressive, and urbanely intelligent, territorial secretary and journalist Richard C. McCormick proved a formidable political rival and antagonist to Allyn during the whole of the judge's Arizona career.

After Allyn's grand jury address, the editorial columns of McCormick's paper were filled with ready sarcasm. The judge's charge was referred to as "strictly erroneous from first to last." The newspaper insisted that there had been no vote-tampering, that the charge was an insult, and that it did injury to "our fair Territory abroad."[108]

Whether because of the *Miner* or other persuasion, or because

---

paper moved to Prescott three months later, where McCormick combined his political and journalistic careers.

After November 1864 the secretary of state's political involvements eclipsed his newspaper work, and E. A. Bentley took over as editor. He was joined by R. Meacham in February 1867, when John H. Marion became owner-editor. Marion, famous for his vitriolic editorials, continued to have an interest in the *Miner* until 1876. The paper combined with the *Arizona Journal* as the *Arizona Journal-Miner* in 1884, then continued under a variety of titles until its demise in 1934. (Estelle Lutrell, *Newspapers and Periodicals of Arizona 1859-1911*, pp. 41–44.)

[108] *Arizona Miner,* October 5, 1864. However, a set of resolutions was signed by the military garrison at Fort Whipple, in which officials of Goodwin's administration were accused of "various shortcomings, such as selling for their own profit stores furnished by the Government." (Bancroft, *Arizona and New Mexico,* p. 522.)

no indictable frauds were found, the grand jury did not act to invali-
date the elections. The young judge's crusade was stillborn, and he
did not again preside in the third district court.

Late in November 1864 Allyn rode to Tucson via Wickenburg
and the Santa Cruz valley. He spent most of December and January
in the Tucson area, visiting mines and ranches, and then made his
way westward through the Papago Indian country to Yuma and on
to his La Paz headquarters. In the spring of 1865 he went by steamer
up the Colorado River to the highest point that could be reached at
that time, near present-day Hoover Dam. His letters describing this
trip are the last of his Arizona correspondence.[109]

Allyn made no mention in his letters to the *Press* that he was
running for the office of delegate to Congress in the general election
of September 1864.[110] Although losing to Governor Goodwin, he
did surprisingly well, outpolling Poston, the incumbent, and running
ahead of Governor Goodwin in populous Pima County. The results
showed Goodwin, 707 votes; Allyn, 381; and Poston, 260.[111] Allyn's
outspoken Union sentiments may have cost him votes and friendships
among Southern sympathizers. When he had given, on request, a
formal Fourth of July address at La Paz in 1864, he told a largely
pro-Confederate audience, "I know most of you did not, as I did,
vote for him [Lincoln]; but he is your President and mine."[112]

But the real reason for Allyn's loss was probably the bitter feud
which had developed between him and the combined forces of Goodwin and McCormick, dating at least from the time of his charge to

---

[109] These letters are the last of the Arizona "Putnam" letters. Actually,
brief, undated, unsigned news items appeared in the *Hartford Evening Press*
for January 5 and April 4, 1866, under datelines of Fort Yuma and La Paz.
These simply mention such news items as food supplies for Prescott and disputes between Indian tribes on the Colorado. They were probably sent by
Allyn.

[110] There has been some confusion as to the date of this election. It was
held to fill the office of delegate for the term beginning in March 1865.
Wagoner logically dates it as September 1864. (*Arizona Territory*, p. 61.)
But for some reason, possibly to allow time for his own campaign, Goodwin
left the delegate's chair unfilled for five months. The congressional election
was not called for until August 4, 1865, at which time he proclaimed that it
was to be held "on the first Wednesday of September next." (*Journal of the
Second Legislative Assembly*, p. 257.) Allyn considered Poston a "secesh at
heart . . . ," and he had doubts about Goodwin because he favored the "dis-
loyal." (Allyn to G. Welles, May 4, 1864; also Allyn to G. Welles, January
27, 1864, in Welles Papers.)

[111] *Arizona Miner*, October 4, 1865.

[112] Joseph Pratt Allyn, Address: *The Fourth of July 1864 at La Paz, Arizona*, p. 11.

the territorial grand jury at Prescott a year previous. In announcing the election returns on October 4, 1865, the *Miner* gloated over Goodwin's victory and wrote the most vicious accusations and innuendos (if not directly, then evidently) against Allyn:

> The defeated candidate and his tactics have afforded infinite amusement. . . . It was early understood that this gentleman came to the Territory for the express purpose of running for Congress. . . . The support of the Judge for Congress was the test of loyalty and political orthodoxy and opposition to his claims converted the undiscerning and unlucky culprit into a rank secessionist. . . . His eminent fitness for office, probably from his extreme modesty, had not been appreciated and recognized by the people among whom he was born and raised. Perhaps his ineffable excellence did not dawn on its fortunate possessor until his elevation to judicial honors. . . . Now a Judgeship may be a very pretty plum for a young gentleman who never practised law a day in his life, and though a commission from Uncle Sam may make a man a judge, only the study and practice of the profession, or a special dispensation of divine providence, can make him a lawyer.

In this same editorial, the *Miner* attempted to appease the other defeated candidate by professing that it had great respect for Colonel Poston and that his defeat was due to "local causes," which, in the opinion of the paper, were "groundless." However, Poston would have none of the *Miner's* consolation or support. He had been elected in July 1864 to fill the congressional term ending in March 1865 and had decided to run for office again. In a December 1, 1865, statement on the election addressed "to the people of Arizona," Poston stated that he had been given the pledged support of McCormick and Goodwin at the outset of the campaign and had assumed all along that Goodwin was working "zealously and honestly for my re-election."[113] But the governor, according to Poston, with "an infamous falsehood and forgery, made without the shadow of right or color of truth, and in violation of all courtesy, decency, honor and law" struck the incumbent's name from the list of candidates.[114] Goodwin thereupon, with *Miner* support, ran for the office himself, while Poston, remaining in Washington, was unable to make any sort of campaign.

Poston pulled no punches. He stated that Goodwin had been "repudiated by his neighbors in Maine and was pensioned off on

---

[113] *Arizona Miner,* February 14, 1866.
[114] Ibid.

Arizona as a political pauper." He then quoted a letter he had received from "one of the highest federal officials in the Territory" (who sounds very much like Allyn): "The Governor is supposed to have the inside track, having been all through the Southern portion of the Territory with General Mason[115] on a political campaign free of expense. . . . The Governor is odious among Union men here."[116]

In a formal statement to the United States House of Representatives on December 5, Poston protested the election and challenged Goodwin's right to the congressional seat.[117] His challenge was based upon several alleged irregularities: that soldiers, not citizens of the territory, voted; that Brigadier General John S. Mason had campaigned for Goodwin; that a large majority of Mexicans and Indians had illegally voted; that polls had been illegally placed on Indian or military reservations; that Goodwin was never a resident of Arizona but remained a citizen of the state of Maine; that the governor himself had, in effect, counted and certified his own votes and declared himself elected.

In reply, the *Miner* explained that it had abandoned support of Poston because Judge Allyn had entered the campaign and "when it was apparent that for reasons too numerous to mention, defeat stared us in the face, and that a particularly odious man, his opponent and ours, would be elected (as we still firmly believe), we turned our support to Governor Goodwin, a more popular man at the time, whom we knew it was possible to elect."[118] Poston, however, remained hostile. Abandoning all attempts at reconciliation, the *Miner,* in an editorial as acrimonious as those against Allyn, made the break complete by accusing Poston of attempting "to bully his election through. Having no merits of his own to commend him to popular favor, and no claims, he is attempting to climb into power by vilification of others."[119] The House of Representatives, despite Poston's protest, left Goodwin in possession of his seat.

The subsequent career of Goodwin did little to help his reputation for political honesty. After taking office in March 1866, he

---

[115] General John S. Mason, head of the Military Department of the Pacific with headquarters in San Francisco, included Arizona in his command. He visited the territory in 1865, presumably in connection with Indian problems. (Henson, *Wilderness Capital,* pp. 238–40.)

[116] *Arizona Miner,* February 14, 1866.

[117] Ibid.

[118] *Arizona Miner,* January 24, 1866.

[119] *Arizona Miner,* August 22, 1866.

unlawfully accepted both a governor's and a congressman's salary
and made no restitution to the federal government despite repeated
requests from the comptroller.[120] His confidant, McCormick, was
later accused of bribery in the controversial switch of the state
capital from Prescott to Tucson for the alleged purpose of assuring
his own future election as delegate to Congress in a more favorable
constituency.[121]

In its bitterest tirades against Allyn, the *Miner* stopped short
of any accusations of dishonesty or corruption. No such smear ever
clung to the young judge. He had, in fact, little interest in political
or economic intrigue. He respected those who engaged in honest
enterprise but was highly critical of fraud and extortion. He condemned Surveyor General Levi Bashford and Attorney General
Almon Gage for selling food to poor miners at exorbitant prices to
be paid in gold rather than greenbacks.[122] As a member of a wealthy
family, he himself had no need to seek a fortune and may well, at
times, have appeared self-righteous and supercilious, as the *Miner*
so caustically stated. If Allyn was indeed fairly defeated, then his
unpopularity may have been due to a certain correctness of manner
and outspoken bluntness[123] characteristic of his New England background. Colonel Nelson H. Davis said, "Allyn is radical, bitter, and
feels badly because he is not supported for Congress."[124] If a true
canvass of legal votes might have shown that Allyn was after all the
legitimate victor in the election, his bitterness is understandable.

Years later, looking back on Allyn's career, the *Miner* (under
new editorship) observed that "he was most cruelly maligned by that
set of political harpies who were associated with him in the adminis-

---

[120] B. Sacks, "Proclamation in the Wilderness: The Salary Clause in the
Territorial Act, with a Note on Illegal Payments to Gov. Goodwin," pp. 12–13.

[121] *Arizona Miner,* January 18, 1868.

[122] B. Sacks, "Arizona's Angry Man," p. 97.

[123] In a letter to Gideon Welles, Allyn prophetically remarked, "I never
yet hesitated to denounce wrong even among party friends." (J. P. Allyn to
Gideon Welles, March 21, 1863, Sacks Collection.)

[124] Sacks, "Arizona's Angry Man," p. 96. Colonel Davis was inspector
general of the Military Department of New Mexico, which included Arizona
in 1884. For Davis to General Carleton *re* Allyn and other officials, see U.S.
War Records Office, *War of the Rebellion,* series 1, vol. 34, part 2, p. 593 and
part 3, p. 210. Allyn was also quite bitter about the "intensely corrupt" territorial government, the exploitation of the Indian, and the greed and material-
ism of Arizonans. (Allyn to Mrs. G. Welles, October 30, 1865, in Welles
Papers.)

tration of the affairs of the Territory during the first two years of its territorial existence."[125] As for the *Miner's* earlier aspersions against the judge's legal talents, the members of the bar of the second judicial district were later to testify to his having "challenged the respect and won the esteem" of his colleagues.[126]

Last Days in the West

Following his loss of the congressional election, Allyn seems to have begun to entertain thoughts of leaving Arizona. The vitriolic editorial attacks of the *Miner* may have convinced him that he could not pursue successfully an official career in the new territory so long as the chief newspaper and the governorship were in the hands of his enemies. He could well have decided to attempt to remedy either or both of these situations, and failing that, to return home.

He was, after all, undoubtedly homesick. Looking back on his journey out west he was to write, "We found that each mile of lengthening distance travelled from home added a heavy link to the chain we drew after us."[127] Part of this chain was perhaps some New England love affair of which Allyn speaks cryptically: when he had arrived in Santa Fe with the territorial party in 1863, he wrote that there were in his mail no "small white envelopes with delicately traced addresses thereon. . . ." And he lamented that "if there was a pang of jealousy or envy towards those more fortunate, or a single thought of her 'whom to have loved was a liberal education,' it must be charged to two months of camp life."[128]

Social life in the territory was indeed bleak for an eligible young bachelor like Allyn. Even society in the capital, Prescott, was dull. According to one observer, no ladies were present at the first celebration of the Fourth of July in 1864 because "there were none in the country."[129] There were, of course, a few ladies, mostly wives. But

---

[125] *Arizona Miner,* July 10, 1869.

[126] *Arizona Miner,* October 30, 1869.

[127] *Hartford Evening Press,* July 13, 1866.

[128] *Hartford Evening Press,* December 24, 1863. In a letter early in the following year Allyn chided a correspondent for not saying "something about my little Quaker girl." (Allyn to Mrs. G. Welles, April 4, 1864, in Welles Papers.) Ben Sacks speculated that she may have been Anna Elizabeth Dickinson.

[129] Quote from D. E. Conner, last surviving member of the Walker party, appears in Berthrong, *Joseph Reddeford Walker,* p. 247.

cultured, unattached young women were a rarity. And La Paz was no better. Those who could escaped at times by round-trip boat excursions to San Francisco or Los Angeles. They and new immigrants told and retold stories of the glamour and excitement of California society.

Many of Allyn's fellow pioneers found Arizona life uncongenial. Allyn's colleague, Judge William T. Howell of the first district court, had remained at his post for only five months before leaving Arizona forever.[130] Jonathan Richmond, a court clerk in Allyn's territorial party, wrote, "Everything is upside down, most of the officials having left the country."[131] Many of them had come as office-seekers or as searchers for gold, silver, and fame. Often they were disillusioned.

Allyn had been in Arizona two years. He now took steps to combat the political and journalistic dominance of Goodwin and McCormick. He must have made his situation known to some of his influential friends in Connecticut. When Goodwin had won the congressional election, a vacancy was left in the office of governor. President Andrew Johnson had various names under consideration for the post. On January 16, 1866, William Faxon of the Navy Department sent a letter to "His Excellency, the President of the United States:"[132]

> I respectfully recommend for appointment as Governor of Arizona, Hon. Joseph P. Allyn, now one of the Judges of the United States Court in that Territory. I am well acquainted with the feeling in Connecticut and know that his appointment would be highly satisfactory. Mr. Allyn's residence in that Territory during the last two years must have eminently fitted him for the Governorship.

----

[130] Goff, "William T. Howell and the Howell Code of Arizona," pp. 226–27. Howell officially took a three-month leave on grounds of his wife's illness. He later stated that he would return to Arizona in February of 1865 but resigned his judgeship March 8, 1865. Despite his brief Tucson residence, the code he compiled, known as the Howell Code of Arizona law, has remained a monument to his territorial career (see note 16, this section). He was replaced as associate justice by Henry T. Backus, a lawyer and legislator from Detroit. (John S. Goff, "William T. Howell and the Howell Code of Arizona," p. 227; John S. Goff, "The Appointment, Tenure, and Removal of Territorial Judges: Arizona — A Case Study," p. 215.)

[131] Farish, *History of Arizona* 3: 245.

[132] Copy in Connecticut State Library. Allyn's friend General Hawley wrote an endorsement which commended him as one of the ablest young men of the state and of the highest honor and integrity. (J. Hawley to G. Welles, Jan. 18, 1866, in Welles Papers.)

To this letter Secretary of the Navy Gideon Welles added the following endorsement:[133]

The writer is Chief Clerk of this Department, is honorable, trustworthy and reliable. Judge Allyn is a gentleman of integrity and ability who has remained at his post whilst most of the Federal officers have absented themselves from the Territory.

Shortly after, on January 19, the editor of the *Hartford Evening Press* wrote to President Johnson:[134]

I beg leave to commend to the favorable notice of Your Excellency Hon. Joseph P. Allyn formerly of this City, now Associate Justice of Arizona, for the position of Governor of that Territory.

He is a gentleman well read in the law, well versed in political history, with a memory of surprising range and accuracy, excellent judgement, and views on national affairs, entirely honest, and scrupulously faithful in the discharge of any public or private duty.

I have heard repeatedly from unprejudiced observers that he was the ablest man in the Territory, and I do not doubt that his appointment would be for the interests of the Territory and a credit to your administration.

But Allyn was passed over by the president in favor of the secretary of the territory, Richard C. McCormick.[135] Doubtless President Johnson's action was a crushing blow to the judge, naming, as it did, his old enemy to the high post.[136]

Allyn also had thought of breaking the *Miner*'s newspaper monopoly by bringing in printing equipment from California. In February the *Miner* reported sarcastically, "Allyn has gone to San Francisco . . . to buy a printing press to start a paper. If so, this is evidence of the Judge's confidence in Arizona which does him credit."[137] Allyn did go to the Coast, having plenty of time to make the journey before the beginning of the spring court term. He took advantage of the opportunity to send additional letters to the *Hartford Press* giving his impressions of the Golden State.[138]

---

[133] Copy in Connecticut State Library.

[134] Warner to Johnson. Copy in Connecticut State Library.

[135] McCormick was appointed April 10 and took the oath of office July 9, 1866. (Wagoner, *Arizona Territory,* p. 65.)

[136] Allyn's bitterness may have been openly expressed. The *Arizona Miner* for November 10, 1866, perhaps maliciously reported of the judge, "That worthy, when he was in San Francisco, lately spoke in most disparaging terms of Andrew Johnson."

[137] *Arizona Miner,* February 28, 1866.

[138] These letters are discussed and quoted from in the Epilogue of this book.

Whatever his original intentions may have been, Allyn returned to Arizona for only one brief visit, to preside over the spring term of the district court at La Paz. He makes no mention of this journey in his Putnam letters, and a reader would suppose that he had continued to reside and travel in California during April, May, and June. The only hint is a break in the datelines between March and July 1866.

It is known that Allyn returned to Arizona in April,[139] but his route and means of travel are a matter of conjecture. A likely assumption is that the judge took the then-popular passage on a steamer running from San Francisco to the Colorado River and from thence went on to La Paz by a riverboat such as the *Esmerelda,* which had taken him upriver the previous year. Certainly, this sort of journey would have been cleaner and more pleasant for a seasoned ocean traveler like Allyn.

One may surmise that this return to the scenes of his lonely and controversial life in the territory was made strictly as a matter of duty and that Allyn left reluctantly the excitement and culture of San Francisco about which he wrote with such enthusiasm. There remains the possibility that he actually intended to stay in the territory and establish a newspaper in opposition to the *Miner.*[140] But one finds no indication of Allyn's actually carrying out such a plan. In any case he returned to Los Angeles and San Francisco in July[141] and never appeared again in the territory.

Allyn had served only two of the four years of his appointment as associate justice of the Arizona Supreme Court. On March 13, 1867, after he had returned to Connecticut in a serious state of health,[142] he wrote the following letter to President Andrew Johnson:[143]

The condition of my health renders it impossible for me to return to Arizona, and being unwilling to longer hold an office the duties of which I am unable to discharge, I beg leave to tender my resignation of the Office of Associate Justice of the United States Court for the Territory of Arizona, to take effect from this expiration of my present leave of absence.

---

[139]*Arizona Miner,* April 25, 1866.

[140]*Arizona Miner,* February 28, 1866. At the time the *Miner's* only competition was the *Arizona Gazette,* published in La Paz. (Lutrell, *Newspapers of Arizona,* p. 44.)

[141]*Arizona Miner,* July 11, 1866.

[142]Allyn's return trip and his subsequent activities are discussed in the Epilogue of this book.

[143]Copy in Connecticut State Library.

He was replaced on the court that same year by Harley H. Cartter, a brother of the chief justice of the District of Columbia.[144]

During the whole of his Arizona assignment, Allyn had taken an active and intelligent interest in the welfare of the territory and its citizens. Shortly after arriving at Fort Whipple, he wrote to General Carleton in Santa Fe suggesting that Granite Creek would be a superior location for the new capital and that the fort itself might be moved there (both, in fact, were later established in this area).[145] He repeatedly chided General Irwin McDowell in San Francisco, who had become responsible for security in Arizona, over his failure to send troops for protection against the Apache.[146] And he proposed the establishment of direct steamship service from New York to Sonora or the Colorado River ports to avoid the delay and expenses involved in the transshipment of goods from San Francisco.[147]

We must assume that throughout his travels and strenuous activities Allyn was living with a case of arrested pulmonary tuberculosis. But that handicap and the threat which it posed to his life seems never to have deterred him for a moment from doing things in the most rigorous fashion. When most in the official party chose to ride west from Fort Leavenworth seated or lying in a wagon, Allyn went on horseback and lengthened the arduous journey by detouring to whatever place struck his interest. When he might have taken a relatively comfortable residence in Prescott or La Paz, he chose to ride over and explore much of the territory. He complained of illness only during the cold and windy Prescott spring weather. At other times, he habitually conveyed a sense of the joy of life and even of physical well-being.

This perennial optimism is a part of the bright side of Allyn. With it goes his love of conviviality, his ironic humor, and his intense interest in all aspects of the life around him. These qualities

---

[144] John S. Goff, "The Appointment, Tenure and Removal of Territorial Judges: Arizona — A Case Study," p. 215; Tutorow, *Records of the Arizona Territorial Court*, p. 37.

[145] Published in the *Santa Fe Weekly Gazette*, June 4, 1864.

[146] (Allyn to McDowell, March 7, April 7, 20, 1865; U.S. War Records Office, *War of the Rebellion*, series 1, vol. 50, part 2: 1,187, 1,204; Connecticut State Library, Allyn File.) At this time McDowell's formal jurisdiction included Arizona.

[147] See Letter 18.

contrast sharply with the judge's more introverted side — his sense of loneliness, introspectiveness, and personal reserve.

An account of Allyn's death from tuberculosis, which occurred only three years after he left the West, is contained in the Epilogue of this book. Had he lived he might have become a great novelist: as it was he gave us what is surely one of our most interesting and sensitive descriptions of the life and land of Arizona in the 1860s. Western literature owes much to the talents of Joseph Pratt Allyn, young man from Connecticut.

II. The Letters

Letter I

A WILD CHRISTMAS EVE — VISIT TO ZUNI — A MOST CURIOUS RACE — JACOB'S WELL — ARRIVE IN ARIZONA

Navajo Springs,[1] Arizona, Dec. 29, 1863
[Published March 7, 1864]

We left the Rock[2] at sunset to go fifteen miles to the Ojo de Pescado,[3] or Fish Spring, the nearest water. The ride was a splendid moonlight one, and we reached camp by 11 o'clock and got supper. This spring is situated in a cañon, where it seemed as if all the winds had concentrated, for it was the chilliest night I have spent in camp. There was no wood nearer than half a mile, and consequently we got to bed very soon.

We stopped there two days to get our wagons repaired and rest the animals. This brought us to Christmas Eve. Near the camp were some Indian ruins,[4] the traces of recent cultivation and irrigation. The Zuni Indians come there every summer and raise corn.

---

[1] Navajo Springs is about four miles north of Jacob's Well and three miles southeast of Navajo (or Navajo Station) on the Santa Fe Railroad in Apache county. Lieutenant Whipple reported seeing a "fine pool" at the place. Other expeditions, and later the emigrants, regarded the springs as an excellent stopping place. (Byrd H. Granger, *Arizona Place Names*, p. 17.) Throughout these notes the Granger book has been used as the Arizona place names source except in cases in which the Will C. Barnes bulletin contains different or additional information.)

[2] "The Rock" is the well-known Inscription Rock, some twenty miles east of Zuni, New Mexico. The Spanish called it *El Morro*, "The Head." General D. Diego de Vargas proclaimed there his victory over the Zunis in 1692. Coronado had been, perhaps, the earliest European visitor to the place in July 1540. Undoubtedly it was the site of early Indian settlements. (Hubert H. Bancroft, *A History of Arizona and New Mexico 1530–1888*, pp. 49, 145, 201.)

[3] Ojo de Pescado (Fish Eye) or Fish Spring was described by Amiel Whipple as some fourteen miles west of Inscription Rock. He camped there in 1853, referring to it as "a pretty stream, glittering with numbers of the finny tribe. . . ." (Grant Foreman, *A Path-Finder in the Southwest*, p. 135. See also map facing p. 157 in David E. Conrad, "The Whipple Expedition in Arizona, 1853–1854."

[4] There were numerous Indian settlements along the Rio Pescado fork of the Zuni River. It is uncertain which of these Allyn refers to.

[45]

Within a mile of the spring, coal crops out of the hills;[5] some of it
was brought in, and burned well in an ordinary camp fire, and admirably in the forge; it was nearly soft enough to be bituminous, and
flaked off like slate.

We determined to celebrate Christmas Eve, for in this sort of
traveling one never knows what a day may bring forth. A wagon was
sent off for wood and greens; it went three times, and just as we got
all ready *it began to snow.* The wood, however, was heaped up, the
wagons corraled to keep off the wind, and draped with the old flag;
the rear of a wagon served for the orchestra and a feed box for the
rostrum, while a huge cauldron of hot water was hissing on the fire.
Speeches were made that, no matter what was their merit, had attentive, earnest and enthusiastic listeners. Capt. Chacon[6] made a speech
in Spanish, translated by Col. Chavez, that was touching and eloquent; he told of the love he had for the flag, of his sacrifices and his
aspirations for the republic; it thrilled the mixed audience that stood
in that pelting storm, and three rousing cheers went up. The toddy
proved excellent, though we had no eggs. The music was admirable,
the John Brown chorus carrying the New Mexicans off their feet,
and a German soldier gave us "I fights mit Sigel."[7] The whole affair
was closed just as the moon peeped out of the clouds, by some remarks by the chaplain and a short prayer. On the whole it was
unique, impromptu, and a success.

Christmas day we got under way, but the snow made the roads
so heavy that we only got the train within four miles of Zuni. The
same stream that rises at Fish Spring here forms the Rio de Zuni,[8] or

---

[5] The coal of this Zuni area is the same formation as that found in the
modern coal mines of Gallup, thirty miles to the north.

[6] Captain Rafael Chacón was commander of the thirty men of Company
E of the New Mexico Volunteers who had joined the territorial party at Albuquerque. Chacón was an experienced Indian fighter. The First Regiment, New
Mexico Volunteers, was raised in 1862 as a defense against the Confederate
units and for operations against the Navajos. The regiment took part in
skirmishes with hostiles on Hassayampa Creek, December 15, 1863. (Frederick H. Dyer, *A Compendium of the War of the Rebellion* 3: 1366.)

[7] General Franz Sigel was a Union Army commander who organized a
volunteer infantry regiment of German immigrants and served throughout
the Civil War. He had migrated from Germany to New York City in 1852.
An equestrian statue of him stands on Riverside Drive in New York. (*Webster's Biographical Dictionary*, p. 1363.)

[8] The "Rio de Zuni" in Valencia County rises in the Zuni Mountains and
flows west across the Zuni reservation, eventually joining with the Little Colorado in Arizona. (Thomas Matthews Pearce, *New Mexico Place Names;
Webster's Geographical Dictionary*, p. 182.)

is supposed to, for it disappears under the lava, and one comes up out of the lava. This miserable stream, not large enough to irrigate the land and not navigable for canoes, was once the subject of an appropriation from the federal government *for a survey of its fitness for steamboat navigation.*[9] Of course the money was expended much as a good deal more has been in New Mexico. About two miles from the Pescado is quite an extensive village built of stone,[10] inhabited by the Zuni Indians in the summer to cultivate this valley.

Several of us rode on to Zuni,[11] Christmas Day. Pretty much all the population turned out to see us, the males and children crowding round us, and the women on the tops of the houses. They were all poorly clad, having scarcely anything on but the ordinary black and white blankets similar to the Mexicans. We saw the governor, an old man quite proud of an old captain's uniform he sported. He did not seem either shrewd or dignified, but, rather childish and infirm. He said they were in the midst of a ten days fast in which they neither buy nor sell, make as little fire as possible, do not even sweep out their houses, etc. He apologized for not asking us to his house, saying it was high up, small, and that he was poor. And then [he] took us to a house occupied by a Mexican who was temporarily staying in the town, who received us hospitably, that is, gave us the best he had for a fair price, viz.: some cornstalks for our horses and a dinner for ourselves. He hadn't much crockery, and the cooking was primitive.

While the dinner was preparing, the large room was quietly filled up by curious Zunis, who watched our every motion. I lighted a pipe, while waiting, and a great sensation was created; there was

---

[9] Sitgreaves refers to the Zuni as "a mere rivulet and not worthy of the name of River." (L. Sitgreaves, *Report of an Expedition down the Zuni and Colorado Rivers*, p. 5.) The survey Allyn refers to may have been the Sitgreaves survey, authorized by Senate resolution July 28, 1852 (Sitgreaves, p. 3). However, the Sitgreaves expedition itself was no boondoggle.

[10] Again it is unclear as to which of the many Zuni settlements is meant.

[11] The word *Zuni* is the Spanish form of *sunyi' tse* of the Keresan language. The original Indian word possibly means "casting place pueblo" or "Rock Slide pueblo." The Zuni pueblo seen by Allyn is located thirty-six miles south of Gallup. It was first seen by Europeans in 1539 when Fray Marcos de Niza and his dark-skinned companion Estevan visited the place. The pueblo was regarded as the "middle ant heap of the world," or the heart of the Zuni universe. Francisco Vázquez de Coronado, Chamuscado, and Espejo all stopped there (in 1540, 1580, and 1583 respectively). The latter explorer was the first to use the name *Zuni*. (Pearce, *New Mexico Place Names*, p. 182.)

buzzing about, the governor was consulted, and at last by means of double interpretation, I learned the reason of their alarm. One of the strictest requirements of the fasting season is that no fire shall be carried out of the house, and they were afraid I would go out with the pipe lighted. Upon my promise to empty it before going out, they were quite satisfied. Whether if I had lighted it outside it would have violated their notions I did not learn. But our dinner was ready, there were but three plates, and but three cups for six of us and no table, so we had to make a table of the floor and seats of some small boxes, and two of us take a plate and cup together, all of which was accomplished successfully in the midst of the curious gaze of fifty Indians.

One of them was an *Albino* or white Indian; he looks for all the world like an Irishman, barring his Indian costume, has blue eyes, tan hair, very fair complexion, rather a silly expression of the face, and cannot bear the light well. He wore a hat, which none of the Indians do. I was utterly baffled in finding out anything definite about these singular creatures, that in small numbers were found in the Pueblo, when the first Spaniard came here 300 years ago. At present there are two men, four women, and some half a dozen children of this race — those I talked with counted up the children differently. Mariano, the governor, being asked about them said there was a tradition that they were the relics of a race once forming a powerful Pueblo at El Morro or Inscription Rock, that they were all gone save these. Another story is that a company of Welsh miners came here to work some mines, and were driven off and murdered by the Zunis, who, *a la* the Romans, seized the women. It is singular that you see no crosses, no half white, and it is asserted that when Albinos intermarry, they do not have Albino children, and one of our party saw the mother of this Albino, and declared she was a pure Indian woman. It is a singularly inexplicable phenomena; the earliest Spanish writers mention finding them in about the same numbers as now.

The houses at Zuni are built in the manner of the other Pueblos of New Mexico, but have more stories, many being three stories high. They are large, roomy and comfortable, many rooms being 15 by 30 feet high between joints, with pavements of smooth, well laid stone, and very large fire places. Their extraordinary durability testifies both to their solidity and the absence of rain and frost in the country. I have never read any account of new houses being built, and the Pueblo is just about the same size now that it was in the earliest times. There is a Catholic church, much dilapidated, and never used, there being no priest residing there. Outwardly the Zunis still claim to be Catholics, but you casually say Montezuma within their hearing, and a very careless observer will see where the heart is.[12] They still retain all their old traditions and worship, and take Catholicism in addition, because it is barely possible it may be true.

We returned to camp about sundown. Near the camp is one of the sacred springs[13] of the Zunis, at least Whipple describes it as such, and it may be so. We used it, and found it good water.

The next day the train went only six miles beyond Zuni, and even then got beyond the water in the Rio de Zuni. Our party spent most of the day in Zuni, and at last succeeded in conquering the aversion to trade, and a lively market day ensued. We wanted *burros,* the Zunis had *burros.* So, counting out silver and spreading out blankets, cotton cloth, etc., negotiations began; pretty much all the asses in town were on exhibition. The Indians were shrewd; just as the bargain for one was nearly finished, it was discovered that he was blind; another had another defect, and so on. After the animals we wanted were picked out, it took a long time to fix the price, and much longer to pay it, for each piece of money was closely scrutinized, and much of the silver we had was in dimes. The reason they will not take greenbacks is a funny one, viz., that they cannot tell one denomination from another; the silver they get will be spent at Wingate. The result of the day's work was some half dozen *burros* and a few skins. During the afternoon the camp was thronged; some came from curiosity, some to sell, but most to avail themselves of our protection from Navajos to cut wood. Nearly every one had an axe. Next morning came more Indians, including Governor Mariano; they sold some ponies, one wild Navajo one that it is worth a man's

---

[12] It was assumed in this period that the Aztecs had originally migrated from the "deserted regions of the far Northwest." (William Hickling Prescott, *History of the Conquest of Mexico and Peru,* p. 14.) But it is very doubtful that the Aztecs were the progenitors of the Pueblo Indians. Bancroft believed that the name *Montezuma* had been introduced by the Spanish and that its recognition was not part of a tribal memory. (Bancroft, *Arizona and New Mexico,* pp. 4–5.

[13] This spring has not been identified. There is, however, a reservoir four miles northeast of Zuni Pueblo which may be on the site of the spring in Allyn's account.

life to mount. They have agreed to send some young men to this place with us to bring back letters for the states.

Just as we were starting it was discovered that one of them was trying to sell a mule, branded U.S. He had tried hard to burn out the brand, but had made bungling work of it. The mule was believed to be one stolen from Wingate. The Indian refused to surrender the animal, and it was taken away from him, and he put in the guard house. He tried to escape, and the sentinel knocked him down, badly cutting his head. There was a nice little row; Mariano, surrounded by about fifty Indians on one side, Col. Chavez and a half dozen soldiers on the other; the Indian, with blood streaming down his face, the central figure. The result was the express did not go with us, and the Indians went back to Zuni, sullen. I am afraid some American will suffer yet, to pay for it. We camped about twelve miles from Zuni, in a fine grove, plenty of wood, no water, several inches of snow, however, on the ground, which, on the grass, does quite as well.

We think we crossed the Arizona line today, but it is difficult to ascertain with certainty.[14] By daybreak we were under way for water; the road led up a ridge from the crest of which a fine valley spread out, covered with grass, but quite bare of trees. In the center of the valley is Jacob's Well, or Ojo Redondo, a very singular reservoir of water.[15] It is a circular pit about three hundred yards in diameter at the surface of the ground, a hundred and fifty feet in depth, that is to the surface of the water; the pool of water is some thirty feet in diameter and it is very deep. A spiral path winds down to the water and the sandy banks are constantly caving in. When we first rode up to it we caught a wolf in it, and it was quite an amusing

---

[14] It seems that Arizona came within just two days of missing the privilege of territorial government. According to the original congressional charge, the government was to be proclaimed on Arizona soil within the year 1863, otherwise the territorial appointments and salaries were void. The date of the proclamation was December 29, 1863. (Benjamin Sacks, "Proclamation in the Wilderness," pp. 3–12.)

[15] Jacob's Well was possibly spring-fed in part, but was replenished mainly by flood waters from time to time. It was an ancient watering place, the Navajos having named it the "Blessing of the Desert." Lieutenant Amiel Weeks Whipple observed that the funnel-shaped, sandy-sided pit was 300 feet in diameter at the rim and 125 feet deep. Lieutenant Edward Fitzgerald Beale and other earlier explorers also camped at or visited the place. By 1938, Allyn's deep pool had been filled by silt, leaving only some five feet of water. (Granger, *Arizona Place Names*, p. 13.)

scene to see the attempts to shoot him from the top; some twenty shots were wasted before he was killed.

The water was frozen, and in breaking it a horse came near drowning. This strange pool has been here from time immemorial, and Navajos' trails radiate from it in all directions. It was perhaps the most dangerous of all our camps, for it is the great crossing place of the Indians, and a band of Navajos might stumble on us without even intending it. The animals were herded close to camp, guards doubled, and the night passed without alarm. At daybreak we made a short march to this point [Navajo Springs], where there is abundant water, in springs right on the surface, and good grass. We have to bring wood, however, several miles. It is very rare in this country that all the requisites of a good camp come together. From this point we shall send back a military express, and if it escapes the Indians it will reach you.

TERRIBLE WIND STORM —
MEXICAN SOLDIERS —
SINGULAR CAMPING PLACE —
WONDERFUL PETRIFACTIONS —
MAGNIFICENT SCENERY

Camp on the Colorado Chiquito[1]
Arizona, January 5, 1864
[Published March 16, 1864]

My last was sent back by our own express from Navajo Springs, and I now avail myself of some teamsters returning from Fort Whipple to hastily write you this. On the 30th we left the Springs at daybreak, and passing across the splendid valley, carpeted with luxuriant grass, ascended the Mesa, that bounded our view to the west. Here we encountered a terrible wind storm, one of the most disagreeable I have experienced, for the chilliness penetrates the thickest garments; it was scarcely below freezing point, and yet I suffered more from the cold than when the thermometer stood at zero.

We struggled on over the Mesas until we came to the valley of the Rio Puerco of the west, which stream, by the way, was perfectly dry.[2] Here we found an *arraya* or ravine in the wall of the Mesa that afforded a slight protection from the wind. Although it was only noon we camped here, fearing to risk the finding even this slight shelter if we proceeded farther. There was no wood within sight, and

---

[1] The source of the Little Colorado or Colorado Chiquito, is on the eastern side of Arizona in Apache National Forest. It flows generally northwest to join the Colorado at Cape Solitude in the Grand Canyon. It was named the Colorado Chiquito by the Spaniard Garcés. The Navajos referred to it as "Tol-chaco" or "Red stream," which is its color when in flood. (Will C. Barnes, *Arizona Place Names*, p. 248.)

[2] The Rio Puerco of the West — or the Puerco (Dirty) River, rises in northwest New Mexico and flows in a southwesterly direction between Lupton and Holbrook. It joins with the Little Colorado a mile east of Holbrook. (T. M. Pearce, *New Mexico Place Names*, p. 135.) Allyn probably reached the Puerco somewhere between Navajo and the Petrified Forest.

we had to be contented with the sage brush, which was abundant, and makes a comfortable fire if you only have enough of it. By arranging the wagons to shut off the wind, we managed to make ourselves at least comparatively comfortable. While we were husbanding sage bush and shivering, we were astonished at the arrival of several of the Mexican soldiers with huge back loads of fine dry wood; they had found it within three hundred yards of the camp. It was not because they knew the country better, for they had never been here before, but simply that they are accustomed to this sort of travel; one of them is worth here two American soldiers. They remind me of the French Zouaves[3] in their imperturbably good nature and faculty of making themselves comfortable under all circumstances. Fortunately the wind went down at sunset. Mica was found in the greatest abundance on the sides of the *arraya,* so transparent that it was difficult to avoid thinking it broken glass left there. As we were still over thirty miles from certain water, orders were issued to feed the animals corn and sound reveille as soon as the moon rose.

At about midnight the bugle notes roused us, and all was confusion; about half our beef cattle and several of the horses, including both mine, were missing, having wandered off after water, owing to the carelessness of those in charge. The cattle were soon found near by, but before the horses were overtaken, they were half way back to Navajo Springs, trotting along under the lead of a pony bought at Zuni, who instinctively knew the way to water. We crossed the dry bed of the Carizo creek,[4] swept over mesas entirely bare of trees, and at day break reached Lithodendran creek, which, like the Carizo, is a tributary of the Puerco. Here we rested for breakfast in the midst of the strangest and grandest surroundings of even this country of startling novelties. We stopped right in the bed of the stream where it was over a quarter of a mile wide near a little frozen

---

[3]The French Zouaves were light infantry originally recruited from the Zouavoua people (Kabyle Tribe) of North Africa. Some Union and Confederate regiments wore colorful adaptations of the Zouave uniform during the Civil War. (*Oxford Universal Dictionary,* p. 2474.)

[4]Carrizo Creek (or wash) is dry most of the year. After a rain it flows southeast into the Puerco between Carrizo and Adamana. The Carrizo parallels the Lithodendron (Greek for *stone tree*), both lying north of the Puerco. The Carrizo (Spanish for *reed grass*) was named by Lieutenant Whipple. (Barnes, *Arizona Place Names,* pp. 78, 248.)

water under the rocky edge of the bank, which when melted was red as brick color. All around, the country was broken into mesas of fantastic shapes; there were huge cathedrals with symetrical cones and sturdy towers, bastioned castles; gigantic tables supported by dome crowned buttresses as uniform as though formed from a common mould; canons and *arrayas,* with rugged, gnarled and broken sides filled with dense thickets, and now and then a cottonwood tree; strewn all around were petrifactions of the most gorgeous colorings and hard enough to strike fire.[5] I saw one nearly perfect trunk of a tree, some six feet in diameter and about twenty five feet of its length uncovered; every seam, knot and fiber of its transverse section, as well as the shaggy bark, as perfect, as when its vital flood flowed, before the mighty and subtle breath of nature had frozen its pulsations and hardened it into immortality, radiant with all the tints of the rainbow.

Broken sections of huge trees were found in every direction, and near to the centers many quite perfect crystals were found, mostly white, but some colored like rubies and emeralds. It was very difficult to break open to them, except you found an open seam, and then the silex cracks off. Near petrifactions the ant hills are uniformly roofed with small stones and crystals, mostly white, but frequently red and orange, and sometimes green, which not unlikely are gathered from the crystals that fall from the petrifactions. Some one having said that these sold at a high price in Denver, large quantities were gathered, but I apprehend the gatherers were sold. Trying the white crystals over the slight heat of a candle they turned red. It is said the ants seek out these to cover their hills with, against the rain, because their specific gravity is less and they can move them.

At noon we left Lithodendran and passing another creek with a little water, and a range of hills, we reached the Colorado Chiquito and camped on New Year's eve, in a fine *bosque* or grove of cottonwoods, which extends as far as the eye can reach on the banks of the river. Here we have remained, only moving camp a few miles

---

[5]The governor's party evidently had reached the area of the modern Petrified Forest National Park, fifteen miles east of present-day Holbrook. Whipple referred to it as Lithodendron Park. The "forest" of eighty thousand acres was created some two hundred million years ago, when volcanic ash covered a forest. Mineral deposits gradually replaced the organic, ultimately creating this phenomenon. (Byrd H. Granger, *Arizona Place Names,* pp. 19–20.)

as the grass was eaten off, recruiting our animals and waiting the arrival of the slower trains behind us.

The distance from Navajo Springs to the river we estimate at over forty miles, but it is impossible to locate certainly the streams mentioned on the maps and in the itineraries of those who preceded us. We crossed more dry beds of streams than are mentioned by any of them, and Lithodendran is the only one that identifies itself. All of them certainly are tributaries of the Chiquito or little Colorado, which at seasons of the year must contain an immense volume of water, for the *bosque* in which we camped, although on a bank some ten feet high from the present level of the water, is covered with dry flood wood, some of it black walnut. On the river near here are the ruins of two modern ranches, like the one at the Pescado, which I believe were erected at the time an attempt was made to have one of the overland mails go this way. Back from the river, on the mesas, a very extensive view can be obtained; off to the east you can see where the river cuts its way through a mesa by a steep canon, and way south of that the Sierra Blanca, covered to the base with snow;[6] to the west, peerless, the San Francisco mountain[7] rises over twelve thousand feet above the sea, its central peak, a beautiful pyramidal one, also covered with snow; everywhere else mesa stretches out beyond mesa in the sunlight, bathed in rich velvety purple.

For miles I have traced, along the mesa bordering the river, at every point where water has worn down to a certain strata, a vast petrified forest of giant trees[8] such as, barring a few in California now, nowhere exist. They lack the rich tinting of those at Litho-dendran, being all a whitish wood color; where they have been long

[6] The Sierra Blanca range is now known as the White Mountains. The highest elevation is Baldy Peak at 11,590 feet, just south of Greer.

[7] "San Francisco mountain," known locally as the San Francisco Peaks, is actually the high rim of an ancient volcano. Agassiz Peak is 12,300 feet; Fremont 11,940 feet; and Humphrey, Arizona's highest, is 12,655. To Allyn, approaching from the east, they would have looked like a single peak. (See Andrew Wallace, *Image of Arizona*, p. 55.) Hopis consider these peaks the sacred home of the kachinas and call them "The High Place of Snow." Spanish settlers called them Sierra Napoc or Napao, Sierra Cienaga, and Sierra de los Cosninos. The present name was probably originally applied by Marcos de Niza in 1539 and finally put into usage by Franciscan missionaries around 1629. (Barnes, *Arizona Place Names*, pp. 383–84, 405.) For contemporary views, see Wallace, *Image of Arizona*, pp. 31, 51, 54ff.

[8] Allyn was skirting the edge of Marcou Mesa on the north side of the Little Colorado. Jules Marcou was a geologist with the Whipple party. (Barnes, *Arizona Place Names*, p. 263.)

exposed the chips scattered about resemble so perfectly the remains of chopping that you would ride over them almost unnoticed, but for the cracking under your horse's hoofs. I rode my roan horse, the largest one in the outfit, right on to the butt of one and his entire length from nose to tail did not span the diameter! It is difficult to get the exact diameter by measuring, as they are frequently broken off. One we measured was over ten feet in diameter certainly, at the last whole place, and at ninety feet from that measured five feet in diameter, and could then be traced for another hundred feet. The largest one I have seen I found yesterday and although much broken the bark having cracked off, it still measured a trifle over twenty feet in diameter.

Not a single evidence of animal life have we discovered. One or two pieces were thought to be fossils, but close inspection usually placed it beyond much doubt that they were something else. The mind is staggered when one undertakes to fathom the antiquity of these forests. Those familiar with the mammoth trees of California pronounce these the same species, from the grain and knots. We searched likewise in vain for anything that indicated the presence of larger bodies of water. In Colorado the remains of fish are said to be found; the only thing that was said to indicate water that we found, were some opal crystals. I am not geologist enough to know. Hugh Miller[9] would have gone crazy years before he did, had he attempted to decypher the magnificent history of the creation nature has here spread open to the student. The cañon and the volcano have in Arizona wrenched from the secret hiding places of the earth the mysteries that have baffled the explorer, and given wide field for speculation, to the charlatan and the enthusiast.

---

[9] Hugh Miller (1802–56) was a noted Scottish geologist and writer. His work with fossils came to the attention of leading geologists in 1837, after which he developed a career in the field. Miller did not become deranged as a result of his labors, but died by suicide because of despair over ill health. (*Encyclopedia Britannica,* 11th ed., 18: 463–64.)

Letter 3

THE COLORADO CHIQUITO —
A FINE COUNTRY —
SAN FRANCISCO MOUNTAIN —
THE CANINO CAVES —
THE FIRST ASCENT OF THE MOUNTAIN —
EXCITING NIGHT ADVENTURE —
DANGER FROM INDIANS —
ARRIVAL AT FORT WHIPPLE

Fort Whipple, Arizona, Jan. 18, 1864
[Published March 21, 1864]

I wrote you lately in camp on the Colorado Chiquito, bringing
this narrative up to that point. We spent the first days of the new
year slowly moving along the sixty miles the road follows this river.
The valley of this stream is one of the richest, indeed *the* richest, I
have seen since I left the states. For the entire distance we passed,
it is lined on either side with a *bosque* of alamos or cottonwoods at
least a half a mile across; back on the mesas there is abundant grass
for miles. I do not suppose there is water enough in the stream to
irrigate all the bottom land, but by constructing banks to retain the
water, there might be nearly as much land cultivated here as there
is now in all New Mexico, if the estimate of the Pacific R. R. reports
is correct. There cannot be a doubt but that all this soil would produce cotton.[1] For grazing, you can scarcely conceive a better place.
The road along the river is a good one, and the crossing is not difficult. It diverges from a direct line to the San Francisco mountain,
both to reach water frequently and to avoid a steep and utterly impassable canon only three hundred feet wide, which could easily be

---

[1]Allyn's views regarding the suitability of the Little Colorado basin for
cotton production have not been borne out. The severity of the winters and
the short growing season have proved conducive only to grazing and to limited Indian farming.

bridged for a railroad.[2] You come on this chasm without the slightest warning, and Whipple traced it twenty four miles without finding a place to cross it.

During these ten days the weather was mild with one slight exception — rain that changed into snow, and fell to the depth of two or three inches. This was the only rain I have seen, with one single exception, in Kansas, since I left Philadelphia last August. Altogether our several camps on this stream were really beautiful; plenty of water, wood and grass, mild weather and splendid views of the mountain capped with snow.[3] The cottonwood trees were thrifty and resembled perfectly an apple orchard in the east.

On the 10th January, we left the river at the Canon Diablo which can be crossed where it debouches,[4] and swept on over a vast mesa covered with loose stones for about two miles, and then descended into a rolling prairie with scarcely a tree, and no water, but covered with excellent grama grass. The decomposed lava mixed with a little vegetable matter makes the soil best adapted to this wonderfully nutritious grass. We camped near where a lava ridge crops out, and named the place Lava Ridge.

Next day, about five miles on, we passed a canon that had evidently had water recently, in which was quite a grove of black walnut trees.[5] From this point we commenced the ascent in earnest of the spur of the San Francisco mountain we were to cross. A vast avenue lined with conical volcanic hills on either hand, some of which had once been craters,[6] led straight toward the vast pile of the central mountain itself. The road was good and the ascent gradual. Turning to the left, we passed into timber on the hillsides that shut out the

---

[2] This is Canyon Diablo or Devil's Canyon. The Santa Fe Railroad built a bridge across this canyon twenty-six miles west of present-day Winslow. The canyon is generally dry and in places more than 250 feet deep. (Will C. Barnes, *Arizona Place Names,* pp. 75–76.) See Andrew Wallace, *Image of Arizona,* p. 173, for a contemporary plate.

[3] The party was approaching the San Francisco Peaks directly from the east.

[4] Canyon Diablo enters the Little Colorado six miles northwest of Leupp.

[5] This may have been San Francisco Wash, which receives the flow of Walnut Creek about eight miles east of Mount Elden. (Will C. Barnes, *Arizona Place Names,* p. 474.)

[6] The series of cones is in an area known as the Lava Beds which includes to the north Sunset and Merriam craters. They were generally the product of ancient volcanic activity, although Sunset erupted as recently as 1066 A.D. An Ives Expedition illustration of the cones east of the San Francisco Peaks may be found in Wallace, *Image of Arizona,* p. 51. See also Barnes, *Arizona Place Names,* p. 242.

river, and in a few miles reached what Whipple calls the divide of the waters flowing into the Gila on the south and the Little Colorado to the north.[7] A fine run of boundless forests stretched off toward the south. The ascent to this point from the river is fourteen hundred feet. Passing down a little descent we came into a magnificent park, set like a lake in the mountains, resembling those I tried to describe in the Zuni mountain. The trees were larger, and there was the imposing mountain overshadowing all. Across this park we struck the Canon Diablo again, which shows that Whipple was mistaken in locating the divide. In the canon here we found an abundance of water, but it was very difficult to get down to it. About a mile beyond our camp here in the canon are the Canino Caves, which are one of the great landmarks of the journey.[8]

They are numerous on the right side of the canon, and are evidently natural caves enlarged and rendered habitable by persons having some mechanical knowledge. They are shaped like a huge oven, and were probably ten feet high, although the rubbish now has filled them up so that you have to stoop a little in them. They were plastered and had mud floors; very well laid walls of stone in some places supported projecting roofs. From the outer cave other little caves branched off, looking something like the cells in a beehive; small circular holes led into them, and they seemed to be shaped like the larger outer room as far as we could ascertain by thrusting in sticks. I suspect these inner cells were used as store rooms. These caves are said to have been occupied by the Canino Indians.

Our next day's march was an exceedingly provoking and perplexing one. Whipple makes the distance to San Francisco spring,[9]

---

[7] Presumably, Allyn is referring to the area of Doney Park at the base of Mount Elden. Various washes, including San Francisco Wash, rise on the east side of Elden and the San Francisco Peaks to flow into Canyon Diablo or the Little Colorado. To the south of Elden the branches of Oak Creek flow southwesterly to the Verde River, which meets the Salt River about twenty-four miles northeast of Phoenix. The Salt then flows into the Gila southwest of Phoenix. (Barnes, *Arizona Place Names*, pp. 304, 379, 404.)

[8] The "Canino Caves" are probably the Cosnino Caves near Turkey Tanks, located a few miles east of modern Flagstaff. The canyon was the site of extensive ancient Indian dwellings. Lieutenant Beale named them Cosnino for the Cosnino or Havasupai Indians who were presumed to have lived there earlier. (Granger, *Arizona Place Names*, p. 67.) Grant Foreman, *A Pathfinder in the Southwest*, p. 160, includes a photo of caves.

[9] San Francisco Spring was probably located just east of Schultz Pass on Macmillan Mesa in what is now east Flagstaff, or it may be the Bear Spring of Lieutenant Beale or modern Elden Spring four miles to the northeast of Flagstaff. (Barnes, *Arizona Place Names*, pp. 41, 245.)

the next water, about fifteen miles, and four miles farther to Leroux's spring,[10] where we are to leave the Whipple route and go south. General Clark,[11] who went through last August, gave the distance to the first, twenty-three miles, and five more to the next. Our road passed on through a succession of sloping parks of the same general type, every mile or so opening a new view of the mountain.[12] When we had gone some fourteen miles we suddenly came to where the roads forked, both with fresh wagon tracks on them. Part of us went to the right and part to the left. I went to the left, and the road passed over a mesa almost in a circle, very rough from the loose lava stones or *mal pais,* as the Mexicans call it.[13] We expected that these roads would soon come together, or that we should find water. We followed this road for five or six miles; the trail seemed fainter, and to turn straight back down a valley that would cross the road the other party had taken, and although a very faint wagon trail, still led on.

We had found no water at all. A council was held: should we go down the valley and try to reach the other road that way, or go

[10] Leroux Spring was located in Fort Valley about seven miles northwest of Flagstaff. It was named by Sitgreaves for Antoine Leroux, the French guide with his expedition. (Paul Reicker, "Map of Arizona Territory, 1881"; David E. Conrad, "The Whipple Expedition in Arizona 1853–54," p. 162–64.)

[11] John A. Clark was surveyor general of New Mexico. He had investigated the gold regions of the Hassayampa and Lynx Creek in August 1863. He worked in close cooperation with General Carleton who also had Walker District gold interests. Clark's trip was a hurried one, and it would appear that Whipple's distances are more trustworthy. This is confirmed later by Allyn himself. The original Fort Whipple in the Chino valley was renamed Camp Clark when the territorial government moved to Prescott. Clark returned to Prescott again in 1865 and informed the town commissioners that the foundation of the town was illegal and without the consent of the federal government. Prescott did not have clear federal title to its site until 1871. (Pauline Henson, *Wilderness Capital: Prescott, A.T., 1864*, pp. 11, 53–56, 154, 176–78; Harwood Hinton, "Frontier Speculation: The Walker Mining Districts," pp. 249–50.

[12] The trail referred to passed south of Macmillan Mesa which generally divides east and west Flagstaff and then southwest to Volunteer Spring. From Volunteer Spring there was a road to Snively Spring (or Holes), east of Bill Williams Mountain, crossing Rattlesnake and Hell Canyons and descending into the Chino valley, north of Prescott about twenty-five miles. This road appears on modern maps only as a trail or not at all between Bellemont and White Horse Lake. (Reicker, "Map of Arizona Territory, 1881;" Barnes, *Arizona Place Names,* pp. 412, 471.)

[13] *Mal pais:* Spanish for *bad ground.* Allyn probably rode to the left around or over the south spur of Macmillan Mesa which presently divides east and west Flagstaff. The righthand route probably went over what is now Schultz Pass at the north end of Macmillan Mesa. Mount Elden rises to the east of the pass.

clear back round the circle. Our horses were tired. We were not at all certain that the valley would take us to the road, and if it did not we should have to still come back here; then we had found neither of the springs. Part of our little party started back round the road we had come. I waited with two or three others, while two, having fresh horses, determined to make a last attempt to find water farther on. It was arranged that if they succeeded they were to fire a pistol three times in rapid succession. In just about ten minutes the sound of the shots were heard. By hallooing we were enabled to call back the party that had started, and then we all galloped on to the water, which proved to be a miserable little spring, that our dozen horses soon drank nearly dry. What spring was it? It wasn't large enough for a train. Go back we must, and of course the old question, how, came up. We separated about as before, myself and two others trying the valley. Riding about a mile, we caught sight of a smoke, and in a few minutes more we met a Mexican soldier that Capt. Chacon had sent up the valley to find us and tell us that he had found water about two miles from the point where the roads first separated. It was two or three hours before the others got in camp.

What was this water? It was about sixteen miles from the caves, and it was southeast of the little one some four miles. We came, therefore, to the conclusion that the smaller one was Leroux's, and the larger one, where we camped, San Francisco. Still these conflicting trails, all comparatively recent, annoyed us. If this was the San Francisco, it was the head of the *Rio Verde* or San Francisco river, which empties into the Gila.[14]

We stayed here two days, and a party made the ascent of the mountain, which rises about four thousand feet above the valley where we camped.[15] They were out one night, and succeeded in reaching the top of one of the highest peaks. They had a map and glass, but their observations added very little to our knowledge of the geography of the country. They said the whole country looked like a vast

---

[14]Allyn may be confused here, understandably. The smaller spring probably was San Francisco, also known by Beale as Bear Spring. San Francisco is possibly the modern Elden Spring, which is now dry. It lay four miles northeast of modern west Flagstaff. The larger spring, where camp was made, was Leroux, which lies about seven miles northwest of Flagstaff, near modern Fort Valley. (Barnes, *Arizona Place Names,* pp. 41, 167, 245; Reiker, "Map of Arizona Territory, 1881.")

[15]Actually, the San Francisco Mountains rise over five thousand feet above the Flagstaff area where Allyn camped.

plain, and they were unable to trace any of the rivers running south.
They identified some of the mountains and traced the little Colorado
to where it disappeared in a canon. This is the first party of white
men known to have ascended this mountain. San Francisco mountain is the most beautiful mountain I have ever seen; it stands peerless and alone, a vast pile of decomposed lava and granite, and rises
twelve thousand feet above the sea. It is covered with tall pine trees
and the most luxuriant grass, nearly to the summit.

In twelve miles from this camp we found Volunteer spring,[16]
the first water on the Clark route to Fort Whipple, and the new mines.
Volunteer spring is in the centre of the finest park I ever saw, belted
with hills covered with the largest timber, and five or six thousand
acres of valley pasture land, the soil all formed of decomposed lava.
From this point the view of the mountain is perfectly superb. I thought
the others the finest I had ever seen, but this infinitely surpassed them
all. As the lava seems increasing on the road, a rest of a day was
made here, to shoe animals and repair wagons.

It is but fifty-nine miles from here to Fort Whipple, and four
of us arranged a party to go straight through. For an escort we had
six men of the 1st California infantry, who had been left behind
when their company went on to establish Fort Whipple, and were
anxious to rejoin their comrades. We packed provisions and blankets
on two burros, and I had an extra horse. The soldiers started at the
first streak of light and we waited until sunrise before following on.
The day was superb, and there was a feeling of lightness and independence in the idea that we were no longer to wait for wagons in
order to get dinner or a bed. We trotted off briskly, the slight snow
crisping under the horses' hoofs. Much of the road was rough from
mal pais. The road passed through timber over a sharp ridge and
opened into another of the vast natural pastures. As we were descending the hill we caught sight of some deer, but not near enough for a
shot. The absence of game on the road has been remarkable. Two
wild turkeys are the only things killed on the entire route, and these
deer are the first we have actually seen, although occasionally we
have seen their tracks. Crossing this valley, which was five or six

---

[16]The Clark route to Whipple has been discussed in Letter 3, note 12.
Volunteer Spring was located approximately twenty miles south of modern
Bellemont. (Reiker, "Map of Arizona Territory, 1881;" Barnes, *Arizona
Place Names*, p. 471.)

miles wide, we entered the timber, and finding the evidences of a large camp we looked for water, which we found near the road.

A mile or so beyond we found stuck on a tree a note addressed to the commanding officer of our escort which we at once opened. It was dated Depot at Canon Springs,[17] January, 1864, and signed by Lieut. Pomeroy[18] of the very company of our little escort. It informed us briefly that the road ahead was nearly impassable, that the Tonto Apaches[19] had stolen forty of his mules and were in open hostilities; that twenty miles on, the road passed through dense woods, where the greatest watchfulness would be necessary. I had very attentive listeners as I read this brief note deposited in this strange post office. We had not yet overtaken our escort. Had they noticed this note? What did the word Depot mean? Why did not Lieut. Pomeroy say camp? Had we better send it on to Col. Chavez? All these queries were almost simultaneously put. Instinctively one felt of his rifle and pistols. We added a brief note to inform Col. Chavez when we passed and put the paper back on the tree. A short distance on explained what depot meant, for we found abundant evidence that Maj. Willis[20] had lightened his wagons here and left the stores in the depot. There were the thousand little evidences of the stay of a body of men, of the game they had shot, the nice shelters they had constructed, etc. But we had no time to waste and pushed on.

---

[17] Canon Springs was probably Snively's or Snively Spring, located just east of Bill Williams Mountain. It seems to have been named later for Jacob Snively who had been General Sam Houston's private secretary during the Texas Revolution. Later he prospected and mined in Arizona and was killed by Indians in 1871. (Barnes, *Arizona Place Names*, pp. 412–13.)

[18] Second Lieutenant Edgar Pomeroy was with Company C, First California Volunteer Infantry of the California Column. He returned to California in August 1864. The *Miner* recorded that he was an "amiable and obliging gentleman. . . ." and a "general favorite." The paper thanked him for "many courtesies." (*Arizona Miner*, August 10, 1864.)

[19] The Tonto (Spanish for *fool*) Apaches were a band of the Western Apache people. They were neighbors of the Yavapai, Coyotero, and Mohave. Early Arizonans frequently confused them with the Yavapai. They were moved to a reservation at Camp Verde in 1873 and to San Carlos in 1875. The origin of the term Tonto is conjectural. (Barnes, *Arizona Place Names*, p. 447.)

[20] Major Edward Baker Willis was born in New York in 1832. He was an officer of the First California Infantry and commander of the expedition which founded Fort Whipple in the Chino valley, December 21, 1863. Willis made supplies available for the Woolsey expedition of 1864. (Arizona Historical Foundation Biographical File, Arizona State University Library; *The 1864 Census of the Territory of Arizona*, p. 118.)

The road was so rough that we could go little faster than a walk. After a couple of hours' riding, we noticed a deuce of spades stuck on a tree, and examining it closely found written on it, "plenty of water in the canon to the left." Was this the point where Clark laid down a camp as fifteen miles?[21] Our foot soldiers either had not seen it, or had concluded that it was not it, for they had not stopped. Proceeding on through timber, over roads rougher than ever, we began to ascend a sharp hill, almost a mountain. At the summit we found our fellows, pretty tired, waiting for us. They meant to reach the fifteen mile water but had concluded they must have passed it. Making a fire we stopped here for dinner; without tablecloths, plates, forks and other things, one usually thinks somewhat essential to a meal, we managed to dispose of an enormous quantity of beef, bread and coffee. From this point the view was very extensive both north and south. With the glass we tried to find Fort Whipple, but did not succeed. We did not know exactly where to look for it.

We rested here a couple of hours and then pushed on. It took us two hours to reach the point Gen. Clark measured as fifteen miles from Canon Springs, or twenty-six miles in all; we estimated it, however, at over thirty, and began to think that if the remainder of the fifty-nine miles were to be as long as these that it was doubtful if we could make it in two days.

This spring identified itself;[22] there had been a very large camp near it, and the boys had killed a bear, at least we found his bones. Our soldiers were in good spirits and wanted to go on. Just as the sun was setting we struck the thick timber Lieut. Pomeroy had spoken of. On we went, the road fearfully rough. Fortunately the moon was very bright. There was no place to camp, and we must go through the wood. Just then someone cried "light." Sure enough, there was a fire off to the right. "Hush," passed along the line. We all gathered in a group, and with a night glass examined the fire. It was unmistakably an Indian one. Our Californians were for going across to it and trying to surprise it. More prudent counsels prevailed, and we went on. It was pretty certain the Indians had not seen us, or they would not have built a fire. On we went, slowly toiling over the rough, sharp,

---

[21] This was possibly Dragoon Creek, which cuts across the Clark trail south of Snively Springs. The creek is a branch of the Verde. (Reiker, "Map of the Territory of Arizona, 1881.")

[22] This was possibly Bear Spring on the Clark trail, having received its name from the bear whose remains Allyn saw. (Reiker, "Map of the Territory of Arizona, 1881.")

rolling lava, up hills and down, watching every fitful shadow of a bush. The poor tired horses would lie down; my lead horse came into play by taking part of the load and carrying one of the footmen all the time, alternating, so that all got rest; the wood seemed interminable. If we had not, from the hill, seen the end of it, we should have thought it would reach clear to the post. The soldiers strode gallantly on, but one could see that they stumbled more, that halts for rest were more frequent and longer. Other Indian fires were seen, still we went on. Before midnight we debouched into an open plain, where a sentry could watch the horses, and stopped to bivouac. We had no water. The other side of the hill there had been snow enough to melt, and not a canteen was filled. Supposing the Indians had not seen us, we did not make a fire. Cold and supperless we rolled up in our blankets and slept. Fortunately we brought corn enough for our horses, and they got their supper.

The last relief of the guard made a roaring fire before daybreak, and we were roused to saddle up. A very short march brought us to Rattlesnake Spring,[23] which Gen. Clark makes forty-four miles. I think we marched more than that yesterday, but this fixed the distance to Whipple at fifteen miles, and we made a very leisurely breakfast. As we lay smoking our pipes and digesting our enormous meal, for it was really an enormous one, in every direction smokes could be seen. Which could be Whipple? Were these miners' camps? What were they? Several bets were made as to the location of Whipple. About ten o'clock we got under way and an hour brought us to the most infernal canon for wagons I have seen yet.[24] It was about 300 feet deep and the sides were nearly perpendicular, and covered with rolling stones. I doubt if wagons can get down except by letting them down with ropes. However, we led our horses down and up, and from there in we had a good road to the post, which we reached in time to get dinner. Here we learned that the smokes seen in the morning were Indian signals, telegraphing our movements. Our welcome was of the most cordial character, and reports from the mines are the most favorable.

---

[23] The Allyn or "Clark" trail crosses Rattlesnake Canyon, which parallels the Chino valley. The watering place called Rattlesnake Spring or Rattlesnake Tanks is located near this place. (Reiker, "Map of the Territory of Arizona, 1881;" Barnes, *Arizona Place Names*, p. 356.)

[24] This is the aptly named "Hell Canyon" southwest of Bill Williams Mountain. It drains into the Verde River. (Reiker, "Map of the Territory of Arizona, 1881;" Barnes, *Arizona Place Names*, p. 204.)

Letter 4

DELIGHTFUL WINTER WEATHER — GAME PLENTY — PURE ATMOSPHERE — EXTERMINATING INDIANS — VISIT TO THE MINES — THE CELEBRATED CAPT. WALKER

Fort Whipple, Arizona, Feb. 6
[Published April 12, 1864; April 18, 1864]

Two weeks of rest, of idleness, save in reading up old newspapers, and writing letters, two weeks of superb weather in an incomparable winter climate, a climate where simple existence becomes luxury; a winter climate where one needs constantly to refer to the almanac to reassure himself that it is indeed winter. The nights are cold enough to make three or four blankets comfortable, and a moderate fire is pleasant until 9 or 10 o'clock in the morning, and in the evening; at mid-day it is warm enough to drive one to the shade, and make a tent hot, and yet there is uniformly a gentle breeze. In these two weeks there has been one slight flurry of snow, that disappeared in a few hours. The northern slopes of the neighboring mountains still are white with the heavier fall there.

This post[1] is only temporarily located at this point, which is about 25 miles north of the gold mines, 140 miles southeast of Fort Mohave on the Colorado, and about 400 miles west of the Rio Grande at Albuquerque. It is very near mid-way between the Rio Grande and the Pacific Ocean at Los Angeles. There is an abundance of water, the richest grass in every direction, timber some twenty miles away, and firewood within a mile or two. At present the post

---

[1] The first territorial capital was established temporarily at Del Rio Springs in the Chino valley. It does not seem to have been called Fort Whipple, although it was referred to as such in the *Arizona Miner*. In 1864, when the government and the military moved to Prescott, Robert Postle, an officer, remained at this site. The Postle Ranch was well known to travelers and later was acquired by the Fred Harvey interests. (Byrd H. Granger, *Arizona Place Names,* p. 342; *Arizona Miner,* March 9, 1864.)

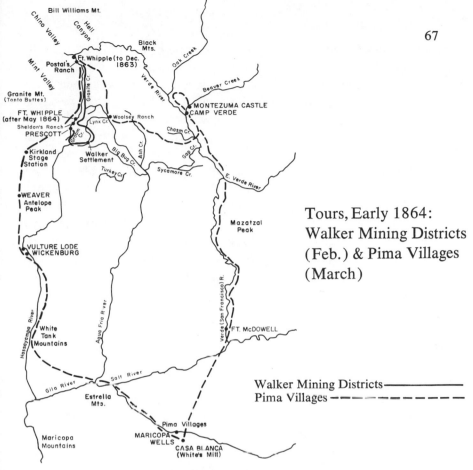

Tours, Early 1864:
Walker Mining Districts
(Feb.) & Pima Villages
(March)

Walker Mining Districts————————
Pima Villages —·—·——·——·——·—

is little more than a permanent camp; quite a respectable building is finished for the company storehouse, and a corral for the stock.

Deer and antelope are very plenty in every direction, and within three miles is the head of one of the branches of the San Francisco river, where beaver dams form a succession of ponds that are literally filled with fish. On the maps this valley is called Val de Chine; here it is called Cienaga.[2] It is so pure in this country that there is no such thing as decomposition; dead animals and the offal that surrounds camps here simply dry up without offensive smell. The air is so transparent that you are continually deceived as to distances; mountains a hundred miles away seem close at hand, and seem draped with a rich purple haze that conceals their ragged barren sides. About

[2]Val de Chine or the Chino valley was named by Whipple because of its lush grama grass, which the Mexicans called *de china*. The name *Cienga* (Marsh) was later applied to another ranch and creek located between Camp Verde and Prescott. (Granger, *Arizona Place Names*, p. 338.)

fifteen miles from the post is an isolated pile of red granite, perhaps
a thousand feet high, that from here is a most beautiful warmly-tinted
mountain, apparently only three or four miles away; when near it, it
appears barren, rough, and really a great deal lower than it seems
here.

The permanent garrison of the post consists of two companies
of California infantry and a detachment of cavalry, which with the
escort that came through with us makes quite a formidable array of
force, at least the Indians think so. The Indians immediately about
here are the Tontos, or fool Apaches, the meanest and dirtiest Indians
I have seen yet. Soon after my arrival a hundred or more of them
came in to hold a council with Major Willis, the commanding officer,
and I think I never saw a more miserable set of human beings. In
addition to the Tontos, the surrounding country is swept by the warlike Apaches of the country east. Stock is not safe anywhere, either
in the mines or on the ranches; it has to be watched carefully in the
day-time, and corraled at night. These repeated depredations have
so thoroughly aroused the animosity of the settlers that a war of
extermination has in fact already begun. Indians are shot wherever
seen, and quite recently a party of whites went into the country east
on a scout, and failing to find the Indians at a safely accessible place,
invited them in to a council, gave them food, and while they were
eating, at a given time fired on them, killing some thirty. But one
white man was killed, he having missed his Indian, the Indian killed
him with a lance. This Indian, however did not escape, being almost
instantly killed.

It will readily be imagined that this sort of a warfare is not
likely to make the country very safe for white men at present. Perhaps
it is the only way to deal with Indians; at any rate the settlers think
so, and once begun it is too late to go back.

I have spent several days in the mines[3] this week. We started
with a couple of ambulances last Tuesday, taking our bedding, a few
provisions, arms, &c. A fine road leads over the rolling prairie

---

[3] These mines were those of Lynx Creek, Big Bug, Turkey, Agua Fria,
Groom Creek, and the Hassayampa. Placer gold mining had developed there
in 1863. Deposits were discovered by the Joseph Reddeford Walker party and
others in the Prescott area. The surface placers were largely exhausted by
1864, although deep shaft mining continued for many years. These mines
were a primary reason for the location of the capital at Prescott. (Harwood
Hinton, "Frontier Speculation; The Walker Mining Districts," pp. 245–53;
Otis E. Young, *Western Mining,* pp. 144–45.)

country for about twenty miles when we came to the first settlement, on Granite creek. The log cabin was not quite finished, and the three or four men here were living in their wagon bodies. Some five miles up the creek, through a beautiful valley, brought us to Sheldon's ranche,[4] where we remained for the night. This is so far as wagons go at present. Sheldon has a large roomy cabin, with a grand, large fire place, one table, two rough beds and some seats; a large strong *corral* of logs set on end with a huge gate immediately adjoining the cabin door, so that if the Indians try to run off the stock they have to come right in front of the cabin. Saddles, bridles, rifles, pistols, and venison were hung all over the walls inside and out; there was no window, the door and chimney letting in enough day light.

It was near sundown and the herd was just being driven in. The shadows of the mountains were stretching over the valley and the last rays of the sun played prettily in the tree tops on the opposite hills. A group of men stood near the door, tall, stalwart, symmetrical men, roughly dressed, with intelligent, handsome faces. We met a cordial welcome and eager inquiries passed for the news. Had the mail got in at the post? Heard anything from California? What about the Indians? See any sign on the road? Sign is footprints or other indications of red-skin presence. These and other queries are rapidly put, while you are getting in by the fire. Meanwhile fresh wood is heaped on, and the coffee-pot is put on the coals. As the water boils and the venison begins to fry, the conversation continues of horses stolen and tracked, new quartz lodes discovered, some rich crevice or pocket hit by a lucky placer miner.

By this time supper is nearly ready; the single table is moved into the center of the room, and the tin plates and cups spread out, two huge piles, one of bread and the other of fried venison, are the central figures on the table, and in less time than it takes to write it as many hungry men as there were plates are seated around. — What appetites you get, out in the open air. I used to have a foolish prejudice that it wasn't best to see cooking if you wanted to enjoy a dinner, but now I think, watching the slow process, for it always seems slow, only gives a keener zest to the appetite. Four times the table

---

[4]James G. Sheldon, a pioneer with the Walker party, established a cattle and farming ranch in 1861, located about a mile south of Whipple near Prescott. The house was a stout, windowless log affair with attached log corral. Sheldon was well known for his open-handed generosity to travelers. He was killed by Indians in 1869. (Pauline Henson, *Wilderness Capital: Prescott, A.T., 1864*, pp. 122–23, 152, 154, 162, 173–74n.)

was re-set before the entire number of persons who happened there for the night were fed, the plates and cups had to be washed each time, and the cook was busy all the time. I do not believe they required a single cent from any one, I know they refused to allow us to compensate them for our entertainment, and if this isn't hospitality, especially when you recollect that flour is worth thirty dollars per hundred and bacon from 50 to 60 cents a lb., payable in gold, I don't know what it is!

The Governor is meditating an exploring trip from the country east of here, reputed to be rich in minerals and agricultural resources. This is a portion of the country so infested with Apaches that prospecting has been impossible. During the evening persons were constantly coming in who wished to join the party, one and all believing and talking of nothing but killing Indians. It is difficult to convey to you an adequate idea of the intensity of this feeling. A miner seems to regard an Indian as he would a rattlesnake.

At bed time every one makes his own bed, either on the floor or the ground outside, and in a few minutes all were soundly asleep. Next morning we were up with the sun; the herd was driven out to graze, accompanied by an armed mounted man. So insecure is stock in the mines that the miners hire their animals herded at the ranches. Breakfast over, preparations for our further trip began. Very few of our mules had ever been under saddle, and none had been packed. We however made up the packs of our bedding, provisions, &c., and placed them on one who fortunately proved docile; indeed, she seemed to like carrying a load that way better than working in harness. This packing a mule is considerable of an art; to get the load properly balanced, sufficiently strongly lashed, &c., is very difficult for a tyro.

It was quite nine o'clock when we got under way, seven of us mounted on mules and the pack animal. A little Indian boy, a Navajo's captive, whose life Major Willis saved some four months ago, and who has remained with the Major ever since, refusing to return to his own people, whom we had determined to leave here until our return, looked so sorrowful and lonesome that the Major relented, and allowed him to get up behind him on his mule. So off we went, Indian file, on the trail, a light-hearted merry party; indeed it is difficult to be otherwise in such a climate as this; Annache, (I spell this as near to the sound as I can,) the Navajo, all beaming with pleasure.

These young Navajo captives are exceedingly interesting. You
see a great many of them in New Mexico. I always took the story of
their unwillingness to return with some grains of allowance, but in
the present instance I know it. Maj. Willis says he has never known
him to show any signs of homesickness, save once, when he was
badly beaten by a little Mexican boy of the same age, some twelve
years, at a foot race, and afterwards in wrestling; the truth being that
Annache, from high living, had grown so fat that he couldn't run
as he used to. He is the best natured boy I ever saw, and the most
willing, but he can't learn English, although he tries hard. Dressed
in a miniature suit of soldier clothes, you have to look twice to know
he is an Indian. There is one little trait that he always retains, that
of laughing at every accident, no matter how serious. If I hear him
laughing, I am sure something has gone wrong, somebody's horse
stumbled, the pack mule got stuck between trees, or an ambulance
stuck. It seems as though he couldn't help it. He is most devotedly
attached to the Major, and sticks to him like his shadow, watching
every motion and noting the slightest wish indicated by a gesture.

The trail wound up a beautiful little valley sprinkled with
timber, the wild grape vines growing luxuriantly on the side. About
six miles of hilly road brought us to the gulch. A gulch is a rocky
ravine or valley, or in this case something between the two. Here we
struck our first miner's cabin. I rode over to it; there was a fire burning and a pot boiling on it. The cabin consisted of two upright poles
supporting a ridge pole from which boughs and poles stretched to
the ground on one side, the other being open; in front was a stone
fire place. No person came in sight. I lighted my pipe and rode on.
The trail winds along the sides of the gulch, rarely completely leaving the creek, in which was a moderate supply of running water. It
passes over steep and craggy hills, covered with timber. Miners were
at work down on the edges of the stream, and cabins made of logs
and quite roomy became more frequent. Six miles of the climbing
brought us to Captain Walker's camp, as it is called, being a collection of log houses with one store, on the site of the original camp
made by the first party led to this country by Capt. Walker,[5] about

---

[5]Captain Walker or Joseph Reddeford Walker (1798–1872) was one
of the most famed of the mountain men. His first trapping expedition was
made about 1820 to the Rockies and the Southwest. It was on this trip that
he gained the title Captain, the result of aid given to the Mexicans against
the Indians. In the 1820s and 1830s he helped to pioneer many of the emi-

a year ago. We rode up to the store, unsaddled, deposited our arms and other traps within, picketed our mules on the mountain side, shook hands with all the people about, answered and asked questions. The Governor's arrival created some little sensation of course.

After resting a few minutes, we started to call on Capt. Walker, whose cabin was across the creek a short distance. I had met the old gentleman before at the post when I first arrived, and he greeted me kindly. Presenting the rest of our party to him, we entered his cabin, and after a toddy the conversation became brisk.

Leaving the party here, a brief, very brief, resumé of the adventures of the Walker party in finding the place may not be out of place. Capt. Walker is over sixty, and is getting somewhat infirm; in personal appearance he reminds me more of the secretary of the navy than any man I have ever seen; he has the same beard, wears glasses, and his height and build is that of Mr. Welles.[6] In manner he is not unlike him. Capt. W. has spent his life on the mountains, and knows them as well, if not better, than any man living. His memory is wonderful of the geography and topography of portions of the country he has not seen for thirty years. Very recently this has been markedly tested. It seems that nearly thirty years ago he was leading a party toward the Little Colorado; they had been some time out of water, and after dark they came suddenly upon a chasm that when descended proved to contain running water. With great difficulty the animals were got down and watered. When morning came it proved they were within one-quarter of a mile of the falls of the Little Colorado, above which they could have crossed easily. At the falls the river plunges into a canon, from which it is not known to emerge. In '49, when gold first began to be found in California,

---

grant trails, ventured into California, and made the first Anglo discovery of Yosemite (1833). His initial visit to Arizona occurred in 1837–38, and in the 1850s he served as a guide and railroad surveyor. In 1863 he led the well known Walker party to Hassayampa Creek and discovered gold. (Hinton, "Walker Mining Districts," pp. 245–53.) Walker was described as six feet tall, "strong built . . . dark complexioned . . . brave in spirit." (Le Roy Reuben Hafen, *The Mountain Men and the Fur Trade of the Far West* 5:363. See also Donald J. Berthrong and Odessa Davenport, *Joseph Reddeford Walker and the Arizona Adventure*.)

[6] Gideon Welles was Allyn's Hartford friend and secretary of the navy, who later recommended Allyn for the governorship of Arizona.

Allyn's obvious regard for Joseph Reddeford Walker may have been partially due to
the fact that the mountain man reminded
him of his good friend Secretary of the
Navy Gideon Welles.

some specimens were shown to one of the men[7] who happened to
be with the party which stumbled into the canon. If that's gold, said
he, I can show you where you can load mules with it. He believed
that he had seen gold in that canon. Various attempts were made
to organize parties under his lead to go to this point, and two actually got under way, but some of the accidents peculiar to gold countries prevented their success. At last this man died, and, dying,
particularly charged that this attempt should be renewed, and recommended Walker as the person to lead them.

Two years and a half ago Capt. W. and a party started for the
falls. They reached the place without serious mishap and found
there was no gold, the men having been probably deceived by copper. Capt. W. was sanguine there was gold farther south and wished
to try and find it. They had not provisions enough, and the question

[7]This was probably Jack Ralston, who had been part of the Walker
party, which had penetrated the area of the Little Colorado. Ralston convinced
George Lount that the Little Colorado was rich in gold after seeing some
specimens of California ores. An 1858 expedition was abortive, then in 1861
Lount and other prospectors reached the area but found no gold. (Henson,
Wilderness Capital, pp. 43–44.)

was whether to go back to California or forward to the Rio Grande. It was determined to go to Albuquerque and refit. They went to Albuquerque, over the same road we came out, the falls being about fifty miles on beyond where we left the river at Canon Diablo. They reached the Rio Grande just at the time the Texan advance was showing the imbecility of the military commander, the treason of the American population of New Mexico, and the general loyalty of the Mexicans.[8] Everybody fled north to Fort Union, the Texans taking Santa Fe. Capt. Walker went on to Denver, and most of the party went to work in the mines in Colorado Territory.

A year ago they again started and proceeded down the Rio Grande to the Mesilla valley,[9] thence they crossed the Gila, and overcoming all sorts of difficulties, dangers, and delays, got through to the Pima villages.[10] Here they turned north, penetrated these nameless mountains, and found the object of their long and weary pilgrimage. A journey of over two thousand miles, most of it through a country almost unknown, occupying nearly three years, can scarcely be paralleled in the annals of private enterprise, and when you recollect that there is no other than a voluntary obedience to the authority of the leader in such parties, it is certainly striking testimony to the ability of Walker that he kept it together.

Leaving Walker's cabin we returned to the store and dined. After dinner, spent the afternoon among the miners.[11] I hardly know

---

[8] The Confederate army of New Mexico advanced from Texas under Brigadier General H. H. Sibley in 1861 and 1862. The conquest of Union posts and territory was accomplished with embarrassing ease and notable federal incompetence. Fort Union, under Major Donaldson, however, was saved by the timely arrival of a northern expedition. In March 1862, Colorado Union volunteers bolstered General Canby's battered federal forces and decisively defeated the Confederates. (Martin Hardwick Hall, *Sibley's New Mexican Campaign*, pp. 29–160.) Arizona had been declared a Confederate territory in February 1862. (Rufus Kay Wyllys, *Arizona: The History of a Frontier State*, p. 143ff.)

[9] The Mesilla valley of New Mexico includes the area around Las Cruces. (T. M. Pearce, *New Mexico Place Names*, p. 100.)

[10] The Pima villages were a series of settlements inhabited by the farming Pima tribes. Some of the communities have survived on the Pima Indian reservation. Pima territory was concentrated along the Gila, just west, and about fifteen miles south of present-day Phoenix. The villages were well known to early travelers, owing to their extraordinary friendliness and hospitality to Americans. (Frank Russell, *The Pima Indians*, pp. 30–33.)

[11] This camp of Captain Walker's, also known as Walker's Gulch, was founded on Lynx Creek in 1863. The settlement later known as Walker is now a ghost town. (Granger, *Arizona Place Names*, p. 361.) Walker's first discoveries were on the eastern tributary of the Hassayampa known as Ookilsipava Creek. (Hinton, "Walker Mining Districts," pp. 246–49.)

what placer-mining is like; great square holes or shafts are sunk in
or near the bed of the creek where there is water, ultimately down
to the bedrock, and the miner is at work breaking the rock and
throwing up the dirt from the bottom to where the rocker is; the
rocker is a succession of sieves or boxes on rockers; the original dirt
is thrown on top and the machine washes back and forth while
water is poured on; the larger stones are left on top and the earth
and dust works through and falls on to another sieve, where it is
still further separated; finally the black sand plentifully sparkling
with yellow is thrown into a pan. It is quite a matter of dexterity to
work out a pan of earth; you dip it into water and keep shaking it
so that the particles may be separated and the gold by its specific
gravity sink to the bottom. One accustomed to it does it in a few
minutes without losing any gold. Of course this is mining in its most
primitive shape, altho' many here haven't even the rocker, panning
the earth just as they dig it out.

Mining here as everywhere is uncertain business. You strike
a crevice, or pocket, and you get a hundred dollars out of a single
pan; the man alongside may be getting perhaps ten cents a pan. In
California with plenty of water and machinery one cent a pan makes
a very valuable claim. While we were here a man took sixty dollars
out of a single pan from an abandoned claim right in front of the
store, that he had paid forty dollars for. Afterwards I watched him
panning out two pans on the same claim; the first paid twenty cents,
the second a dollar and ten cents. While patience and industry bring
their reward in mining as in everything else, the element of chance
or luck plays a much more conspicuous part in it than in most of the
other pursuits of life, and this is the real element that makes mining
so fascinating. I should judge that the work was harder than that
of the ordinary laborer at the east; it is certainly more disagreeable,
down in mud and water, shut out from much sunlight. Even in the
mild climate, only four or five hours a day are suitable for work. The
water freezes hard at night and it is scarcely thawed out at eleven
o'clock, and it gets too cold to work it before sundown. On this gulch
one claim is pretty much like another in general appearance, only
differing in the size of the shaft. There isn't water enough for the
extensive works one hears of in California.

It is difficult to estimate the average results of mining labor
here, but from the general tone of talk I think men who work make
from ten to twenty dollars a day. The last claim taken on the gulch

has proved infinitely the richest; the owner, Mr. Coulter,[12] has already realized a handsome fortune and remitted it to California. We were at his cabin; he said most of his gold was cached where we wouldn't want him to get it; but he would show us some; just slipping his table one side, right under the leg, he poked aside the dirt and produced a little tin canister holding five or six hundred dollars; saying, that next time we came it wouldn't be there. There were some quite large lumps, as large as walnuts for instance, among what he showed us.

There are more prospecters than miners on the gulch, and large stories are told about the rich indications of quartz all about the country. The stock of flour and bacon on hand here is exceedingly small, and should not a train come in soon prices may go high; venison, beef, and mutton are plentiful and worth only 12½ cents a pound.

In the evening there was quite a gathering at the store, and the governor in a brief speech took all by storm by advocating the extermination of the Indians. King Woolsey,[13] the leader of the scout that resulted in the killing of the large number alluded to before, was present. He is a small, well-knit, handsome man, and the last person you would pick out for the hero of such an affair. He says the chief of the Apaches when he came in wanted him, Woolsey, to brush the dirt off for him to sit on, and that it was hard to control himself; he

[12] George Wilson Coulter (1818–1901?), sometimes known as "General" was a native of Pennsylvania, married, and the father of five sons and a daughter. He served for a year with the Missouri Mounted Infantry in the Mexican War. After his discharge in Santa Fe, Coulter went to California, engaged in mining, and founded Coulterville. In 1863 he was a member of the Walker party and had several claims on Lynx Creek. (Arizona Historical Society Biographical File; *Arizona Miner,* June 19, 1866, June 12, 1869.)

[13] King S. Woolsey (1832–79), a native of Alabama, was a member of Captain Walker's party. He mined along Lynx Creek, and his ranch on the Agua Fria River was near the present-day town of Mayer. Woolsey led expeditions against the Indians in the Prescott area and elsewhere in January, March, and June of 1864. His most famous exploit involved the massacre in January of Tontos and other Apaches at "Bloody Tanks" near the modern town of Miami in Gila County. Apache mistrust of Anglos stemmed in part from this incident. Woolsey's policy toward the Indians is stated in a letter to General Carleton, "I fight on the broad platform of extermination." (Typescript of letter to General James H. Carleton from King S. Woolsey, Lt. Col., Arizona Volunteers, March 29, 1864, in the Arizona Historical Society Files.) Woolsey was also prominent in state politics. (Clara T. Woody, "The Woolsey Expedition of 1864"; James A. Barney, "Col. King S. Woolsey, Famous Arizona Pioneer.")

gave the Indian a blanket to sit on but he never rose from it! Woolsey is the proprietor of a large rancho on the Agua Fria, about 14 miles from the mines. It is the very outpost of the line of settlement, and he has suffered much from depredations. There is much talk of a large party under Woolsey accompanying the governor's expedition east in order to fight the Indians. The only difficulty is rations and ammunition, but for this you would think every man would go, either to prospect or to hunt Indians.

The belief in the mineral wealth of the country east rises to the confidence of faith in every man I have seen. In general appearance these miners are a striking body of men. I think I never saw as many handsome men in the same number before; they are all fine specimens of the physical man, and with a single exception all were Americans. They are quick, intelligent, shrewd men, and very many had superior educations. I saw one woman in the creek; she was a Mexican and came out from the Rio Grande with Major Willis's party.

Next morning we started over the mountain to Hassayampa Creek under the guidance of a Mr. Smith, who told me he was once a clerk in Day, Griswold & Co. in Hartford.[14] He is a man of influence among the miners and interested in some valuable quartz lodes. The trail was very steep up the ascent; near the top we left it and climbed to the top on foot to get a view of the country. The view was an extensive panoramic one, swept to the San Francisco mountain on the north and to the range on the east that shuts out the valley of the San Francisco or the Rio Verde rivers.[15] The country is rugged and broken with occasional *cienagas* surrounded with rich

[14] Van C. Smith was at this time the recorder for the mining district. (See Henson, *Wilderness Capital*, pp. 59, 124.) The firm Allyn mentions was actually two companies — C. G. Day & Co. and H. Griswold & Co. Both were prominent textile-producing establishments in Hartford and Griswold respectively. Early in the Civil War, Connecticut's quartermaster and adjutant general were dismissed on charges of having favored these and other Baptist-owned firms with fat war contracts. (John Niven, *Connecticut for the Union*, p. 366n.)

[15] The Verde River was known as the King's River by the Spanish. It was called the San Francisco on the Disturnell map of 1847, the Bill Williams Fork by Whipple (1853). Indians called it the Green, due to malachite on its banks, and the name was translated to *Rio Verde* by the Spaniards and Mexicans. (Granger, *Arizona Place Names*, p. 361.) The range "that shuts out the valley of the San Francisco" was Mingus Mountain above the city of Jerome.

pasture land. It looks as though the trip east would be a rough one, but with pack animals you can go almost anywhere. A couple of hours slow riding over hills, and most charming scenery, brought us at last to the Hassayampa, in a deep gorge, where the sun shines but a few hours. The mountains south all had snow on the sides. Near where the trail debouched was a small cabin, the owner, however, absent. We camped here under some fine old trees and ate with great relish a cold lunch. There is more water here than at Walker's, and it was clear and cold.

After lunch we went up the creek a mile or two on foot, passing several cabins, and many unworked claims. On a hill to the right are the ruins[16] of an extensive stone house and corral; the walls are built in the same manner as those ruins on the top of Inscription Rock. These buildings have been so long in ruins that the earth fills up about halfway up the rooms, and large pine trees, one hundred and fifty feet high, are growing in the center. Near by are many piles of broken quartz, showing that somebody prospected there before the present parties were in the country, but whether twenty or two hundred years ago you cannot tell.

It is the universal opinion of the miners that the placers here have been worked before. There is no particular agricultural temptation for such a settlement as the ruins indicate, and I should think the balance of probability was that whoever built them was there for the precious metals. Yet I think the quartz was broken long since the buildings were in ruins, and very probably by some party from Sonora that we have never heard of.[17]

During the evening quite a number of miners came to our camp, and the universal testimony was that the placers were not worth working there; twenty miles below they said some parties were doing well, and that the quartz lodes were as rich as any in the world. Next

---

[16]Anthropologist Robert Euler of Prescott College states that these nameless ruins have never been adequately examined but that they should probably be dated twelfth century or earlier and that they were probably abandoned in the fourteenth century. (Interview, November 26, 1971, Museum of Northern Arizona, Flagstaff.)

[17]Miners from northwestern Mexico had been active in Arizona, but the Apache menace tended to confine their mining activities to southern areas, where the Spanish and Mexican military presence could provide some protection. (James H. McClintock, *Arizona: Aboriginal, Pioneer, Prehistoric, Modern* I: 101–2.)

morning we crossed a spur of the mountain about three miles to a branch of the creek on which is the cabin of Mr. Croame,[18] the recorder of the district, who has quite an extensive cabinet of quartz specimens from the different lodes, which he believes to be rich in gold and silver; samples have been sent to San Francisco, but the returns have not come to hand. There is no question about the abundance of quartz in the mountains; it only remains to demonstrate its richness, and this country will be developed like magic.[19]

From this point we followed the trail back to Granite creek, about seven miles, over a hilly country, covered with timber, and came out at an embryo town called Granite City.[20] It is beautifully situated where the valley widens, there are three log stores owned by Mexicans, and three or four houses. Here we were treated to an abundance of champagne, in the usual Mexican style. I suppose they were not unwilling to have the first legislature called here. From thence a couple of miles brought us back to Sheldon's, where we spent the night, returning to the post in the morning.

---

[18] "Croame" is Allyn's misspelling of the name Robert W. Groom, the first recorder of the Hassayampa Mining District established on December 6, 1863. (Henson, *Wilderness Capital*, p. 60.)

[19] The placers of the Hassayampa and Groom and Lynx creeks yielded fairly substantial treasure, although their development was dominated by speculators and later by some of the territorial officials, including the governor and McCormick. Allyn does not seem to have dabbled in the mines himself.

When the placers were worked out by the mid-1860s, miners turned to the more costly hard-rock lodes located on the slopes of Davis, Spruce, and Union southeast of Prescott. Many of these mines continued to be worked well into the twentieth century. They were profitable though not of bonanza quality. The value of their ores was depreciated by the high cost of transport and the scarcity of water. (Hinton, "Walker Mining Districts," p. 3; Henson, *Wilderness Capital*, pp. 124–25; Young, *Western Mining*, p. 144.)

[20] Granite City was an early name for Prescott suggested by the local granitic geology. (*Arizona Miner*, July 20, 1864; Granger, *Arizona Place Names*, p. 355.)

Letter 5

AN EXPEDITION OF DISCOVERY —
TRIUMPH OF THE SPENCER RIFLE —
INDIAN FIGHTING AND EXCITING ADVENTURES

Pima Villages, Arizona
March 16, 1864
[Published April 26, 1864; April 30, 1864]

My last, if it reached you, fully described a trip to a portion of the new gold fields, and informed you of a projected exploration of the country lying east of Fort Whipple, in the valleys of the Rio Verde or San Francisco and Salinas or Salt rivers, occupied by hostile Indians.[1] The object of the expedition being the finding of a more suitable place for the permanent location of Fort Whipple, the development of the mineral and agricultural resources of the country, and on the part of the citizens designing to accompany the party, the punishment of the Indians that had been committing depredations on the settlements. Our preparations were completed, and the 11th of February was designated as the day of departure from the post. For a day or two before it had been cloudy and windy, so that anyone else would have been certain a severe storm was gathering, but in this rainless country few of us feared it.

Just as the advance of the party was mounted, ready to start, it commenced raining smartly, and our departure was countermanded. It rained unceasingly two days and one night, and then turned to snow which fell to the depth of several inches. When it cleared off, the ground was so soft that animals mired at once, and in consequence we were detained until the 18th. It was hoped that

---

[1] This is the only letter of this series actually written while traveling. Letters 6, 7, 8, 9, and 10, describing the rest of the expedition, were written after Allyn's return to Fort Whipple.

the storm had commenced soon enough below to prevent the rendez-
vousing of the citizens at Woolsey's.[2]

On the 18th we started with some fifty soldiers as an escort, a
dozen or so cavalry men, the rest infantry, and a train of pack mules.
The command only made fifteen miles the first day, making a dry
camp, the animals much exhausted, as the ground was not yet hard,
and the American horses and mules were all those brought with us
from the states, unacclimated, accustomed to corn; at the post there
is nothing but grass, and that of course is poorer at this season of
the year than at any other time.

Major Willis and myself rode through to Woolsey's that night,
and found some dozen or fifteen citizens waiting, who had most of
them been there the whole week. They were wearied with waiting,
and cordially welcomed us. Thirty miles ride, part of it after sundown, usually sharpens appetites, and my impression is that I do not
exaggerate when I say that a large quantity of venison was speedily
consumed.

Woolsey's rancho is called the Agua Fria and is upon one of
the bends of this waterless stream that runs to the Gila parallel to
the Rio Verde; it is situated just above a deep-cut canon upon a
cienaga and upon the site of an extensive Aztec ruin which furnishes
the materials for the two large loop-holed houses, and wall breast-
high that encircles them.[3] Water is reached easily by sinking wells,
and one is dug within the enclosure. The land near the *cienaga*, Mr.
W. believes, can be cultivated without irrigation, and it is now being
plowed; the soil turned up looks very rich. Woolsey's is the outpost
settlement, and the Indians have twice stripped him of stock.

---

[2]This party of citizens was representative of the human flotsam and
jetsam common to mining camps of the time. Possibly some of the members
had heard of the governor's expedition during the evening of conviviality at
Sheldon's ranch described in Letter 4. Besides searching for Indians to kill,
these men were out to find rich farmland, grassy range, or gold.

The expedition made its way across the Black Mountains and then very
likely down what is now known as Chasm Canyon. The exploration of a
month or so found Indians but no gold, although the area was to produce rich
mines in later times. (Pauline Henson, *Wilderness Capital, Prescott, A.T., 1864*,
pp. 127, 128, 132; Department of the Interior Geological Survey map of
Prescott, Arizona.)

[3]The reference to Aztec ruins was in accord with the widely held view
of the times that the Aztecs had originally come from this region. See Letter
10, note 7, for McCormick's views on this. Hubert Howe Bancroft, *History
of Arizona and New Mexico, 1530–1888*, pp. 4–5; William H. Prescott, *History of the Conquest of Mexico and Peru*, p. 15.)

The new stone houses were covered with dirt roofs, admirable in a dry climate, but not calculated for long storms like the one of last week. Mrs. Woolsey gave me a most ludicrous account of their miseries, not alone that the roof leaked, but it leaked dirty water and mud, and was no respecter of persons or things in dropping either. The citizens were camped outside in some willows. Major Willis and myself slept on the stone floor of one of the houses, with an abundance of blankets, however. As the room we slept in was kitchen and dining room, we were roused by sunrise, and I had an opportunity of learning that castes and distinctions of social rank had quite as full play out here in the wilderness, as in the statelier mansions of Beacon Street or the 5th Avenue. Capt. Walker slept here with us, and the first thing he did was to concoct a toddy which, notwithstanding my New England Maine law education, I confess I relished. It was quite chilly, and lighting my pipe I sat down in the chimney corner, and chatted with the cook, a rough, blunt specimen of a mountain man, who evidently considered he was one of the main spokes in the wheel of this establishment.

Said he, "The meal I got for you last night was the sixteenth time that table was set yesterday." I asked how that could be. How many there were on the place, etc.

"O, there's not many folks here," said he, "but they don't eat together. First, there's the black men, i.e. Mexicans, the herders; then there's the white men, i.e. the carpenters, masons, etc.; then there's Mr. King, i.e. Woolsey and his friends; and last, I and my family."

"What the deuce is your family?"

"O, my family is me, the Indian girl, an Apache captive, who is the personal attendant of Mrs. W., and the dogs."

By this time the chimney began to smoke, and listening to the maledictions of the cook on the boys who built the chimney too large, I escaped into the open air to see the sun creeping over the mountains, crimsoning the valley, the little smokes in the willows showing the citizens were stirring, the herd in the corral ready as soon as the herders got their breakfast to go out for the day, and the little Apache girl gathering wood to make her mistress's fire. The contrast between the temperature before day and during the day here is wonderful; water freezes almost solid in the night, and at 2 o'clock the thermometer will mark from 80 to 90.

Judge Allyn introduced Arizona frontiersmen to the Spencer seven-shot carbine rifle, a gun which was proving invaluable to the North in the Civil War. "I could have sold a dozen on the spot at very near a hundred dollars in gold apiece," the young judge comments.

Soon this little frontier establishment was all alive, the herd was moving afield, workingmen busy laying walls, and digging wells, the plough was moving through the soft soil, and a wagon was ready to go after fuel which has to be brought several miles. At noon Gov. Goodwin and the advance rode in, and by sundown the whole party was gathered in, and camped in the willows.

We rested the next day to arrange details, fit pack saddles, assort and equalize packs, etc. The note of preparation was heard everywhere, mules being shod, saddles and bridles repaired, balls cast and cartridges made. The citizens were trying their long rifles at a mark at about a hundred yards. It was a small board painted black, with a bit of white paper, an inch square, in the center. All frontiersmen are curious about new weapons, and at the same time prejudiced against them. The fame of my seven shooter, the Spencer, had got abroad, and they wanted to see it shoot.[4] I didn't much like to waste ammunition when no more can be got, and to tell the truth I had no great confidence in my marksmanship to do justice to the weapon. I never fired a rifle in my life until I left the Missouri, and I never fired anything but the Spencer. This last gave me great advantage, for the weight in the Spencer is very different from any other, and usually annoys a stranger in firing it at first. I advanced into the ring, and at the first shot had the good luck to hit the paper in the center and split the board. I concluded it was not best to try again, and others fired off the other shots.

As a weapon for fighting Indians the Spencer has no superior. Its seven shots can be loaded in less time than any other rifle can be

---

[4] The Spencer seven-shot carbine rifle was just coming into use in the Civil War. It brought a revolution in infantry tactics, for it proved to be murderous when used against the advancing close-ranked Confederates. It saved the day for Union units at Olustee in northern Florida and elsewhere on many occasions. (John Niven, *Connecticut for the Union*, pp. 180, 182, 358.)

loaded and capped, it can be fired more rapidly than a revolver, and re-loaded in a tenth of the time it would take to re-load a Colt; in fact, in an Indian fight, close quarters, I think a revolver never was re-loaded. The fixed ammunition has immense advantages, as soon as it can be easily obtained, say at San Francisco even, for it never wastes, and cannot be injured by transportation. So completely were the soldiers and citizens convinced of this that I could have sold a dozen on the spot with two or three hundred rounds of ammunition each, at very near a hundred dollars in gold pieces, if I had had them.

On Sunday, the 21st, we started about sunrise and made about fifteen miles over an Indian trail, upon which a portion, at least, of the stolen stock had been driven. There was no particularly difficult road this day, but our animals, unaccustomed to packing, were difficult to keep in order, some trotting furiously ahead, others hanging back, some shaking their packs off, or nearly so, for our soldiers were about as green at packing as the mules. The day was fine, everybody was in good spirits, and we hoped soon to get the machine in good working order. This travelling with pack animals is about the perfection of independence; you can go anywhere, and you can go rapidly; of course you have to dispense with tents, mattresses, and much crockery, or a great variety of cooking utensils, but in this climate you don't want the tent, and if you are luxuriously inclined there are boughs and grass enough to make soft beds. We camped quite early, and loafed away the afternoon under improvised shades of blankets, listening to the gossip of old mountaineers.

I have described Capt. Walker to you before: a cool, reticent, courteous man, careful what he says, and impatient of contradiction. Captain Weaver, from California, a man older than Walker, who led a party into the mines about the same time that Walker came from the Rio Grande and settled at Antelope and on the lower Hassayampa, is also with us; and he is the opposite of Walker in every respect; garrulous to a fault, tells large stories until he has the reputation of a sort of Arizona Münchhausen, impulsive, and with a failing memory.[5] Walker and Weaver are both old trappers, and had

---

[5]A famous mountaineer and onetime Hudson Bay trapper, Pauline Weaver was a discoverer of many of the gold regions, including Colorado River, La Paz, and Granite Creek. He does not seem to have become rich himself, however. He was considered to be the first settler and miner on the site of Prescott. Though he led parties of prospectors to Arizona in the early

both explored all the mountain streams for beaver twenty years ago, but neither know anything about the country between them. They looked for beaver, not gold or silver of rich valleys. Then there is Woolsey, in the prime of life, brave as a lion, quick eyed as an Indian, and thirsting for revenge. In his party are men from Washoe, now Nevada, who prospected the rich silver lodes there before they were famous;[6] from the head waters of the Columbia in Idaho, who have worked in the rich placers near Bannock City, and disliking the fierce winters of the north, hope to find here equal mineral wealth, that can be got out all the year; old Californians with yarns of '49 and '50, when the pistol and bowie-knife were judge and jury.

Next day we followed the tract farther and camped at Ash Spring.[7] We were now in a country where no white man is known to have been before. We made some ten miles today, about half of it up a rocky canon. At night the wind blew fiercely, but we slept soundly under the shelter of bushes. Directly to the east of us was apparently a low pass in the mountains that would take us directly to the Rio Verde.[8] On Tuesday we went a mile or two on the trail and messed at the mouth of a canon. We bore south to cross and expected to find an easy path to the river. We crossed two canons, working south, and striking one heading north, followed it up to water, one mule giving out. Woolsey had been north of us on a scout on the Indian trail, found a practical road for wagons and had seen the sign of a large body of Indians going in toward the settlements. There was some excitement. Had the Indians seen us? Would they turn back if they had? Or would they think it more favorable for an

---

1860s, Weaver had visited the area as early as 1832. Late in his life he farmed and was a military pensioner. Tradition has it that he was an ex-army officer and was given a military burial by the Whipple detachment in the late 1860s. His grave is located on the grounds of the governor's mansion at Prescott. (Alpheus B. Favour, *Old Bill Williams, Mountain Man;* Sharlot M. Hall, *First Citizen of Prescott: Pauline Weaver, Trapper and Mountain Man.*)

[6] Washoe County, Nevada, was the setting for the Comstock Lode silver discoveries after 1859. Prospectors pushed up the slopes of Sun Peak and discovered first gold and then enormous quantities of silver. This became one of the greatest silver strikes in history and provided substantial financial aid to the Union cause in the Civil War. (Otis E. Young, *Western Mining*, pp. 234ff.)

[7] A number of places were so named because of the presence of ash trees, which were used for the making of bows and arrows by the Indians. Allyn was probably somewhere on Ash Creek, which flows near Mayer.

[8] This "low pass" can be seen today by looking east from the Mayer area toward Gap Peak.

assault and keep on? Conjecture was useless. Next morning we went
up the canon a half mile to where we could climb the side to the top,
where we saw the divide, being shaped like a horse shoe, smooth,
sloping toward us. We passed up on a clearly defined Indian trail
that had no sign of animals; a bad sign for us, for an Indian foot trail
almost invariably leads to jumps that an animal cannot make.

Over the divide the waters plunge into a canon more ragged
and precipitate than any we had yet seen — the trail led along the
north side about halfway up the mountain. On we went, barely getting footing to keep the animals from rolling headlong into the gulf
below. The rock was crumbling lava like that which is worked up
into jewelry at Naples, and of rich fawn colors. On one side was a
ragged mountain touching almost your elbow as you led your mule
along; on the other, from your feet almost perpendicular was a chasm,
the bottom you could not see, save in the tops of the tall trees that
fringed the stream whose rich music, as it plunged along, echoes
melodiously through the gorge.

Grand points of projecting mountains we would wind; what a
place for an assault; fifty Apaches could have annihilated us by
rattling down stones, for we had scarcely footing enough to take an
aim up. Suddenly, halt! rang along the line; every man and every
animal stopped where he was. The poor pack mules stood, the
crumbling lava under their feet giving way. Fortunately, I was near
the advance and right at the point of a projecting spur whence I
could see the whole party. I sat down, lighted the unfailing pipe,
looked at the fine specimens of lava, cut some with my penknife.
From the front word soon came that Woolsey and the advance had
reached one of their jumping-off places, a perfect *cul de sac*. They
had turned and worked down to the bottom, where they found the
stream so filled with driftwood, fallen trees, etc., that they could
not get over, and had sent back for an axe, which was passed on to
them. The pack animals had stood still an hour; something must be
done; turn round we could not. It was determined to try to climb
to the top diagonally, perhaps a way to get on would then be visible.
We got up with the train and had to go back to the head of the canon
and camp.

We hoped to hear from Woolsey if he got through. No word
coming in several hours, scouts were sent to the north. Weaver went
south, and a couple of citizens were sent on Woolsey's trail. From
the north they reported no route out. Weaver saw the sign of a large

body of Indians passing into the settlements. This added to our apprehension about the safety of the miners. The two men who went down into the canon did not get through to Woolsey, but found a way by which with some labor a trail could be made to the bottom, whence there appeared no further serious difficulty.

It was determined in the morning to try to go through. His party had no provisions, and it was evident they supposed we were coming on after them, or they would have sent back. Next morning we started and reached the bottom of the canon, over a trail made by a fatigue party ahead, without serious accident, and yet if mules were not immortal, or, at least, like cats, endowed with any number of lives, it could not have been done.

Those of us in advance led our animals to the bottom without much trouble, and there waited the descent of the train. Such a sight, mules stumbling and recovering themselves, mules with heavy packs rolling two or three hundred feet, first heels up, then packs, over and over, until they landed plump against a tree; stones following them seemingly large enough to crush them, which never happened to hit; one came so near doing it that it lodged like a shelf over a mule's head, and she could not get up until it was removed; and it took hard lifting of several men to do that.

At last all were gathered on the bed of the canon and we started on, crossing and recrossing the stream, over fallen trees, huge boulders, rolling stones; under branches of trees that threatened to serve us as Absalom once was; vast palisades of lava and granite piled up for hundreds of feet above us; the stream leaping from rock to rock until at last it plunged near a hundred feet, forming a beautiful cascade. Before reaching the river, the trail left the canon which turned south, and crossing a spur of mountains we came upon the camp of our pioneer party. Exhausted and hungry, they had caught a fish or two the night before, but had no salt to cook them with.

This camp was some little distance from the river. We proceeded to the bank and camped. The Verde here is a fine rushing stream, some fifty yards wide, and not fordable; it is dammed just below with drift wood. We have struck the river in the canon between the upper and lower valleys, and it will be difficult to get out.[9]

---

[9]Allyn's party appears to have descended either Gap Creek or Chasm Creek canyon. This was a pioneering expedition into the Verde, and Woolsey and the others were obviously unfamiliar with the terrain or they might have chosen to follow a more northerly route down the canyon.

Off to the south the country is volcanic, broken into canons and gulches, barren and desolate. A good many fish were caught today, tolerably good-sized and of good flavor.

To get out of the canon we had to go back to the hills, and in an hour we reached a point whence the upper country could be seen spread out as far as the eye could reach toward the San Francisco mountain. But intervening canons made it take us three hours more to reach the river at the lower end of the valley. We saw fresh Indian signs as we crossed the hills, and before we reached the valleys, signal smokes, on the hills around, were telegraphing our arrival. We unpacked when we struck the river and rested a few hours, and then went on to good grass a few miles farther up the stream. The terrible floods of two or three years ago have furrowed this valley with channels, paved it with smooth round stones, and strewn it with drift wood. The volume of water must have been immense, the stream there perhaps a mile wide. There is an abundance of cottonwood trees and mesquite bushes.

Near our camp that night an Indian came on the hills and hallooed at the guard; toward morning one was caught crawling through the bushes, near Lieut. Robinson's[10] bivouac; but both escaped. In the morning the tracks of several others were seen, that had been prowling around.

On Saturday, the 27th, Woolsey and a party crossed the river to look for trails east, and scout up the bank to join us in camp. The main party had gone on without much to note for some eight miles, when looking ahead, I was very near the advance. I saw Col. Chavez and Major Willis both spurring furiously ahead with drawn pistols and unslung rifles. I started as fast as I could after them, and was perhaps thirty or forty yards behind when they commenced firing at something. I had seen nothing. I rode up.

"Got your rifle?" I had lent it to cross the river.

"For God's sake get under cover, you'll get hit."

An arrow took Maj. Willis's horse right through the ear, and I saw a large stalwart Indian just falling back from the bank of the stream facing us, and discharging his arrows. Chavez had fired his rifle and was down in the willows firing his pistols. When they first came up, the Indian was on this side of the river and his squaw

---

[10] First Lieutenant Frank Robinson commanded a detachment of Company K, Eleventh Missouri Volunteer Cavalry, which was serving as escort. (*Returns from U.S. Military Posts 1800–1916,* Fort Whipple, February 1864.)

with an infant was on the other side. The Indian made a brave, noble fight to give her time to get away.

By this time others came up and the scene beggars description. Chavez and Willis crossed the river, followed by a half dozen soldiers. Everybody saw Indians, shots were flying thick and fast. I didn't see any, other than the one I have described. Not having a rifle I waited till one of the footmen handed me a Sharps'.[11] Just then someone on the other side hallooed for some men to follow up the west bank as the Indians were on that side. A half dozen of us galloped for a mile up without seeing anything. Then there came a cry for more horsemen to cross, and three of us crossed the river. Riding a half mile toward the voice, we found private Fisher of the California cavalry badly wounded with an arrow under the arm.[12] He was very much excited, and the wound bled copiously.

We dared not open the coat to get at the wound lest the sight of it would make him faint. This Fisher started from the post, as I learned afterward, with a presentiment he was to die; he dreamed about it, and had talked wildly about it. A litter of a blanket was made, and he was carried to the river. The force we had could not get him across, and I started back for help, and, unluckily, plunged right into a quicksand, the mule up to her belly in the sand and on one of my legs, which her struggles soon released. I then got off, and being very strong, she worked herself out. The sand closed half up to my knees as I waded. In the excitement, I forgot the rifle which was just thrust through a socket attached to the saddle. On shore I found it was gone; wading back for it, there was just one little ring of it visible above the sand. I pulled it out, cocked it, and to my surprise fired it, as well as though it had not been buried under water and sand ten minutes.

Riding on to camp, we sent help back for Fisher, and began to gather particulars of the fight; there had been three Indians killed, besides the squaw and child, who were killed with the same shot by a soldier who mistook her for a man; there is little difference in

---

[11] The Sharps was the first successful breechloader and the most popular shoulder arm in the West during the 1850s. In calibers from .36 to .52, this single-shot carbine and rifle was used extensively for buffalo hunting. (Robert Easton, "Guns of the American West," pp. 385–86.)

[12] Private Joseph Fisher could not be saved; he died of his wound before reaching Fort Whipple. A native of Germany, he was only twenty-four when buried at the fort. His death was the first at Whipple. (*Arizona Miner*, April 6, 1864; Henson, *Wilderness Capital*, p. 139.)

dress. Two, and perhaps three, others were seen to get away. Woolsey
and his party came in; had seen a trail east with signs of stock on it,
some very extensive ruins, and an ancient burying ground.[13]

This evening two Mexican boys came in, having been two days
in coming from the Agua Fria Rancho, over our trail every step of
the way, with the news that the Indians had again stripped Woolsey
of every hoof, except the oxen ploughing near the house. About
sixty Indians made a rush on the herd at mid-day; the guard fired
at them, but did not kill any, and they drove the stock off.

We followed this upper valley up some twenty miles to where
it forks, one stream coming from Bill Williams, the other from San
Francisco mountain.[14] The general characteristics of the valley are
similar to those of the Rio Grande and there is nearly as much water
in the river as there was in that stream when I first struck it coming
from Santa Fe. With irrigation it would yield as the Rio Grande
does. There is grama grass on the mesas on the west side, and large
timber at both San Francisco and Bill Williams mountains, within
from 20 to 40 miles. The bluffs on the east bank are all white lava,
and the country is generally a lava country.[15] There is not the slightest
sign of minerals of any kind on the river thus far.[16]

---

[13] Woolsey's group probably saw the ruins later known as Montezuma's
Castle National Monument, on the north side of Beaver Creek. There are,
however, other large ruins in the general area, including a sixty-room stone
pueblo on the east side of the Verde on the M. Talbot ranch and a somewhat
smaller structure with thick stone walls on private land some fifteen miles
west of Camp Verde. (Department of the Interior Geological Survey map of
Congress Quadrangle, Yavapai County; Arizona State Museum Archaeological Survey map of site nos. 0:5:11; 0:5:13;0:5:14.)

[14] This was very likely the junction of the Verde River and Oak Creek
just below present-day Bridgeport.

[15] Allyn's "white lava" bluffs were not volcanic rock but eroded limestone.
There are, however, many darker lava formations in the area.

[16] Allyn was unaware of the vast copper deposits at the nearby site which
would later become Jerome.

Letter 6

EXPLORATIONS — AZTEC TOMBS — TRACES OF GOLD — PETRIFACTIONS

Fort Whipple, April 5, 1864
[Published June 3, 1864]

My last from the Pima Villages brought the resumé of our trip to the Rio Verde up to the point where the skirmish with the Indians took place. It was the original intention when we left the post to have gone east from the point to strike the upper waters of the Salinas river, thence to follow either that valley or the divide between the two rivers, as was most practicable, to the junction of the two, and then to return in the most direct way to the post. This would have led us into the heart of the country of the Pinal Apaches, and into a country that the traditions of hundreds of years have uniformly pointed out as the El Dorado of the country. Few white men have penetrated its mysteries, and they have uniformly been driven out by the Indians. It was here that the Indians used gold bullets and exchanged them with Mr. Aubrey.[1] All the streams that empty into the Gila from the north, east of the Rio Verde, are known to be rich in minerals, and they all head into this country, and rise in the neighborhood of the Mogollon and Sierra Blanca mountains.[2]

A consultation held at the time of the skirmish alluded to showed that the unfortunate delays in reaching the upper valley of the Rio Verde had so far exhausted our provisions and our animals that to make the trip designed was simply impossible. It was therefore determined reluctantly to cross the river, strike southeast, see as much of the country between the two streams as we could, turn

---

[1] Felix Aubrey was the first to explore the feasibility of a wagon route over the thirty-fifth parallel. He drove his wagon from San Jose, California, to Santa Fe, New Mexico, and was prominently identified with the Santa Fe trade and early Arizona history. (Thomas E. Farrish, *History of Arizona* I: 353.

[2] The Mogollon Mountains refer to that portion of the rim of the Mogollon Plateau which lies east of Camp Verde, extending through the area of Strawberry and Pine. The Sierra Blanca later became known as the White Mountains.

southwest, visit the lower valley of the Rio Verde and return home. This decision created much dissatisfaction among the citizens, who, furnishing their own provisions and animals, had accompanied us in the hope of prospecting in some small degree this unknown gold region, or at least of having a fight with the ruthless savages whose forays made their homes unsafe, and that we knew were even now behind us, on the warpath among the comparatively defenseless settlements.

On the 29th of February we crossed the river and traveled down the east bank of the trail leading along under the shadow of the white, chalky-looking lava bluffs that form the wall of the Mesa above, on which were very extensive ruins of masonry fortifications, like those seen on our route from Albuquerque, at Inscription Rock, for instance. In the bluffs about midway were many caves externally resembling those we saw at Canino caves; they were the same size, and the projecting lava roofs were supported by the same regularly laid walls.[3] Time seems to have destroyed the trail leading to them, and no one climbed up to see what was inside of them. We camped as we supposed near the Aztec burying ground, passed by Woolsey on the scout several days before, and intending with pick and shovel to invade the mysteries hidden for centuries beneath those trenches. After dinner the party started out, but somehow they had mistaken landmarks, and after walking four or five miles and not finding it, most of us returned to camp. Two or three who had seen it before persevered and at last found it, but not until after sundown, when it was too late to explore it. So nobody's sleep was haunted that night by visits from indignant Aztec spirits disturbed from the slumbers of a thousand years. Science and curiosity lost the possible additions to our knowledge this vandalism might have furnished, and these individuals of the Montezuma race still sleep in graves as dark and mysterious as the hieroglyph recorded story of the ancient magnificence and rapid downfall of that once imperial nationality.[4]

---

[3] Allyn is doubtless describing the ruins which later became Montezuma Castle National Monument, seen earlier by Woolsey's party (see Letter 5, note 13).

[4] Early American settlers assumed that such Indian ruins had been left by the Aztecs. This view was reinforced by Prescott's historical work. Later archaeological study was to discredit this view. The ruins referred to are doubtless those now known as Montezuma's Castle. Indians occupied them from the eleventh to early fifteenth century. (Harold S. Gladwin, *A History of the Ancient Southwest*, pp. 221–22; William H. Prescott, *History of the Conquest of Mexico and Peru*, pp. 13–15.)

Next day we started east, passing over a smooth bench of the valley that might easily be reached and irrigated by an acequia from farther up the stream, which is a rapid one, and would furnish considerable water power. In the afternoon we crossed a beautiful little valley well timbered with pine, oak and cottonwood, in which after a vain attempt to proceed farther south, which was barred by apparently impassable canons, we camped for the night. The next morning we followed a trail east that led up the valley and over a hill that opened a frightful canoned country, with very high mountains, but the trail proved easy down into the canon and along its course. Leaving this, passing over a small hill, we opened a view of the main eastern fork of the Rio Verde, lined with cottonwoods all leaved out, the first I had ever seen, and a most beautiful tree it is, symmetrical, and the leaves of rich bright green; the stream was rapid, leaping from rock to rock, with steep banks, and the valley was covered with fine grass. We stopped here for nooning, and it was in this stream that we found the color of gold, as it is called, which is when you wash out a pan of earth to find particles enough to show the existence of gold. This fact is a striking confirmation of the theory of extensive gold fields to the east, the first stream you find heading toward the Mogollon, and away from the streams of lava; the San Francisco mountain in its volcanic days deluged the country, which attests the presence of the precious metals.[5]

On the banks of this fork we found an abundance of curious petrifactions, dead leaves petrified, single and in bunches, as they had fallen in the autumn, every fibre, vein, and stem hardened to stone, and yet so thin that they broke at the touch, and it was impossible to carry them away. When we got under way we crossed this fork and wound up the mountain, not a bad trail but a long, long pull which made some of the mules give out, and one was shot to prevent the Indians getting him. We camped at the end of the ascent on the top of an extensive mesa covered with grass and small pines. There had been a large camp of Indians here recently, as shown by the trees cut, traces of fires and lodges.

We had quite an excitement in camp this evening. About sundown Col. Chavez' Mexican boy and three Californians stumbled on an Indian *rancheria* about two miles from camp. Instead of com-

---

[5] Allyn's estimate of rich gold deposits in the area of the east Verde River was not confirmed by later developments.

ing back to report the fact and get force sufficient to destroy or
capture the whole body, they dashed in alone firing and killing
nobody. The Indians turned on them and drove them off, in fact
they did some tall running to get in. Off went a party of volunteers,
mostly citizens, but it was too late and too dark; they found the
fires, and gathered any quantity of baskets and other traps left in
the hurried flight, but the prey had gone. There was cursing loud
and deep that night on the poor unfortunate wights whose bravery
had led them into the indiscretion of that fatal assault. Here was
an opportunity to have redeemed our whole expedition, thus far a
failure, and give us something to turn the sharp edge of ridicule
when we got back, and it was lost.

From this Mesa by going northeast, we could have kept upon
level ground and apparently could have turned the terrible canon
that stretched athwart our path south, but this it was thought would
interfere with the programme of working toward the lower valley
of the Rio Verde. Several volunteered to go ahead and explore the
canon, and see if we could get our pack train in and out of it again;
they were to halloa to us and our course was to be determined by
their decision. We packed up and went to the bank of the gorge,
saw [Van C.] Smith waving his hat and shouting, but it was impossible to hear what he said, so a soldier was sent down to hear and
report what he said. The soldier halloaed that Smith said there was
a good trail out of the canon, come on! Down we plunged, the largest
and steepest of the hills we have tried yet, having to lead our saddle
animals.[6]

I was very near the advance of the long file, when my mule
twitched back and lost footing, fell backwards upon my only free
hand, right on to a "devil's pin-cushion,"[7] the meanest prickly
arrangement of the cactus species, not excepting the Spanish bayonet
or prickly pear, that I have yet seen; the little needles literally pinned

---

[6] Allyn's party was descending into the canyon of the East Verde a short
distance above its junction with the main fork of the Verde.

[7] The cactus generally known as "devil's pin cushion" or "stout needle,"
Mammillaria robustispina, occurs only in southeastern Arizona and does not
grow on the Verde. Allyn apparently applied the name mistakenly to some
other common "pin cushion." (Lyman Benson, *Cacti of Arizona,* pp. 112,
113.)

my leather glove to my hand, and when I pulled it off, the blood spurted. I lost a spur at the same time, and, to add to my intense disgust, while I was trying to pick the largest prickers out of my bleeding and smarting hand, the train had closed up behind me on the narrow trail, and someone behind yelled out, "What's that stopping for down there?" I pushed on and never stopped until I got to the bottom of the canon. That morning so many mules had given out that our mess had put everything on one pack animal, making a large, clumsy pack, our tin plates, cups and limited table furniture being rolled up in the bedding. The result was that the bedding, disgusted at our slow progress, rolled off and down the hill straight on its own hook, so far that after we reached camp for noon at the bottom, it took two men a couple of hours to find, and then a large bottle of ground red pepper was found crushed, everything else, however, safe.

At the bottom we found Smith, and *he had shouted to us not to come.* Here was a scrape; there was no trail for pack animals out of the atrocious *cul de sac* we were in. On both sides the mountain rises a thousand feet at least, and almost perpendicular. After consultation it was determined to work down the stream to the Rio Verde, probably not over seven or eight miles off, but such miles probably!

At half past two o'clock p.m. we started; had to make a trail, cross and recross the stream, creep under the low sweeping branches of living trees, climb over the debris of dead ones, force our way through tangled thickets of willows, every little while have to leave the stream and climb up on a bench or terrace, then down it again. The canon grew wilder and wilder. I saw places where I think the perpendicular rock was a thousand feet, and the canon fifteen hundred feet high. It has been reported that Indians had been seen while the men were out looking for our roll of bedding, and everybody was on the *qui vive,* and Indians were seen watching us out of range, probably wondering what consummate fools we were to be in such a place, what we were after, and where we were going.

There is no more comical spectacle than a pack train climbing one of these steep, rough, stony mountain trails. I had learned by experience that the safe place in such a party is to be either in front or clear behind, so today, being tired at this endless walking (for you couldn't ride), and leading an obstinate brute of a mule, I stopped under the shadow of a big rock, lighted my pipe and watched the outfit defile by. I hadn't much more than got merely stretched out when a soldier leading a pack mule came plunging through the stream. I was right on the bank in an exceedingly picturesque spot. He caught sight of me, and with sincerest alarm depicted on his face, rushed toward me, saying, "Are you hurt? How did it happen?" I assured him nothing had happened. "Why," said he, "I thought you had been thrown against that rock," the poor innocent rock that was affording me a delightful shade. On the file went, occasionally a huge boulder loosened by the repeated tread would come crushing down, cutting right across the path below, and land with a splash in the stream, then a mule pack and all would get rolling, and never stop until it landed against some friendly tree, when it would lie just as though it was dead. Three or four men rush at it, lifting by the head, the tail, the pack, perhaps prying him up with a long timber if you can find one in this forsaken country, until at last he is on his feet and off he trots as though nothing had happened. I used to think a cat had more lives than any other animal, but it's a delusion, the mule decidedly gets the nearest to the frontier of immortality.

But the train is all by save a mule or two back that won't stir, and I suppose most likely will be shot; and it's not the safest thing to stay here moralizing in the Apache country, if you value your scalp. So up and on after the party. I soon overtook it at camp. We had traveled four hours, had not reached the river, and camped, perforce, because we couldn't go any farther. The sixth mule since we started was shot today. It's too bad. They are only tired and would bring a hundred dollars in gold, if red tape would let them be sold. Vegetation is quite far advanced, trees leaved out, new grass started, etc.

Next day we made the Rio Verde; the trail much better than yesterday; signs of spring abundant; tiny wild flowers were just peeping out under the stones. We followed down the stream three days, crossing and recrossing the river, following the trail on up to the mesa and down again, passing some extensive ruins on the mesas, one large building containing twenty or thirty rooms with extensive stone corrals for stock.[8] Wild flowers increasing in variety and rare beauty. One day we passed a finely preserved ruin; the walls were twenty feet high, and at the top two and a half feet thick. It must have been several stories high once. The mesa upon which it is built strikes me as a richer soil than any above, and was doubtless cultivated when this building was inhabited. Col. Chavez left us this day, March 7th, for the post, not deeming it prudent to go farther with animals. He has to get back to the Rio Grande. We go with the Californians, under Major Willis, determined to reach the lower valley if possible.

---

[8]The party has been traversing the canyon of the Verde below the East Verde junction. The ruins observed by Allyn appear to be those left by the Pueblo Indians described by Gladwin: "At about A.D. 1350 . . . a few groups of evacuees worked their way westward to the Verde Valley, probably by way of the East Verde and Fossil Creek. . . . The Verde was literally the last ditch for any Pueblan refugees from the east, as the Yuman Yavapai, west of the Verde, strongly objected to any invasion of their domain." (Gladwin, *The Ancient Southwest*, p. 326.) Anthropologist Emil Haury says that these were probably the Limestone Ruins or nearby sites and that the structures in this area on both sides of the Verde River are definitely of pre-Spanish origin. The fourteenth century is the best approximate date. The evacuees could well have fled westward as a result of conflict with other Pueblo tribes to the east. (Interview, November 10, 1971, Tucson, Arizona.)

NOTES ON MULE-BACK — THE CACTUS — TRAVELING IN AN INDIAN COUNTRY — EXTENSIVE RUINS

Fort Whipple, April 5, 1864
[Published June 6, 1864]

March 8th — It grows warmer every day, the trail improves, the grass grows poorer and poorer, and the starving mules are ready to eat firewood. We are now upon a well-defined Maricopa[1] war trail, which leads straight through the valley we want to see to reach their villages; no more danger of impassable canons there, the Indian never goes that way. From the top of a high hill today we got a fine panoramic view of the mountains on the east bank of the Verde; they were barren, desolate, impassable enough; there was nothing to relieve the repulsive grandeur of the view, save in one place where the light green leaves of some cottonwood trees indicated that there a little sickly stream of water trickled. Cactus alone seems to find a congenial home there. Where anything grows the wild flowers peep out; many new and richly-tinted varieties showed themselves today. We were terribly annoyed by a new species of cactus called Choyas;[2] it grows two or three feet high, branching out into a sort

---

[1] The term "Maricopa" was used to designate all the Yuman-speaking peoples of the Gila and Salt river valleys. Ezell states that the term did not appear in any document until the records of the Kearney expedition in 1846. "Maricopa" refers to different populations with cultural similarities. (Paul H. Ezell, *The Maricopas: An Identification from Documentary Sources*, pp. 9–10.) According to Bancroft, the Maricopas numbered five hundred in 1858. They were honored with the Pimas in being given the first reservation and gifts in Arizona in 1859. Bitter foes of the Apache and other marauding tribes, they served in the Apache wars and were present at the Woolsey Bloody Tank massacre. (Hubert Howe Bancroft, *History of Arizona and New Mexico, 1530–1888*, pp. 501, 548.

[2] While there are several species of cholla ("choya") in Arizona, Allyn's description would indicate that he encountered *Cylindropuntia bigelovii*, commonly known as the "jumping" cactus. Benson's distribution maps show the jumping cactus range beginning barely north of Phoenix and extending south and west. (Lyman Benson, *The Cacti of Arizona*, pp. 32, 34.)

of bouquet, or perhaps more like a branching candlestick, forming at the end of each separate branch a ball exactly like a chestnut burr, only that the burrs are needles, both in sharpness and strength. The slightest jar sets these rolling off, and they are murderous if they happen to stick on to a poor beast. If you try to pull them off, if the animal will let you come near enough without kicking, the needles will break right off in the flesh, or rather pull off from the ball. Animals used to a cactus country avoid them with wonderful dexterity, but our American horses and mules must needs smell of them, get one or two of them in their nostrils, and then, frantic with pain, plunge right into an acre of them, sticking them into every part of the body. One poor horse accidentally got one lodged under the stirrup leather, broke from the person leading him, and plunged frantically down a trail, when the train was all strung out on a side-hill, dashing the whole length, fortunately not hitting anyone.

This country is the paradise of the cactus[3] in all its manifold shapes, and the fit home of the Apache, but even he won't stay in it. The cactus is manifold in its varieties, all alike nuisances. There is the towering Seguarro, the monarch of the family and grim sentinel of the desert, a tall, straight fluted column from one to two feet in diameter, and those I have seen, some thirty feet high, of a rich green color, all cased in a mail of needles. Sometimes at ten or fifteen feet high one or two branches start out the same size and shape as the parent column, and grow alike perpendicular and parallel to it. There is the "devil's pin cushion," I have feelingly alluded to before, the prickly pear, the Spanish bayonet, and the fishhook, as it is called, from the bent prickers that envelop it; this is about the size and shape of a bee-hive, and is the only variety I know of that is good for anything; inside is a white pulpy substance from which water can be squeezed to quench thirst, and of which,

---

[3] Identification of cacti which have not previously been mentioned are as follows: The saguaro ("seguarro"), *Cereus giganteus,* grows in southern and western Arizona. There are several species of *Opuntia,* to which the name "prickly pear" is applied, that Allyn could have encountered in his northern Arizona travels. The Spanish bayonet, or yucca, is not a cactus but a lily, producing brilliant clusters of white blossoms on a tall candlelike stock. The "fishhook" cactus is doubtless *Ferocactus wislizenii,* the common barrel. Another species popularly called fishhook cactus is *Mammillaria microcarpa,* but this last is a southern and western Arizona species not found where Allyn was. (Benson, *Cacti,* pp. 72–76, 35–36, 95–99, 120–21.)

boiled with plenty of sugar for several hours, a splendid citron preserve can be made.

Still no signs of the lower valley; we hope to reach it to-morrow.
Next day fourteen miles more of desolation and cactus brought us
to the head of the famous long-sought lower valley; a valley all on
the west side of the river with deep sandy bottoms, plenty of cottonwoods, mesquite, and elder, and not a blade of grass. After resting
at the head a day or two we went on below to get to grass if possible,
but there was no grass worth naming. It is time to be turning toward
Fort Whipple, distant as near as we know, 120 miles. The poor mules
grow weaker and weaker, the eleventh was shot today. The soldiers
have burned up their extra clothing, broke up their ovens, almost
invaluable here where they cannot be re-placed, to lighten the packs.
As near as we can estimate it is between forty and fifty miles to the
Pima villages on the Gila, right south, and from them there is a
wagon road to the post, passing settlements. The train is to go back.
Mr. [Van C.] Smith proposed to go with me to the Pima villages,
rest there ourselves and animals, and then go home by way of Antelope[4] and Weaver. I agreed to go.

On March 11th we parted company, the Governor and entire
party starting for the post, Mr. Smith and myself going toward the
Gila. We had our riding animals and a burro, upon which was
packed our blankets and a limited supply of provisions, consisting
of flour, coffee, sugar and salt, and the smallest quantity of each, for
provisions were so scarce we were unwilling to take the least thing
from the main party, who had the longer and more difficult route.
Ours was considered much the more dangerous, as it passed the trail
of Apaches bound for the Gila. I do not however so regard it, for I
think generally in an Indian country the small party is the safest.
You can travel at night, are not under the necessity of seeking large
quantities of water or grass, and it is the merest accident if an
Indian sees you at all.

As this was my first experience in traveling as mountain men
do, and the novel incidents are so fresh in my mind, I am sure they

---

[4]Antelope is Antelope Peak adjacent to the mining village of Weaver,
which later became a ghost town. Weaver was situated about eighty-five miles
northwest of present-day Phoenix. Rich deposits had been discovered there
by Mexicans in Weaver's party in 1863. (Byrd H. Granger, *Arizona Place
Names,* p. 331.)

will interest you. The usual cooking outfit in such trips consists of a tin quart cup tied to your saddle and a large hunting knife at the belt. I had neither, but Smith had both, and we thought we could get on two days, which was the time we expected to be in reaching Pima. We waited till they were all gone before we packed up, and then loading our donkey, strung out. We determined to follow the trail referred to before which passes down the valley. It led us down as far as some quite extensive ruins, parallel to the river, and then bore about south while the Verde bears to the east to join the Salinas[5] at the eastern base of a red granite mountain, to the west of which this trail passes. Directly opposite this valley towers up a great landmark of the Apache country, the Massassl [Mazatzal] mountain.[6] Behind it a great chief with the significant name of Big Rump,[7] lives in a fine valley where there is plenty of gold; at least captives say so. Neither the Maricopas or the Pimas in their campaigns have ever been able to reach it.

The trail passed an almost imperceptible divide and at 12½ o'clock we were on the banks of the Salinas, some seven or eight miles below the junction of it and the Verde. Here we rested, grazed our animals, caught a fine large fish, (fish were quite plenty in the Verde,) and when the sun was lower got our dinner. I made the

---

[5]There are a number of extensive ruins, including mounds, ball courts, and pueblos, in the area of the lower Verde River. Possibly Allyn was referring to an extensive mound site one-half mile south of old Fort McDowell. There is also a pueblo and mound site of large size located 2.2 miles south of the fort. (Department of the Interior Geological Survey map of Ft. McDowell Quadrangle, Maricopa County; Arizona State Museum Archaeological Survey map of site nos. U:6:9; U:6:10.)

The Salinas or Salt River is the Gila's largest tributary. Kino named it Salado, but it was known variously as the Matthew and the Asunción until 1852. After this date the name Salinas or Salado applied again. The brackish taste of the river water at low ebb was responsible for the name. (Granger, *Arizona Place Names*, p. 115.)

[6]"Massassl" or Mazatzal Peak (7,888 feet) does indeed dominate this region east of the lower Verde River. Pioneers said the name was of Apache origin meaning "bleak, barren." (Will C. Barnes, *Arizona Place Names*, p. 270.)

[7]Thrapp identifies Big Rump as follows: "Not only the white Indian fighters, but the more prominent Indians became widely known to the pioneers, and none was more famous at this time than Wah-poo-eta, or Big Rump, so named presumably for his most prominent feature. According to the early newspapers, Big Rump roamed an enormous portion of Apachería, probably because almost any depredation was blamed on any Indian whose name was known, or could be spelled." (Dan L. Thrapp, *The Conquest of Apacheria*, p. 59.)

fire, put the tin cup filled with water on the coals and poured the coffee into it, while Smith was kneading the dough for our bread. This you draw out about as you would molasses candy and wind it round a stick an inch or two in diameter spirally and hold it over the coals, turning it round until it browns; or if you are lazy, sharpen the end of the stick and drive it slanting into the ground and leave it to bake. But there was the fish; we hadn't any nice bark like you have in northern woods to make a gridiron or rather grid-bark of, and we could not make it stay on a stick, so perforce it had to be thrown on the coals, and broiled. The cooking done I improvised a small tin yeast-powder box for my share of the coffee. We each had a stick of bread, a clean stone answered for a plate for the fish, and my pen knife and fingers for the rest of the outfit. It is useless to say that meal relished, if you don't believe it reader, try it yourself, with a trusty Spencer by your side and latent apprehension every time the wind stirs a bough that an Apache is near.

Just before sundown we started again, crossed the Salinas, a wide but rather shallow stream, and struck the same trail which in a short distance brought us to the remains of a great *acquia*[8] [acequia], which I had heard of before but regarded as a fable. It is really a work that must have rivalled all the old aqueducts, hardly excepting those that span the Campagna,[9] in the labor spent on it and the volume of water it carried. Recollect it is not a masonry work, and was a ruin before the first Spaniard reached the Gila, three hundred years ago. I rode across it as it is now, and I think it fifty feet at the top and twenty-five feet on the bottom. Wouldn't that float any canal boat on the Erie Canal? We rode along by its side, our animals' hoofs striking the ruins of the city near it two hours and a half, and could not have gone less than seven miles in a straight line.

---

[8]*Acequia* is Spanish for *aqueduct*. Turney has published detailed maps and descriptions of this ancient irrigation system, showing its relationship to present-day Phoenix area canals which still use parts of the ancient routes. (Omar A. Turney, "Prehistoric Irrigation.") When Haury supervised the excavation of the great Pueblo ditch at Snaketown nearby on the Gila River, he estimated its beginnings at 300 B.C. or earlier. It was the basis of an agricultural system which flourished for some 1,500 years. For his account of the culture and illustrations of the excavated acequia, see Emil W. Haury, "The Hohokam, First Masters of the American Desert.")

[9]The Campagna di Roma is a low-lying area of wastelands about the city of Rome which was crossed by one of the great Roman aqueduct systems bringing water to the city. Allyn must have seen this during his travels in Italy.

What a population[10] must have been here once! Seven miles on one street! At this point the *acquia* turned to the left and I am told it has been traced thirty miles, then we left it, and in a short time reached the river again, having crossed a bend of it. We did not go to the water lest Indians might be lurking there, but turned away from it and the trail into a clump of mesquit a quarter of a mile off; tied our animals, there was no grass, made a fire of the smallest dimensions and some coffee, smoked our pipes in silence, spread down our blankets, rifles by our sides, in the moonlight and slept to the music of the distant murmur of the water and the tramping of the animals.

Next morning we were up at daybreak, led the animals to the river side to graze on the new grass among the stones on the edge, and prepared our breakfast. Same bill of fare as yesterday, lacking the fish. At about 8 o'clock we got under way, expecting to reach Casa Blanca,[11] the residence of the Indian agent at Pima, before sundown at farthest. We went on bravely for two or three hours when my mule gave out; just walking along and that was all. I blooded the spurs in the vain attempt to quicken her gait, and then got off and walked an hour; Smith laughing at me, and saying I didn't know how to make a mule go. The appearance of the animal was certainly on his side, for she was fat and in good condition. No signs of the Gila yet. We had been expecting to see its fringe of cottonwoods on the horizon for an hour. I said we must stop; he said he would ride my mule; so we exchanged. His was a slim, light Spanish mule, worth about half of the money mine was, but much better adapted to the saddle; mine was large, and had been in our ambulance team from Leavenworth, and was used to corn. The truth was, the grass filled her belly without giving her any strength. We went on bravely for a half hour, and looked behind to see Smith afoot, his long rowelled Spanish spurs in his hand, and he every little while digging them into the mule. The laugh was mine now, and I asked if we hadn't better stop. Yes, was the reply. So the first

---

[10] This population was that of the Hohokam, a Pima term meaning "those who have gone." For a brief illustrated discussion of Hohokam culture see H. M. Wormington, *Prehistoric Indians of the Southwest*, pp. 118–47.

[11] Casa Blanca (White House) was a trading post in the Pima villages run by Ammi Mitchell White, a New Englander. He had a stage station there and later was said to have run the first steam flour mill in the area. (Granger, *Arizona Place Names*, p. 292; *U.S. Census*, 1864.)

patch of grass we came to we camped. Our canteen leaked and we had no water; it was pretty hot and we didn't know how far it was to the Gila; not a sign of it. We had used the last of our coffee this morning, so we lunched on bread baked this morning.

At sundown we got under way again, having transferred our pack from the burro to my mule; it only weighed some forty pounds; Smith agreeing to ride the burro if I would drive the pack mule. Armed with a long stick, wherewith to pound the animal if she was obstinate, I started; Smith in the lead, pack mule next, and I bringing up the rear. The mule seemed to think there was some joke about the pack, that it would shake off, or something, for she trotted a whole hour right smartly, and I began to think she was shamming in the morning. The moon rose in almost tropic brilliancy, the air was bland as Italy, and on the whole I felt quite jolly over my first experience in mule driving. But it is not safe to crow until you are out of the woods, for the pack got to be an old story, and the mule soon got at her old tricks, beginning to go so slowly that she seemed scarcely going at all, and at last deliberately laid down and tried to roll; but a pack saddle and a lot blankets are not the easiest to roll off.

Just at that moment a slight breeze wafted the unmistakable smell of a mesquit fire to me. Was it Apaches? Who else could it be? Smith was ahead, out of sight, trying to get a glimpse of that ever receding stream, the Gila, which I was beginning to think was a myth. I scanned the direction of the smell with eager eye, but could not see anything; a bad sign, if it were white men it was almost certain to be visible; still it might be Pimas or Maricopas. I dared not shout at the obstinate mule, and shouting is an essential part of a muleteer's business. By this time, however, she got up and refused to follow the trail. Off she would go to the right, through a thicket of mesquit, and then go to grazing; I after her, belaboring her with the stick; the next time she would go quite as far to the left, I after her, until I began to be apprehensive that we should lose the trail, not the easiest thing to follow by moonlight. Ever and anon that smell would sweep down on the breeze. At last, however, the mule concluded to go on, and a half hour brought us to an enclosure, a cultivated field, and a steer grazing outside of it; glad sign of the Pimas, but where is the Gila? The mule bolted off after the steer and went

From J. Ross Browne's *Adventures in the Apache Country*

Ammi M. White's settlement, centering around a flour mill, is portrayed by Allyn as an outpost of comfort and conviviality in the midst of an uncivilized desert country. After his intial visit to White's Mill in spring 1864, the judge returned the following winter to find the little establishment flourishing.

to grazing. While I was vainly trying to get her on, Smith came back, having found a camping place on an *acquia*. The Gila couldn't be far off, but it wasn't safe to go on, as the land was cut up with *acquias* and brush fences. We soon unpacked, built an Indian fire, viz. a small one, and baked bread. I nearly forgot to say that we drank two canteens of water before we did any thing else. We were very soon sound asleep.

Almost as soon as we were awake in the morning, a Pima stood noiselessly by our side; he was out with a pick axe to repair *acquias*. He said it was but little distance to Casa Blanca. About ten minutes brought us to the Gila; not a tree on it, the Pimas having cut them all down. We crossed, and had all sort of annoyance in getting across the cultivated fields fenced in by acquias and impassable bush fences. At last we hired a boy to show us to Casa Blanca, and it was a very welcome sight when we saw its hospitable adobe walls and the old flag floating over them. We were soon there and were cordially welcomed by Mr. White, the Indian agent for the Pimas and Maricopas, Col. Poston, superintendent of Indian affairs, Mr.

Ross Browne[12] the author and newspaper man, and some dozen other Americans.

The fatted calf was killed at once, or rather the fatted chickens, and we breakfasted on boiled eggs, boiled chickens, fried potatoes, coffee with milk in it, and other things you will laugh at as luxuries, that I assure were very pleasant to palates that hadn't enjoyed them for some six months. I will try to give you an idea of the Pimas in my next.

---

[12]John Ross Browne (1821–75) was born in Dublin, the son of an Irish publisher and editor who was exiled to the United States in 1833. Browne went to California in 1849. While there, he served as an official stenographer of the constitutional convention. Beginning in 1853, Browne was employed by the U.S. Treasury Department as customs house inspector and as inspector of Indian agencies. It was in the former post that he met Poston and was persuaded to join an expedition to Arizona, one result of which was a series of articles appearing in 1864 in *Harper's,* featuring Browne's original narrative and lithographs. A number of these illustrations appear in this book. (Lina Fergusson Browne, ed., *J. Ross Browne: His Letters, Journals and Writings,* pp. xiii–xvii, xx, 118ff, 182ff, 303ff; Arizona Historical Society Biographical File.)

Letter 8

RESTING IN THE INDIAN COUNTRY —
GOLD HUNTERS — THE PIMA INDIANS

Fort Whipple, April 20, 1864
[Published June 20, 1864]

Never was city, with its glaring gaslights, its radiant shop windows, its thronged pavements, its hotel palaces, its parks, fountains and gay equipages, half as welcome to the wanderer as those miserable straggling brush-hut villages of half-naked Indians, and the — by contrast at least — extensive house of Mr. White, with its tiny fluttering flag, was to us when we rode up. A week slipped by almost unnoted. There were letters to write, agreeable men to talk with, persons coming and going, rumors of fearful Indian troubles around Fort Whipple and the mines.[1] Bishop Lamy[2] stopped a day with us on his return from California; a frank, agreeable, fascinating gentleman, with the *bon homme* of the Frenchman and the earnestness of the zealous Christian; a man of works rather than words, whose field of labor is an empire, his diocese stretching from Denver to Mexico, and from the Rio Grande to the Colorado. Such charming evenings, the full moon's beams streaming in the casement as we, grouped around a tiny fire to destroy the chilliness of the house, chatted. [J. Ross] Browne had roamed over half the world, there were others who had strayed over northern Mexico, with strange stories of a primitive and almost unknown people, of beautiful cities

---

[1] Indian troubles had developed after the arrival of the miners and became intensified after the Woolsey massacre. Yavapais living on Granite Creek also were resentful. Raids on cattle, horses, and settlers occurred with increasing frequency in 1864, especially as the Anglo population increased. (*Arizona Miner*, February 15, March 23, 1864; Pauline Henson, *Wilderness Capital, Prescott, A.T., 1864*, pp. 148–55.)

[2] Bishop John Baptist Lamy was named first bishop of the see of Santa Fe in 1853. He combined the talents of a fine administrator with a capacity for needed reform. Arizona Territory was a part of his mission field, and he visited it in 1863 and 1864. (James Grant Wilson and John Fiske, *Appleton's Cyclopaedia of American Biography* 8:602–3.)

[107]

and mines of fabulous richness; those who could recount hairbreadth
escapes from the Apache and the Texan; those who were going to be
millionaires as soon as some lode could be worked, and who scarcely
knew how they were to get bread tomorrow.

Your genuine gold hunter is a happy fellow; he lives in antici-
pation, discounting his fine house, elegant carriages, his costly dinners and rare wines; he literally takes no care for the morrow; no
anxieties about wife or children or how silver his hair, no agonizing
restlessness as to the issue of battles fought above the clouds or
below the fogs disturb his appetite; the fierce craving of accumu-
lation has never taken hold of him. He gambles with nature; if he
wins, it is well; if he fails, he has lost nothing save the castles in the
air he cherished and a few years, but what are years in the mountains
where one never grows old.

Mr. White could tell us of the customs of the strange people
that surround us and the imagination had full play as to their mysterious origin. I doubt if there is a tribe or people on the globe as
unique or whose past is so mysterious as the Pimas. They are a
single disconnected inexplicable fact. For about three hundred years
we know they have lived on the same land, in the same mean huts,
the same industrious, plodding, virtuous, peaceable people. The
description of the first friar who reached the Gila would answer for
today. They have no ascertainable tradition of change, none of who
built the *acquia* or city alluded to in my last. All this time they have
uniformly built their houses and buried their dead facing the east,
have watched the rising sun for the coming of the Montezuman God.[3]
No Jesus ever shook their faith or led them to baptism.

The Pima villages, eleven in number, stretch along the Gila
about twenty miles. One is a duplicate of another, and a mere
straggling collection of brush huts not large enough to stand in; in
fact they only use them to sleep in, living outdoors except in cold
weather, and then they huddle around a fire inside. There is no
chimney, and diseases of the eyes are common among them, caused
by the smoke. From the villages to the river, a half mile to a mile,

---

[3]Allyn seems to have been impressed by his reading of Prescott. The
"Montezuman God" is doubtless Quetzalcoatl, whom the Aztecs expected to
return after having abandoned Mexico earlier. Because of the god's white skin
it was thought at first that Cortez was this divinity. (William H. Prescott, *History of the Conquest of Mexico and Peru*, p. 39.)

The *olas kih* houses Allyn saw were most often found in clusters, built to accommodate the various members of a particular Pima family. The young judge describes this group of Indians as unique, with a mysterious past and unchanging traditions.

are the cultivated fields. This tract is marked off by *acquias* and perfectly impenetrable brush fences, presenting a striking contrast to the desert that stretches interminably in every direction: outside, sand and bushes; inside, the wheat several inches high and the ground moist and rich.

The transformation one of these tiny threads of dirty water, scarcely observable, makes, is difficult to convey to those accustomed to the well watered regions of New England. The desert literally becomes a garden. These brush thickets around the fields are pierced by apertures through which you have to crawl on your knees, just the reverse of the English style or stile. It's not either a dignified or comfortable mode as I learned one evening, when after taking a walk, I started back in a direct light line and found myself entangled in a perfect network of alternating ditches and fences, which compelled me to go about twice as far, before I got home, as I would have had to if I had gone back as I came. These Indians number about six thousand souls and are rapidly increasing.

During the past year they have raised one million pounds of wheat; two hundred and fifty thousand pounds of corn, besides cotton, sugar, melons, beans, and other small crops. Since Mr. White's first residence among them, they have quadrupled their production of wheat and corn; and, assured of a permanent market, would increase it almost indefinitely.

A more peaceful or industrious community, as a whole, can scarcely be imagined. There is no blood of the white man at their door, and yet the whole southern emigration to California passed through their reservation.[4] After sunset it is so still that it is difficult to realize that you are in the midst of such a body of semi-civilized Indians, and firearms are as useless here as in the most secluded of the villages of the Atlantic states.

Their form of civil government is simple, and seems adequate to their needs. There are eleven villages, nine principal ones, and two similar ones attached to others; the villages are under the general management of a Chief Captain, and in some, they have captains for *acquias,* for the land and for war. The power of the nation is vested in a grand council, the young warrior gets the right to sit silently here, by killing a few Apaches, and further success gives him a voice and a vote. The chieftaincy is not hereditary, although the present chief is son of the preceding one; he was appointed before his father's death, at the father's request, and is now chief in little but name. Murder is punished, or rather avenged, by the family of the deceased. Theft is common, and does not seem to be punished at all, although the stolen property is reclaimed wherever found. The law of descent is simple, all the land is owned by the women, and they alone inherit from their mother. A man's personal property is all burned at his death, even to his house, in the belief that it enriches the deceased in the next world.

When a warrior dies, the nation mourns, and imposing obsequies are performed. After his death, his family take possession of the body, and with a *reata* or hide rope, tie up the body, passing the reata under the knees, around the neck, drawing the legs up to the chin. It is then buried with the head toward the east, and the grave covered with brush to keep the coyotes off. Four days after,

---

[4] The westward route through the Pima villages was pioneered by James Ohio Pattie and his father Sylvester. These two Santa Fe Trail traders and mountainmen established a route to California from New Mexico via the Gila River in the winter of 1827–28. This trail became a major route to the Pacific. The Pima villages were a favorite stopping place for water, rest, flour, and other provisions because of the peaceful, generous nature of these Indians. Hubert Howe Bancroft, *History of Arizona and New Mexico 1530–1888,* pp. 406ff; Byrd H. Granger, *Arizona Place Names,* p. 303.)

processions are formed at each end of the chain of villages in this order: first, women clad simply in the tapa, or cloth wrapped about the loins; second, warriors in the full panoply of war; lastly, men on horseback, i.e., old men, farmers, etc.

The two processions meet near Casa Blanca, the women part to the right and left, the warriors advance to the front and halt; an old man now grasps a tattered banner attached to a long staff which assists his tottering steps as he advances to the open space, and in trembling accents recounts the virtues of the departed. As he proceeds, a prolonged wail goes up from the assembled Nation. Afterwards they proceed to the grave, near which a Ramada is erected (a *ramada* is a brush shed resting on poles), under which baskets of wheat are placed. The circle completed around the grave, the women sow the wheat over it, and sprinkle it over the heads of those present. This is that he may have bread in the next world. Then an old man advances, pulls off his blanket, or some other valuable thing, and throws it down for the beginning of the funeral pile, others follow, and soon the rush becomes general, everyone throws on something: beads, blankets, saddles, and every description of personal property. Sometimes the women strip off their tapa, and throw that on to the blazing pile, which often reaches thousands of dollars in value. This consumed, the ceremony is over. Beads, in some way, are sacred; those unconsumed in the funeral pile are carefully gathered, and buried with the deceased.

Their mode of courtship is for the swain to serenade the damsel, and if she is agreeable, she comes out to him, and they go together to her parents; the lover then makes the family a present, according to his means, for instance a horse. There are a few who have more than one wife, but it is contrary to the habit of the people, and repugnant to their sense of right. The Pima women are proverbial for their chastity. It is against their custom to marry outside the tribe, and constant intermarriage is degenerating them physically. The Maricopas, whose habits and customs differ materially from the Pimas, are a much more robust race, and are vastly more warlike. The Pima has an old custom that compels him to return from a war party as soon as blood is shed, for the reason, he says, that as soon as the Apache knows he is in his country, there is no use following the warpath. The Pimas have a hideous habit of plastering up their heads with clay; malicious people hint that it is to kill lice, and others say it makes the hair blacker.

We were fortunate enough to see the distribution of Indian goods to both tribes, by Colonel Poston, superintendent of Indian affairs. A company of California cavalry happened to be passing, and the captain at once placed his men at Col. P's disposal, to preserve order. The guard inclosed the open space in front of Mr. White's house, and the name of the captain of each village, written on a card, was placed on a column of the portales, and the hardware — axes, hoes, rakes, etc. — designed for that village, was placed around it. All was ready, but no Indians! It was about noon before they made their appearance. Then, from one to two thousand were grouped around outside. As far as we could see, groups were watching the proceedings, even to Casa Blanca, a mile off. The captains were admitted inside the guard. They were fine-looking, venerable men, as a whole; the Chief Antoine Azul was, perhaps, the meanest-looking; there was Juan Chevariah, the great war captain of the Maricopas, fairly weighed down by his enormous epaulettes; a grim, iron-faced man, whom one would rather have as a friend than a foe.

Col. Poston addressed these "principales" in Spanish, and they listened most respectfully to his suggestions about the necessity of increased industry, as the opening of the mines above had made a demand for their wheat, etc., and they promised to increase their productions. Each captain was then allowed to bring in five of his young men to carry off the gifts, and the ceremony was over.

Antoine Azul brought his wife with him, and Col. P. decked her out with medals, beads, etc., intensely to her satisfaction. She is a fine-looking woman; looking, in fact, younger than her son, Antoineto, who is a strapping Indian, got up in the most approved style of Indian dandy, his hair being colored green! This young scapegrace has several wives now.

The Maricopa villages join the Pimas on the west. They are equally industrious and are the relics of a powerful Colorado river tribe that fled for safety to the protection of the Pimas thirty or forty years ago; then only numbering two hundred and fifty souls. Now they are a thousand strong. Juan Chevariah, their great chief taking rank only after Iretaba the chief of the Mohaives, who is now in New York, among the friendly Indian leaders of the country. The Maricopa prides himself on not turning back when on the

Antonio Azul

warpath. We accepted while here an invitation from Col. Poston to accompany him on a trip via Fort Whipple to the Moquis, perhaps the most unknown of the tribes now on the continent.[5]

They inhabit seven cities way north of the Little Colorado and have rarely been visited by white men. Lieut. Ives is the only officer of the United States government who has ever been there, and he only saw *one* of the cities.[6] Moqui was the farthest north the Spanish

[5] Moqui was an older name for the Hopi Indians of northeastern Arizona. One of the Hopi villages, Old Oraibi, is the oldest continuously inhabited settlement in the United States. (Laura Thompson, *Culture in Crisis: A Study of the Hopi Indians.*)

[6] Joseph Christmas Ives (1828–68) sighted the Hopi villages and visited Oraibi (and "Mooshaneh") on May 12th and 13th, 1858. (Joseph C. Ives, *Report on the Colorado River of the West, Explored in 1857 and 1858*, pp. 119ff, 122, 124.)

monks ever got, and but one, possibly two, ever got there.[7] It was
the reported wealth of these seven cities of Cibola, as they called
them, that caused the Spanish military attempts north of the Gila,
which all ignominiously failed. Entrenched as it were in their canoned
mountain fastness they have lived since when? who shall venture
to guess — sometimes preyed upon by the Navajo, but always perfectly isolated from the white man.

---

[7] Cristóbal de la Concepción, Andres Gutiérrez, and Francisco de Porras,
all New Mexican Franciscans, first attempted the conversion of the Hopis,
arriving at the Moqui villages in August 1629. Three churches were built at
Awatovi, Shungopovi, and Oraibi. Tradition has it that priests were thrown
from the Oraibi cliff and the church destroyed at the time of the great revolt
of 1680–92. Bancroft notes extensive Franciscan missionary efforts among
the Moqui (though not in Oraibi) again after 1700. Padres Sylvester Escalante
and Francisco Domínguez, traveling from Santa Fe, reached the Moqui in
1776 and were well received but failed to convert the Indians. The Jesuits
were active in midcentury, though also unsuccessful. Efforts to convert Oraibi
continued to be unfruitful during the Spanish-Mexican period. (Bancroft,
Arizona and New Mexico, pp. 221–346, 349, 362–67, 391–98, 461–62; Odie
Faulk, *John Baptiste Salpointe,* pp. 190, 194, 196, 202. Also consult Edward
H. Spicer, *Cycles of Conquest.*)

Letter 9

AN INDIAN ESCORT — QUEER NAMES —
CALLING THE ROLL — INDIANS FISHING —
ALMOST LOST — INSTINCT OF THE INDIANS —
DRESS PARADE OF INDIAN SOLDIERS —
MUSICAL DONKEYS — VISIT TO WEAVER VILLAGE
A PLUCKY FRONTIER WOMAN —
END OF THE MOQUI EXPEDITION

Fort Whipple, April 20, 1864
[Published June 22, 1864; June 25, 1864]

Col. Poston had been refused a military escort by the military
authorities of Tucson, and had applied to the Maricopas for an
escort. Juan Chevariah promptly promised it. Our preparations went
gaily on for this unique trip, once in a while disturbed, it is true, by
the rumors still more definite of Indian troubles around Fort Whipple, but we put these aside as exaggerated and unfounded. The Pimas
were more disturbed than we, but not for like cause. Their natural
pride was touched; Col. Poston had not asked them for any men.
You could see there was something at work among them, and at
last they came and asked to be allowed to furnish a like number of
soldiers with the Maricopas. Col. Poston said "we were going [on] a
long journey of many days, and he did not want men who turned
back on the path." They promised by all they regarded as sacred
to go wherever Colonel P. went, not to turn back, etc. At last it
was agreed that they might furnish thirty men, and the next day the
men came and had their names all taken down; a splendid set of
men physically; the nation had been ransacked for its best. As a
curious illustration of the habits of this people, among their soldiers
was one fine-looking fellow Mr. White had never seen before. Mr.
White's store is the sole exchange of the tribe, there all their crops
are purchased, and Mr. W. knows almost every head of a family

[115]

in the community. Mr. W. said to him, "Have you ever been here before, I don't recollect you?" The Indian said he lived about two miles above, and had never been there before. He was a farmer, his wife sold their wheat, and in all these years he had never been even to the store; now he proposes a journey of three hundred miles into an unknown country. These Indian soldiers are not encumbered with transportation, for each one carries his own provisions, i.e., a sack of *pinoly* [*pinole*]. (I don't know if that's spelled right, it conveys the sound, anyway). *Pinoly* is parched wheat or corn, ground, and, with a little sugar dissolved in cold water, is very palatable food, as I can testify. The work of grinding up the provisions of the party made the women very busy through the two tribes. It was arranged that we were to start on Monday, March 21st, the Indian recruits to meet us across the Gila, to receive their blankets, knives, etc., and thence we were to go on.

On Monday we started, but owing to a heavy road and weak animals, we were unable to make the rendezvous that night. During the night it commenced raining, and a more chilly, dismal group you never saw; we had no tents. Fortunately it lulled for breakfast, and soon after we got under way, crossed the Gila and came to the camp of our Indian escorts. It was still drizzling. The Indians were grouped, shivering, around small, cheerless fires, a squaw or two about, who had followed them this far, in hopes, perhaps, to steal a blanket, for theft is first nature to an Indian.

The scene was unique; in the background the Maricopa mountain all dressed in rolling masses of cloud, nearer the Gila with its margin of willows and cottonwood.[1] Col. Poston stood under a green blanket, stretched across sticks held by his servant, to keep off the rain, and the Pima roll was called, each one answering to his name, twenty-six in all under an old war captain, Juan Manuel.

---

[1] Maricopa Peak is 4,084 feet and is part of the Maricopa Range. Originally the Spanish referred to the Maricopas and the Estrella Range as the Sierra Estrella. The Sierra Estrella is located south of the junction of the Salt and Gila rivers below the present-day city of Avondale. The name Gila was applied to the province of New Mexico about 1630 by the Spanish, after the idiom *de gila,* meaning "steady going to or from a place." Father Kino seems to have been the first (in 1694) to apply the word to the river. Originally the Gila was the major tributary of the Colorado River and was never dry as in modern times. Modern dams have drained off feed-streams which once poured into the Gila. The river was crossed by Anglos as early as 1539. (Byrd H. Granger, *Arizona Place Names,* pp. 102–3, 294.)

Superintendent of Indian Affairs Charles D. Poston, the colorful "Father of Arizona," accompanied Allyn's party from White's Mill to the Hassayampa, in company with a guard of Pima and Maricopa volunteers.

With them was young Antoine, who, stripped of gay trappings, looked even more thoroughly a stupid boy. Blankets were distributed to each, blue ones to the soldiers and red ones to the captain. Antoineto and the interpreters were provided with sabres; the soldiers likewise received a belt and knife. They were previously all equipped with muskets, cartridge boxes, etc.

Next the Maricopa braves were called, ranged in a line and a list of their names taken down. They were boisterously merry during this proceeding, and the names given were certainly comical enough; some did not seem to have any name and one was manufactured for them, generally relating to some peculiarity of personal appearance or manner; but there were others like "horse," "old pantaloons," "soap suds," etc., which excited rounds of laughter. *Pantalon viejo,* or "old pantaloons," was not, as his name indicates perhaps, an old man, but on the contrary was the youngest Indian along, his father giving him the name apparently as though he had got along so far without one, and on the rainy day in question he certainly had an old pair of pants on, which was quite *distingué* considering that most had no other pants than nature provides. The precocious youth was handed over to Col. P. as a sort of servant, in which capacity he was very useful, as he did not understand either English or Spanish. The equipment of the Maricopas in the same manner as the Pimas over, our novel party got under way. Some dozen of the Maricopas were mounted and formed the cavalry of the outfit. They moved off as the advance guard, followed by Smith, Poston and myself, and then the wagons, pack train, and the two companies of footmen.

We camped on the Gila. The sky was still threatening, and the Indians soon built themselves a complete rancheria or village. It did not rain, however; we tried to persuade them to set a guard over the animals, but they declined, saying they were all sentinels. There was something of the romantic in the idea of three white men quietly going to sleep in the midst of a camp of Indians, and that too, on a journey through a country desolated by an Indian war, to visit an almost unknown nation of the aborigines of this country.

We moved the next morning, and that day reached the Salinas. In camp here, we were in sight of the monument erected at the junction of the Gila and the Salinas by the boundary line commission.[2] While we were here the Indians did some fishing in a novel way. They dammed a "slough" of the river with brush, standing on the dam to keep it firm, and then two or three of them with improvised nets waded in and caught the fish.

The next day we hoped to get water at the White Tank mountains, a little to the left of the road;[3] our animals were weak and we

---

[2] According to the Treaty of Guadalupe Hidalgo, which ended the Mexican War (February 2, 1848), the original boundary was north of the Gila River. At the Salt and Gila junction the line followed down the middle of the Gila to the Colorado. (Rufus Kay Wyllys, *Arizona: The History of a Frontier State*, p. 102.) John R. Bartlett, member of the boundary commission established by the treaty, sent a party under Amiel Whipple and surveyor A. B. Gray to survey the Gila River line. This work was finished in 1855 and the monuments installed. (James H. McClintock, *Arizona: Prehistoric, Aboriginal, Pioneer, Modern*, 1:117.)

[3] The White Tank Mountains lie east of the Hassayampa River and north of the present-day city of Buckeye. (Will C. Barnes, *Arizona Place Names*, p. 485.)

had to make a noon rest. When we got started the Indians moved off with great rapidity, and toward sundown our train was beautifully scattered. Smith had already ridden ahead to see about the water. I rode on alone slowly, thinking I should overtake S. or the Indians, passing our wagon alone, in one place, the pack train farther on, equally unguarded. It grew quite dark, I neither found the Indians or Smith, Poston did not overtake me, I had seen no trail leading to water. I turned back, found the wagon, and pack animals, but no Poston, Smith or water.

The men in charge of the wagons and team only spoke Spanish; I am especially unproficient in that language anyhow! Someone was hallooing way off the road, and at last a gun was fired. I sent one of the boys on a mule over to see if he could find out who was there, but he came back without reaching them. By this time Poston arrived, and we concluded to go on. About a mile brought us right on the camp of our soldiery, fires blazing and everything comfortable, just as though we were not in the world. This may be a very safe way of travelling, but it is new to one accustomed to military routine. It seems the Indians were thirsty, went straight to the water, and thence on to where they camped, not touching the road for six or seven miles.

I suppose, careless as it seemed, there was really less danger of a surprise than with regulars. These Indians have a sort of an instinct that tells them when an Apache is near. To illustrate the keenness of their observation: You walk out in the streets of their villages, call the first man you see, and ask him whose track that is, pointing to a footprint in the dust, and he will tell you the name of the person, with almost unerring certainty, who made it. When you think of a population of six thousand, this verges on the miraculous. But I nearly forgot Smith; he went to the water, returned to the road to show us the way and struck it after we had passed, and came into camp last of all. Of course it was a dry camp; fortunately there was enough water in the canteens to make coffee, and over our supper we laughed at our mishaps.

The next day it was a long tedious drive across the same monotonous desert to the Hassayampa creek, where we found running water.[4] Here we had quite a gay camp. Our soldiery had been prac-

---

[4] The Mohaves named it the Hassayampa River or the "Place of the Big Rocks Water." (Granger, *Arizona Place Names,* p. 183.)

tising slyly at dress parades and at evening we were invited to be present at one. Antoineto and his interpreter have been in San Francisco, and there or at Fort Yuma they had picked up the rudiments of the manual of arms. Arranging their company in double line, they went from order to shoulder arms, then to present, etc., quite creditably. All the orders were in Pima, and Capt. Juan Manuel kept walking up and down the line, talking most volubly to his recruits, scolding them, I suppose, in a manner not unlike a drill sergeant in the states. After this they underwent a careful inspection of their arms and practiced for some time in the loadings. I have seen white recruits who did no better than these Indians. This thing was purely of their own volition. There is quite a brisk rivalry in this matter and there was little to choose between the two.

My friend Smith had invested in a half dozen chickens and a pair of small pigs to stock a ranche he has on Granite Creek, and the trouble they made him was a constant source of fun. More obstinate animals than the pigs it would be difficult to imagine. Tie them up by a long rope to a box, and for an hour I have seen one of them pulling as though it would pull its own leg out. All sorts of expedients were resorted to, to let them out of the box, where they rode all day, and not let them get away. They were hobbled, that is, two feet tied together, side lined or hobbling the legs upon one side, picketed, but every little while they would get loose, and then our young attache "old pantaloons," was set at the pleasant task of catching them. He is a lazy little scapegrace, and it often took him a long while, and then the squealing was terrific. The smaller a pig is the more noise he can make. The chickens were less trouble, but they kept constantly getting mixed up with a lot more the cook had to kill. This difficulty, however, was easily remedied by eating the one lot up. Our model donkey that had come with us from the Verde, now he had got into company, bid fair to lose his reputation as a remarkably good ass by making night and day hideous with his terrible braying. Reader, did you ever hear a donkey bray? I hope you never will, or if you do that you will be in a country where there is no statute against cruelty to animals. Johnny had never opened his mouth, except to eat, during all the long trip before, but now that he was among Indians and asses, he seemed determined to outbray them all.

On the Hassayampa the next day we passed two or three abandoned ranches and camped near the first occupied one we came to. Here we met an express messenger bound to Pima, with letters begging the assistance of the Indians in a campaign against the Apaches. The messenger corroborated the worst reports of the state of things above.[5] Half the population had left for the Colorado to avoid starvation and death; a hundred men under Woolsey were to start at once on a campaign; Fort Whipple was thronged with fugitives; there wasn't an animal fit to use left in the country; and, lastly, he said the governor was only a little way behind him, with an escort, bound to the Pima and Tucson.

In a short time the governor rode up. From him I learned of the safe return of his expedition from the point where I had left, losing only mules enough to make a loss of nineteen in all on the trip. He represented the state of things as deplorable, but seemed to have little hopes of doing much because of the want of provisions. Col. P. offered to lead his Indians to join Woolsey if they could have but a thousand pounds of flour. The governor assured us it could not be got at Whipple, although he admitted there was over five months' supply for the garrison on hand, and the post is within less than two hundred miles of the Colorado, where supplies are abundant. Juan Chevariah was consulted; he said his people had no wheat, that the military had taken all that after the harvest in June; he was ready to go and supply his boys himself; that his party had but five days' supply of *pinoly* on hand. The camp of the governor's escort was about a half mile from us, and many of the Indians strayed over there; when they returned they said they had been told Colonel P. was taking them where they would freeze and starve. They professed not to mind it, but it was evident that it had disturbed them. Col. P. determined to go on to Whipple and make requisition for provisions, and let them then refuse if they would.

---

[5] Indian depredations were attributed variously to Hualapais, Yavapais, and Apaches. Sometime the innocent paid for the sins of others. Early files of the *Arizona Miner* are incomplete. However, the issue of March 23, 1864, reported that on March 16th Indians attacked Sheldon's Ranch, twenty-five miles south of Prescott, and killed Mr. Cosgrove, in charge there, and ran off several head of cattle. The Indian problem influenced the decision to move the capital to Prescott in May 1864. (Pauline Henson, *Wilderness Capital, Prescott, A.T., 1864*, p. 148–55.)

Next morning five of the Pimas went back, and the rest of us pushed on to Weaver,[6] a small mining town at the foot of Antelope mountain, on the top of which is the celebrated Jack Swilling[7] claim, where twenty thousand dollars in gold was taken out in a week with no water, and a simple belt knife, about a year ago. The claim is still very rich, and is worked by carrying water up on donkeys. The village of Weaver is a picturesque little hamlet stretching along Indian Creek in a gorge of the mountain. It is stragglingly built on one street. There are adobe, reed, mud, and stone houses, two thirds of them covered with wagon sheets yet, a large number of stores with considerable stocks of goods, a population as mixed as the houses, Jew and Gentile, black and white, Mexican and American. We camped about a mile from there and walked into town accompanied by the two Juans and a half dozen Indians, creating great excitement. Chevariah was the lion of the hour. The whole population was on the street. Were we bound against the Apaches? was the query. Our fix was soon buzzed round the town. There were sixty good Indian fighters that could "pack their own grub;" they only needed a little flour; Uncle Sam wouldn't or couldn't give it to them; the Governor had gone; how much flour was there in Weaver? This is about the run of the comments.

An inventory showed fifteen hundred pounds of flour in the town, with a population now of about one hundred — there were four hundred there before the outbreak. One man threw an hundred

---

[6] Rich deposits of gold were discovered on Antelope Mountain by members of the Abraham Harlow Peeples party in 1863. Weaver (or Antelope or Weaverville) developed into a small town which serviced the mines on the peak. The ore bodies were worked out by the 1890s, and the place became a notorious hangout for riffraff. (Granger, *Arizona Place Names*, p. 362.)

[7] Jack (John W.) Swilling (1831–78), a native of Georgia, appeared in Arizona with Captain Hunter's Texans. Subsequently, Swilling engaged in mining at Antelope Mountain and at the Vulture Mine near Wickenburg. He is credited with the founding of Phoenix in 1867, when he and a dozen men resurrected the ancient Hohokam irrigation canal about four miles up the Salt River in modern eastern Phoenix. He organized the Swilling Irrigation Canal Company and rebuilt what came to be known as the Grand Canal. The development not only resulted in the establishment of Phoenix but in modern large-scale farm production in the area. Swilling was with the party which met the Apache renegade, Mangas Colorado, and accepted his surrender. Later Swilling was falsely accused of holding up the Wickenburg stage and died in Yuma prison awaiting trial at the age of forty-seven. (Hubert Howe Bancroft, *History of Arizona and New Mexico 1530–1888*, p. 514; Andrew Wallace, "John W. Swilling," pp. 16–19; Boyd Finch, "Sherod Hunter and the Confederates in Arizona," pp. 169–74.)

pound sack of flour down in the street, another covered it, and another, until the pile was a large one, and included bacon, coffee, sugar, salt, etc. A dozen men volunteered to go. Col. P. arranged to unpack and store his Indian goods for the Moquis, and his luggage, in order to furnish pack animals to carry the provisions. Chevariah's interpreter, and perhaps old Juan himself, took considerable whisky and then commenced shouting in Spanish the praises of Chevariah. As I passed up the street his *muy valliante* rang out clear and sonorous, echoing back from the mountain. Altogether it was a scene that it would be difficult to forget. Just in the midst of the excitement a pack train of thirty donkeys, loaded with provisions, came up the street, just arrived from the Colorado, and the donkey chorus was soon in full blast.

I took tea with an American woman from Indiana, the only one left here now. She was a plucky little woman, slept with her pistols under the pillow, and had a little brood of four or five children, who soon announced themselves by rushing in to tell mamma the Indian company was on the street; mayn't they go and see 'em. It proved that our escort was going through the dress parade they had practised. Mother and children went down to see it, and they thought it was splendid.

˙ So the Moqui expedition ended. I and my companion, with mules, pigs, chickens, and Johnny,[8] were left to our own resources again, and about sixty miles from the post. My mule was uncertain; she didn't improve. I had been riding a horse of Col. P.'s so far, which had to go on the Indian hunt. A Mr Halstead[9] with a Mexican bay joined us, who wanted to get through, so we commenced preparations. I had to buy some coffee and sugar and get enough to last two or three days, for five dollars. We got through without accident, save that my mule had to be left, finally, after all. I didn't shoot her,

---

[8] "My companion" was still Van C. Smith, and "Johnny" was the mule.

[9] The identification of "Mr. Halstead" is uncertain. However, in June 1864, about the time of the Allyn account, a James A. Halstead of Yuma was appointed lot appraiser in Prescott. (Arizona Historical Foundation Biographical File, Arizona State University Library. See also Thomas E. Farish, *History of Arizona* 3:193.) An earlier Halstead had a gold mine near Fort Yuma in 1854 (Wallace W. Elliott, *History of Arizona Territory: Its Resources and Advantages*, p. 93.) Farish also notes (from Sylvester S. Mowry's *Arizona and Sonora*), that a Halstead discovered the Colorado River copper mine in 1861 and that he was an "indefatigable prospector." (Farish, *History of Arizona* 2:74, 76.)

but left her where there was good grass and water. One of the chickens died; the rest, with the pigs, survived the packing on the back of Johnny. It was about the most provoking load to pack, for the pigs would not lay still, and kept disturbing the equilibrium of the load; but Johnny got back into our good graces by his behavior now.

To illustrate to you how carefully men travel here: One evening we traveled until 9 o'clock, turned way off the trail, camped without fire, tied our animals, stood guard over them all night, and when dawn came we found another party of about our number had camped within an hundred rods of us and neither knew the other was near. It was a melancholy journey, past burned and deserted cabins. But this letter has already exceeded all bounds, and I am sure any one who reads thus far will be glad I am tired.

SPRING AT FORT WHIPPLE —
PARTING WITH OLD FRIENDS —
PRESCOTT, THE NEW CAPITAL —
MAKING A CITY — A BRAVE FIGHT —
CULTIVATING THE LAND —
RESOURCES OF THE TERRITORY

La Paz, June 29, 1864
[Published August 8, 1864]

Some apology is due to the indulgent reader of these letters for this long interval of silence. I had not neglected thus long my old friends, but for the pressure of multifarious cares and health not over strong. I wrote you once of the delightful climate of Fort Whipple in the winter. Alas, what a change. I returned thither on the 1st of April to find a spring rivaling New England in the rapidity of its atmospheric changes; the fierce winds being really the only uniform thing about the climate. The dust whirled in all sorts of airy flights; rattlesnakes crawled out of the rocks, and bloodthirsty mosquitos made perpetual music in your tents. Two months, passed in intense discomfort, slipped away, the weary monotony only broken by the wrangling of politicians (for in this free country of ours one needs to go further in the woods than this to get beyond the busy intriguings of ambitious men), or the semi-monthly arrival of the mail, by which we get a sort of sideways glimpse of the outer world, most unsatisfactory now, too, when great events are transpiring, and the fortune of millions is staked on the issue of battle.[1]

With the opening summer came the advance of the eastern emigration; trains of white-topped wagons drawn by weary oxen,

---

[1]Allyn is undoubtedly referring to the great engagements being waged before the approaches to Richmond. In May and June of 1864 the terrible battles of Spotsylvania and Cold Harbor had been fought with enormous losses to both sides. In a series of grinding, costly battles, Grant attempted to outflank Lee before Richmond. The result was a slow, sure attrition of Confederate strength. (Bruce Catton, *Never Call Retreat*, pp. 354–59.)

containing the household goods and gods of families moving from one half finished home to begin another, with the ever restless, never satisfied spirit of the frontiermen. Three trains came all the way from Denver, and more are behind them.[2] They bring sad stories of the suffering of the several parties that have gone into the Rio Grande over the same route we traversed so safely in mid-winter. The snow had been deep, animals had died, and, footsore and half starved, the men had limped into Wingate. It was very fortunate that Col. Poston's trip to Moqui was broken up,[3] for it would have been scarcely possible to have escaped loss of life in the storms we surely should have encountered.

During these two months Col. Chavez, with the last of the Missourians that came with us from Leavenworth, have gone back to the Rio Grande. It was like parting with old friends; the severing of the last tie that binds us to the east. Those rough bronzed faces had grown familiar in the long journey; even one came to know the very horses they rode. Together we had endured the heats of September upon the plains, the fierce early snow storms upon the Arkansas, crossed the Rocky Mountains, explored the canoned mysteries of the Rio Verde, and the volcanic surroundings of the peerless San Francisco mountain. I rode out with them a few miles the morning they started, and as the last echo of their three cheers broke on the ear, there was a slight twinge of longing for home, a terrible sense of loneliness that one could not shake off for the moment.

They disappeared over the slope of a hill and I rode wearily back toward the post. Col. Chavez attempts a new route to the east that will save some hundred miles between the mines and Albuquerque, by going to the Little Colorado, avoiding the San Francisco mountain; a route he has already examined, but where wagons have never been taken. It crosses the Rio Verde just above the scene of the skirmish with the Indians where Fisher was wounded. The season is now quite advanced and everything promises a pleasant and suc-

---

[2]No references to these wagon trains were found in the contemporary issues of the *Arizona Miner*.

[3]The reference is to the abortive expedition to the Hopi which broke up near Prescott. (See Letter 9.)

cessful trip. The Governor at last returns from Tucson,[4] and it is definitely announced that the Capital is to be located on Granite Creek, about twenty miles from him, and the post is to be removed thither.[5] All is now bustle and excitement at both places. The surveyor[6] is now at work measuring off plazas, laying out streets and avenues, and creating the city of Prescott[7] on paper. Trains are rapidly moving the accumulated stores from the old to the new post. One by one the buildings are demolished at the one place and re-erected at the other. More troops came in from the Rio Grande that passed Col. Chavez at Navajo Springs, in sight almost of the Little Colorado. Col. Chavez found his progress barred by the Canon Diablo down which he had to proceed in order to get across.

He was three days without water, and his rations were about

---

[4]The Fort Whipple records show that the Goodwin party and its military escort came back from Tucson on May 27. The governor had returned from his Verde River trip on March 17 and in early April left for southern Arizona. ("Returns from U.S. Military Posts," Fort Whipple, March, May 1864. See also *Arizona Miner*, April 6, 1864, May 11, 1864.) Goodwin needed to make a decision on the location of the capital and to survey the territory for which he as governor was responsible. The trips were doubtless also made to increase his political stature.

[5]The first capital was established at Fort Whipple on January 22, 1864. This site was soon found to be unsuitable because of its remoteness and lack of mining activity and population, in spite of rich pasture and a plentitude of water. Traditional Tucson and booming La Paz were obvious candidates for a permanent capital, but the Union-dominated government and the miners had other ideas. Indian troubles, territorial government fears of the Confederate and Mexican influences in Tucson, and the presence of promising gold mines on Granite Creek all contributed to the choice of Prescott. The military left Whipple (renamed Camp Clark) and reestablished the fort near Prescott. (See Governor Goodwin's letter to General Carleton, published in the *Arizona Miner*, April 4, 1864. See also *Arizona Miner*, May 11, 1864; May 25, 1864; June 22, 1864; Pauline Henson, *Wilderness Capital, Prescott, A.T., 1864*, pp. 127, 153–55.)

[6]The surveyor was Robert B. Groom. (Wagoner, *Arizona Territory*, p. 36.)

[7]The name Prescott was assigned by McCormick, who had brought a library (now part of the Arizona State Library, Capitol Building, Phoenix) which included *The Conquest of Mexico and Peru* by William Hickling Prescott (1796–1859). In a series of articles appearing in the May 25, June 22, and July 20 issues of the *Arizona Miner*, McCormick explained his reason for so honoring the famous historian. The territorial secretary believed that Prescott had concluded that the Aztecs and Toltecs had originated in the Arizona region. Actually, Prescott merely says that "the Chichemecs entered the deserted country [Mexico] from the regions of the far Northwest" and that "the Mexicans . . . came also, as we have seen, from the remote regions of the North. . . ." (*Conquest of Mexico and Peru*, pp. 14–15.)

exhausted, when he met these troops. There can be but little doubt but that by going farther to the right, the canon can be avoided, and that a road will yet be made on that route. Last of all, the flagstaff was taken down and removed to the new post. All this time there has been a lull in the Indian hostilities, the great Navajo tribe has at last yielded, and six thousand of them are already in the reservation near Fort Sumner.[8] Late trains met large bodies with flocks and herds on the way east to surrender. This releases a large body of troops for the prosecution of the war against the Apaches, and a formidable campaign is already projected.

The climate of the valley of Granite Creek is in marked contrast to that of the open plain around the old post. The mountains around shelter it from the winds, and the trees shield you from the burning heat, so that it is warmer at night and cooler in the daytime. A more picturesque little valley for a town can scarcely be imagined. The surveyor has staked out blocks, squares and streets. The camps of the new comers are scattered along the stream; a boarding house is opened where you get bread and bacon for ten dollars a week, payable in gold, and an improvised whiskey shop is in full blast under a tree, before a house is erected on the town site.

It was arranged that the town lots should be sold at auction, and on the day appointed a large crowd assembled. Those desirous of securing lots put notices on those they preferred, in the vain hope that there would be no bidding against them. The bidding was spirited, and the entire sum realized for lots the first day was about twelve thousand dollars. The highest lot sold was one intended for a printing office, and about the only one at appraisal was for the whiskey shop. This I suppose indicating the high regard in which the press is held in the mountains.[9]

---

[8] The Navajo had been defeated by forces under Colonel C. (Kit) Carson and Colonel José Francisco Chaves. By April 1864 the remaining Navajos had surrendered and were ordered by General Carleton to be located at Bosque Redondo, Fort Sumner, on the Pecos River in southern New Mexico. Carleton planned to empty "forever" the Navajo homeland. His plan ultimately failed, and the Navajos were returned to a reduced reservation. (Lynn R. Bailey, *Bosque Redondo*, pp. 54–84, 149–57.)

[9] This undoubtedly refers to the future site of the *Arizona Miner*, which claimed to have erected the first building in Prescott. (*Arizona Miner*, June 22, 1864. See also New York *Tribune*, June 1, 1865.) The *Miner's* owner-publisher, Secretary of the Territory Richard C. McCormick, was an early purchaser of and speculator in Prescott real estate. (Henson, *Wilderness Capital*, p. 165.) For more information on the *Arizona Miner*, see Background, note 107.

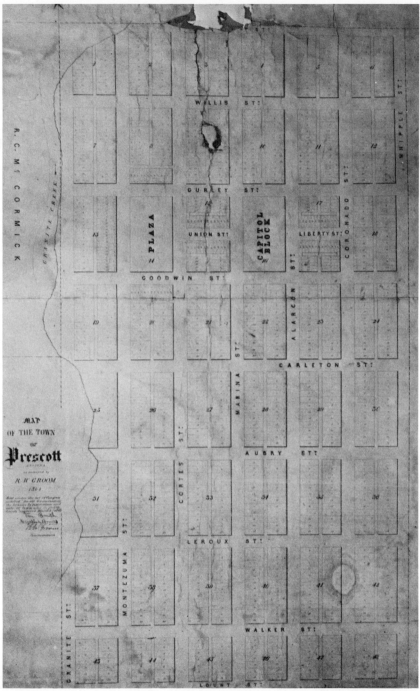

This 1864 map of Prescott shows the streets as blocked out by the surveyor. Allyn describes the spirited bidding for lots in the projected town.

No better illustration of the firm faith of the people here in the future development of the various gold and silver lodes in the neighborhood could be had than this sale. Miners hastened to invest their hard-earned dust, and merchants their enormous gains, in little twenty-five to one hundred and fifty feet lots in a town without a building. If the quartz within twenty miles radius of Granite Creek equals the surface indications, this is incomparably the richest mineral region of the territories, and it requires no vivid imagination to see ten thousand people within a year in Prescott, when a few short weeks ago the only live establishment was a whiskey shop under a tree.[10] The single quartz and saw mill[11] now on the Colorado river on its way hither will do more to destroy the Apaches than all the bands King Woolsey leads, or the columns Gen. Carleton hurls against them. Demonstrated, the accessible existence of gold and silver in the rocks, and all the rest is easy. There is no state so easily built up as a mining state, and perhaps none have so fragile an existence after they are built up.

The Indians have broken the long lull with one of the most sanguinary and brave little encounters on the part of a small body of whites I ever heard of. Five men had carelessly camped on Tuesday week without a guard, and during the night they were surprised, or *jumped,* as the phrase is here, by a large band of Indians. At the first fire every one of them was wounded as they lay sleeping. Seizing their arms, they crawled back to a place better adapted for defense, abandoning their animals and camp. All that day they kept up the fight, the Indians constantly assailing them. Growing weaker from their wounds, they at last determined to send the two strongest for assistance. These left, and traveled to the lower Hassayampa, where a party was at once raised to go to the rescue. They found the wounded men alive, and the Indians driven away. So exhausted were these poor men that they had been twenty-four hours in crawling to water distant only a few hundred yards. An express was sent to the post for a surgeon, and at last accounts all were still living.

---

[10] The "whiskey shop" may have been the first building of logs in the new city. Michael Wormser purchased such a building on Montezuma Street from Rafael Lucero and turned it into a saloon. (Henson, *Wilderness Capital,* p. 165.)

[11] According to the C. B. Genung account in Farish, the first sawmill in the Prescott area was built by George Lount and C. Clark. It operated on the outskirts of Prescott. (Thomas E. Farish, *History of Arizona* 3:215.)

Allyn says that the lot intended for the office of the *Arizona Miner* sold for the highest sum in the Prescott land auction. In the background of this picture stands the "whiskey shop" built on the only appraised lot sold that day.

Now that the frosts are passed, everyone is busy planting a little garden. Seeds are almost worth their weight in gold. No one knows what the seasons are, or how much rain we have. Still a good many acres are spaded up, and a little of everything is being planted. If anything grows it will be remunerative, for anything in the shape of a vegetable will bring any price, there being none here. The later immigrants drove through a good many cows, so that we are beginning to indulge in the luxury of milk. The cost of provisions here is enormous; flour $80. per 100 lbs.; bacon, coffee and sugar 75 cts. a pound, in gold. These high prices are incident to the early history of nearly all the mining countries, and will probably be of less duration in Arizona than the others, for our territory is really less inaccessible than the others. Prescott is less than two hundred miles from the Colorado, a river navigable by steamboats, that empties into the Gulf of California. Beside, there is, near the mines, an abundance of land adapted to grazing, and the Salinas and the Gila valleys would supply a hundred thousand people with breadstuffs. If the mines develop sufficiently to draw a large population, a year will scarcely elapse before Arizona ranks among the first of the stock raising countries. Nothing but the Indians prevents large herds being driven from California now.

Letter 11

JOURNEY FROM FORT WHIPPLE TO LA PAZ — INDIANS — GETTING LOST — NIGHT RIDING — SPLENDID CACTUS — SUFFERING IN THE DESERT

La Paz, July 1, 1864
[Published August 19, 1864]

On the 9th of June I left Fort Whipple with an escort of five men, for the great Colorado river at this point. We had a light wagon, with four mules, and I was mounted on a recent purchase, a half-breed California horse, that had recently been ridden from San Bernardino[1] over the deserts on both sides of the Colorado, showing on the trip extraordinary powers of endurance. Thus equipped, we felt little apprehension about getting safely over the desert; the weather was delightful, the soldiers in the highest spirits; one of them killed a deer the first day, and all went merry as a picnicking party.

Our route takes us to Antelope or Weaver, the little mining hamlet where I left the Pima and Maricopa Indians last March. Having a wagon, we do not however follow the same trail that we took then. We swept round the huge granite mountain[2] that forms so marked a landmark near Fort Whipple, and which I think must be the Tonto buttes of the war department map, there being no other prominent isolated mountain near; over the foothills, covered with fine grass and sprinkled with the endless variety of richly hued and fragrant little wild flowers, so agreeable a feature of this por-

---

[1] San Bernardino, California, at the western end of the San Gorgonio and Cajon Pass routes to and from Los Angeles, was an important point of departure for Yuma and other Arizona points.

[2] The "huge granite mountain" is no longer known as Tonto Buttes but as Granite Mountain. Allyn swung north and west of the range along a route to be followed a century later by the Santa Fe Railway when it relocated its Ash Fork to Phoenix branch line, thus bypassing Prescott.

[133]

tion of the country, and camped the first night in a valley called
the Mint valley,[3] from the quantity of mint that grows near the
spring.

Next morning we crossed over the divide that separates the
Val de Chino from the waters that run to the Bill Williams fork of
the Colorado. The road is a very rough one for five or six miles,
and threads a labyrinthian mass of granite boulders of fantastic
shapes and giant proportions that would have delighted the eye of
the Druids. We stopped to rest during the heat of the day in the
shade of a beautiful grove, and were enjoying the laziness of the
hour, watching the wreaths of smoke rising from our pipes while
the animals were grazing. Suddenly there was a cry, "Indians,
Indians," a grasping of rifles, and an instantaneous springing to our
feet. About twenty-five Indians with bows and arrows were in sight,
advancing, showing a white flag, crying out, "Amigos, Apache
Mohave!" The Mohaves[4] are favorable to the whites.

We advanced toward them, and by signs made them lay down
their arms. They said they were camped some miles below with
their women and children to gather provisions and hunt; that we
were between them and the water. We allowed them to pass to the
spring and forbade their coming into camp. But you might as well
tell the wind not to blow. After getting the water they squatted
down in a body a few rods off, and in a half hour, on one pretext
or another, two-thirds of them were in camp, begging for tobacco,
etc. They were so annoying that we packed up and went on to avoid
the possibility of any quarrel. The whites have quite Indian war
enough on their hands without aggravating another harmless and
starving tribe. We camped in a splendid *cienaga,* where the grass
was up to the belly of a horse.

---

[3] Mint Valley in Yavapai County on Mint Creek, is approximately fifteen
miles northwest of Prescott. An early settler by the name of McKee named
the area in the 1860s because of the mint along the creek. Indians and drought
forced him to abandon his ranch. (Byrd H. Granger, *Arizona Place Names,*
p. 351.)

[4] The Apache-Mohaves, or Yavapais, were related to the Colorado tribes
and to the Apaches in "race and character." The 1,500 to 2,000 members
were generally friendly but had become notorious owing to their connection
with the Oatman massacre of 1851. They were subjected to savage Anglo
attacks during 1866–68. In retaliation, the tribe went to war in 1871–72. In
1874, because of their identification with the Apache, they were sent to the
San Carlos Reservation. (Hubert Howe Bancroft, *History of Arizona and New
Mexico,* p. 546; Rufus Kay Wyllys, *Arizona: The History of A Frontier State,*
p. 134.)

Next day, riding ahead of the wagon, I followed the wrong trail down the banks of the Santa Maria[5] five or six miles. I knew I ought to reach Rutland rancho[6] in about that distance and paid little heed to the direction until I had ridden that far and found no rancho, when I saw I was going nearly west instead of south. I knew the road was to the left of me, and first tried to follow the Santa Maria up, and thus strike across to it, but the country was broken and the banks of the stream frequently perpendicular, and always covered with dense undergrowth, so that I made slow progress. In the midst of my perplexity I heard someone calling. Thinking it my own party, I shouted back, rode toward the sound, and soon discovered an Indian on the top of a hill gesticulating, laying down his bow and making other friendly signs. I think it not unlikely that he was aware that I was lost and wanted to show me a trail across, but I concluded it was best not to trust him, so I turned back on my own tracks and retraced my steps the whole distance and then followed the fresh wagon tracks of my own wagon, overtaking the boys who were a good deal alarmed at my non-appearance at 2 p.m. I had been eight hours in the saddle and was very tired, so that the wagon was a very pleasant sight.

Next day we crossed Antelope mountain and camped near Weaver, which looked the same nondescript picturesque hamlet that it did last March.[7] I saw little change, save warm weather; it was literally infested with flies, everything was black and the concentrated buzz could be heard a half a mile if the wind was favorable, I am sure. This was the starting point of our difficult journey, and the officer commanding the escort was busy obtaining information about the road, water, etc. All seemed to agree that the road was good, grass superb, and the only drawback want of water. It might be eighty miles without water, they said. Only one person told a different story, an American woman, the only one in town. She said her husband tried it once with a wagon and although

---

[5] The Santa María River, named by Oñate in 1604, or the Bill Williams River, enters the Colorado near Parker. Allyn apparently had inadvertently swung west along one of the tributaries of the Santa María. (Granger, *Arizona Place Names*, p. 222.)

[6] The "Rutland Rancho" is not listed in the exhaustive file of Arizona ranches in the Arizona Historical Society Library or elsewhere. Possibly the name Rutland is an error on Allyn's part or a misprint.

[7] See Letter 9, note 6. Weaver was situated a short distance east of what is now Congress Junction and adjacent to Octave, north of Wickenburg. Allyn probably followed a route through Skull Valley.

he got through, always spoke of it as a fearful trip, one that no one ought to try again. Our preparations were very complete. We carried sixty gallons of water. If the road was smooth, this would carry us some eighty miles, and we had learned by experience that distances were overestimated, and did not believe the eighty miles would measure over sixty. A gentleman just in on horseback pointed out to the escort the range of hills that indicated the first water.

Next morning we started and followed about ten miles a wagon road that led toward the points he indicated and found at last that it was a wood road and ran out. This time I had stuck by the wagon, and two of the boys were off on the trail. I rode across the country four or five miles trying to find a place to get the wagon across a canon, until it seemed evident that there was nothing to do but to go back. So back we came to Antelope Creek and camped. It was a bad day's work for mules that had a hard journey before them. I presume the gentleman who pointed out the landmarks to Sergeant Ashby[8] was deceived; either he was, or Ashby misunderstood him. The weather is much warmer this side of Antelope mountain, and if it grows much more so, as it most probably will in the desert, it will not do to travel in the day time. Between here and the Colorado we have to descend several thousand feet. It was always the most difficult problem of the Pacific R.R., how to get down to the river from the table land. Whipple accomplished it by way of Bill William's fork, in the same direction in which I got lost.[9]

By sunrise in the morning we were off on the right trail, which led over vast steppes, between two ranges of mountains.[10] The soil

---

[8] Sergeant Charles Henry Ashby (1834–?) was a native of Massachusetts and had come to Arizona with the California Column (Company C, First California Cavalry), probably joining in 1862. He led an assault against the Yavapais who were attacking the Sheldon ranch near Prescott in 1864. Ashby was mustered out August 25, 1864. (Arizona Historical Society Biographical File; *U.S. Census*, 1864, p. 119.)

[9] At Weaver, Allyn's elevation was about 5,000 feet. He refers to Whipple's 1854 survey of possible railway routes from New Mexico to California. (Amiel W. Whipple, *Report of Exploration and Surveys to Ascertain the Most Practical and Economical Route for a Railroad from the Mississippi River to the Ocean, 1853–1854*, p. 305. See also David E. Conrad, "The Whipple Expedition in Arizona 1853–1854," pp. 147–78.)

[10] Allyn's route to La Paz seems to have followed, in general, the routes of modern highways from Congress through Aguila and Wenden to Quartzite. This route passes through the Aguila valley between the Harcuvar Mountains on the north and the Harquahalas to the south. Early maps show such a wagon road from La Paz to Prescott. (See Arizona Historical Society Map File: "Arizona Territory 1881.")

was a granite gravel, and the growth of grass luxuriant, of a kind
called *sacatane* [sacaton],[11] very nutritious for animals. We reached
Solomon's wells,[12] the first water at noon, and the odometer marked
the distance fourteen miles; it was called sixteen. The heat was intense in the sun, but a gentle breeze swept over the plain and we
improvised a shade with blankets and the wagon that was quite
comfortable. It was not certain that we should find water beyond,
so we filled up our barrels and kegs here, and at sundown started on.

Next morning we were under way before day and found no
water in Canon Springs, pushed on until we reached the turning of
the road to Hockaville,[13] an Indian rancheria three miles off the
road, where there was water. Here we found a party of Mexicans
resting their animals, laying off on a wagon sheet stretched over some
cactus bushes, stripped entirely naked. The road has here diverged
considerably to the south and on to the lower benches of the mountains, which may account for the absence of grass. There seems no
reason why this steppe should not be good pasturage as well as the
other. The air seems to be constantly in motion on these plains,
although it blows in streaks. I have seen a half dozen little whirl-
winds raising columns of dust and marching along.[14] One struck
our Mexican shelter and made quick work of it. These little whirl-
winds are rather pretty features of the river in a hot day. I saw none
of the larger ones, such as we had at Whipple last April. There I
have seen a perfect unbroken column of dust at least two hundred
feet high, with another fifty feet of smoke above it, marching majestically along for miles. I estimated the height by seeing one march
right against the flag staff, the little storm flag strained the halyards,
but they were strong, and in a moment this pillar of cloud passed,
and the colors dropped listlessly to the staff; from the parade ground
it passed to the officers' tents, and taking the surgeon's in its course,
it literally lifted everything up and tossed it off some distance, a
perfect wreck.

---

[11] *Sacaton* is derived from a Nahuatl word and refers to a coarse and
often inedible forage. What was probably meant was *sacate,* which is a type
of grass preferred by cattle and horses. (Granger, *Arizona Place Names,*
p. 305.)

[12] Solomon's Wells was not found in the Arizona Historical Society Files
or in other sources consulted.

[13] Hockaville also was not found in sources consulted. It is possibly a
corruption of the name of the nearby Harquahala or Harcuvar Mountains.

[14] These are commonly called "dust devils" in the West.

The road passed over a low range of hills and debouched into another of these grand steppes, hemmed in by mountain ranges. I rode slowly ahead alone. It was cool, and the full moon was just silvering the plain. All the varieties of the cactus described in my letter from Pima were sprinkled around, now in the full glory of their white flower, which blossoms in clusters at the end of a long stem that shoots out of the center of the plant.[15] As I rode along in the strange solitude of this bewitching night, I passed numerous trees of some cactus species of rare symmetry and beauty. They grew like the pineapple bush, one branching out into another and another, like antique candelabra, until the two reached a height of some twenty-five or thirty feet.[16] The soldiers never had seen anything like it before, and we never saw it again after that night. From description, it resembles the Maguey of Mexico. Some stray seeds, perchance, were scattered here, and thus solitary they thrive. Riding on, I soon discovered I was beyond grass and on a desert indeed. I rode rapidly on two or three miles to see if I could find grass again, but unsuccessfully, so I turned back and stopped the wagon at the grass at about 10 o'clock.

We camped here, sent our animals on to the water and rested all the next day. It was hot, stupid business, trying to find a cool place and keep the flies off. The evenings would have been bearable, but then we must travel. Twenty-five miles on is Granite Wash[17] where there may be a little water, whither we try to go tonight, rest tomorrow, next night go through to first water.

Our barrel is yet untouched, and that ought to carry us one day without suffering. I started ahead with one soldier to go on to Granite Wash, to see if water could be got and wait there for the wagon. We traveled till after midnight and I was taken sick, so that we had to wait for the wagon there. We slept till broad daylight on the sand, only disturbed by the passing of the Mexican party who reported the wagon getting on well, about six miles behind. No wagon came. We were without provisions or water. I was sick. What was the matter? Back I sent the soldier with my horse and lay down

[15] This is one of the yuccas, or Spanish bayonet.

[16] He encounters here the Joshua tree, *Yucca brevifolia*, which ranges northwestward from Allyn's location through the higher elevations of the Mohave Desert of California, and southern Nevada and southwestern Utah. (Thomas H. Kearney and Robert H. Peebles, *Arizona Flora*, p. 187.)

[17] Granite Wash runs through an area near the towns of Hope and Salome.

under the miserable shelter of a mesquit bush to wait. In about two hours another of the boys rode my horse back bringing me some water, cold coffee, bread and whisky. Then I learned that the mules had given out and the wagon must be abandoned, or at least the animals taken on to water. I could not go back to consult what was best to be done, for what little strength I had must be saved for the march to-night, and my horse would be ill fit for the ride to-night if I let him go twice more over that seven miles. Nothing was left but to stay there all day with the horse alone, send my keys back, let the few most needed things be picked out and leave the rest. Reader, I know you think that was a terribly long day, and I am sure if I had read of some one else staying so, I should have thought so too; but I assure you it was not so very disagreeable after all, and a horse is company too. If the flies hadn't been so thick I could have slept half the day away. Really the most uncomfortable thing was the sleepiness, without the possibility of sleep. I amused myself smoking, looking at a pocket sun-dial to see what time it was, eating and feeding my horse. He ate the same I did, bread was all we either of us had on the desert, and I divided the whisky fairly with him, soaking his bread with it which he seemed to relish amazingly. Toward sundown I got quite thirsty myself. When you haven't any water you always do, so I thought I would walk back a little way and meet the boys coming on with the mules.

The moment I began to walk off, Dick,[18] the name of my horse, set up such a mournful neighing at being left alone, that I actually abandoned the idea and stayed with him. The boys came up promptly at about sundown with a two-gallon keg of water, my saddle bags, and a few other articles absolutely indispensable. The plan had been changed, and Mr. Howard,[19] who was with us, and one soldier,

---

[18] "Dick," Allyn's present horse, was obtained in New Mexico to replace the Missouri army mount called "Swindle." (See Background, note 21.)

[19] Mr. Howard is doubtless John Howard of Michigan and New York, who had been a territorial judge in Colorado Territory. He joined the territorial party at Santa Fe, traveling with it to Prescott. Farish reports that he had married in Denver, but his new wife left him shortly after. Howard was nicknamed "Blinky" and was "a most lovable character, full of humor and native wit." He did not enter public life and lived in Prescott until a short time before his death. (*Hartford Evening Press*, October 30, 1864; Pauline Henson, *Wilderness Capital: Prescott, A.T., 1864*, p. 87; Thomas E. Farish, *History of Arizona* 3:249; 4:211; Eva Favour, "Journey of Arizona's Territorial Party," p. 50.) Judge Howard was the brother of a prominent Republican, Mark Howard of Hartford, Connecticut, with whom Allyn must have been acquainted. (Niven, *Connecticut for the Union*, pp. 24, 31.)

staid back with the wagon. The boys left them ten gallons of water, all our rations, and promised to send help to them as soon as we got in. I have little faith in being able to do so. Very few minutes sufficed to saddle Dick, and off we moved, at 9 o'clock, the soldiers marching in drawers and under-shirts. It was a hard, monotonous march; the moon swept clear across the sky and sank, just as the round fiery ball that rules the desert day rose. It was a stern, stubborn march; we had little breath to waste in talk, even the pipe, one in open air life rarely abandons, loses its charm, in the presence of thirst. We had a canteen apiece of water, and whenever I stopped to drink, the frantic mules would dash at it and bite and push; my poor horse would stretch his head round so that his hot feverish breath would strike my cheek, and his round black eye looked so grateful when I poured a little in my hand and moistened his mouth, which I had to do secretly, for thirsty men don't appreciate the feelings of thirsty animals, and the soldiers on foot were more thirsty than I. Indeed, I did not suffer more from this than I have many times in a hot, dusty railroad ride.

At daybreak we struck the range of hills in which we were to get water. I was so sleepy that I nearly fell off my horse, so I let Dick join the mules in going on to water, and threw myself under a bush and went to sleep. Sleep and water, two luxuries that are priceless; one never realizes their relative value to what we call luxuries till he has made a trip like this. When I lay down I didn't care much how far I would have to walk to pay for that snooze. I wanted sleep, the horse wanted water, I took the one and gave him the other.

I must have slept a couple of hours, and then to pay for it, I had to walk two hours in the hot sun. When I met the boys, they had been at the Apache Chief mine,[20] and brought a courteous invitation from the superintendent, Maj. Hammond,[21] for me and Dick

---

[20] The Apache Chief Mine was located near La Paz in modern Yuma County. It does not appear in the comprehensive files of the Arizona Historical Society, the Arizona Historical Foundation, or in other sources consulted.

[21] The superintendent, Major Hammond, was probably Major Lafayette Hammond (1829–73). He was a native of Pennsylvania and arrived at Fort Yuma in 1861. He served at Tucson in 1862 and Fort Wingate in the following year. He was a member of the regular army in 1872 at Ehrenburg and died at Fort Yuma the next year. (Arizona Historical Society Biographical File.)

to become his guests over Sunday, and then he would ride into La Paz with me, which it is almost superfluous to say we accepted. Maj. H. had only been here a few weeks, and had nothing but a cactus shed for a house, but he had a good cook, plenty of barley for my horse, and the coldest water I have seen since it quit freezing at Whipple; all added to the warm welcome of an accomplished gentleman, made it very pleasant to a worn out traveler from the desert.

I passed two days here most agreeably. The Apache Chief is perhaps better known than the other lodes on the Colorado. Its mineral is exceedingly rich and the surface ore has paid thus far all the expense of developing the mine, but the lode is not yet reached, and until it is, and its size and direction ascertained, it is impossible to tell how valuable a property it is. Maj. H. has a gang of hands working day and night, driving a tunnel into the hill, on the top of which, the rock crops out so rich, which in a week or two will determine if the lode is there or somewhere else. On Monday, we rode into La Paz, a thriving town of five or six hundred inhabitants, on the Colorado.

Letter 12

THE HOT SEASON — RAIN — SAND STORMS — A BEAUTIFUL HOME DESTROYED — A SUMMER RESIDENCE — PLEASANT REPTILES

Apache Camp,[1] August 12, 1864
[Published October 14, 1864]

The climate of the Colorado river put its best foot forward to greet us when we arrived at La Paz,[2] and if I recollect right, I was drawn into some indiscreet praise of the weather with the thermometer ranging to 110 degrees. One must live and learn here as elsewhere, and concerning climates as well as other things. As July marches on, the nights grow warmer, and at last it came to be a novel sight to walk up the main street of an evening — the moonbeams silvered by the scene. You were in danger, if you were much attracted by its quiet beauty, of stepping onto some tossing, sleepless, sweating sleeper on the sidewalk — no one could or did attempt to sleep indoors, and even the *ramadas* seemed close. The best place of all, perhaps, to sleep, was on the roof, that is if your house had a roof strong enough to use that way. Every day or two witnessed the departure of some friends "inside," as going to California is called, to escape the heat and pleasure it at Los Angeles or San Francisco for a month or so. The sun each day rises a great fiery ball whose slow march you watch all the day long, and the days are long too. Claret and your dinner begin to lose their charms, accompanied by such profuse perspiration.

The lazy clouds, hanging over the mountains and the occasional fierce sand storms, begin to admonish us that the annual rains are

[1] "Apache Camp" is the campsite of Major Hammond at the Apache Chief Mine described in Letter 11.
[2] For information on La Paz, see Background, note 86.

coming. Commencing on the Mexican coast in the spring they work northward, the rainy season in California being in the fall.[3]

One day, as the dust was whirling in dense clouds along the streets, the fearful cry of fire! fire! broke on the ear. The whole population gathered at once — a motley throng, Jew and Gentile — naked Indian and bronzed Mexican, Germans, Italians and Frenchmen, all languages were chanted, confusion reigned confounded, and if mud walls were not fire proof, I am afraid the day would have chronicled a terrible disaster to La Paz.

Large quantities of powder were stored in the adjoining buildings, and the fire was right in the heart of the town, among the good buildings. Like all the fires, about, I have ever attended, stupid blunders were made by zealous persons desiring to aid in extinguishing it. This fire, let alone, would almost certainly have burned out in the building where it caught, but some one thought the *ramada* over the sidewalk should be pulled down. Down it came, and I never saw so hot a fire — in tumbling down, the mud, that forms the upper coating of these sheds, was shaken off, and the flames had full sweep at the reeds and hay that constituted the bulk of one of these roofs. Dried by the fierce heats of two or three summers, better fuel could not have been provided — The flames madly licked up everything. The wind swept the fiery and crisping mass. Fortunately, it was all burned in a few brief minutes, and the damage was found to be limited to the destruction of the shade trees on the street.

Only those who have been in these burned up tropical countries, can realize how rain is watched for; rain is the key that unlocks the mineral country; all around us are the richest placers, your horse perchance paws in gold dust; without water it cannot be separated; yonder hills are full of veins, perchance, of untold wealth, they cannot be prospected without rain to fill the tanks. Daring men sometimes essay it and fearful stories are told of the terrible suffering, of brains on fire, of wild delirium, of days of wandering they know not whither, and dare not think of after. At last it came, hurled by a tornado that seemed to drive the sand in one vast mass before it — you could not see across the streets —

---

[3] The Pacific coastal winter storms are drastically weakened by the time they cross the southern California mountains and deserts. The lower Colorado River valley thus is dependent for much of its rainfall upon the monsoon-type thunderstorms which sweep in from the Gulf of California during the summer.

La Paz, the headquarters of the second judicial district, had a boom population of 5,000 when Allyn was there in 1864. However, within about ten years, when this picture was taken, the place had already become a ghost town.

first slight puttering — then fiercer and fiercer until the welcome water came in sheets. Houses are built generally without foundations and a stream of water rushing against the walls will undermine them in an instant and then the walls will crumble down into mud. The shower lasted an hour, passing beyond us, and in the evening it was real luxury to tramp round in thick boots and woolen clothes again.

A couple of miles below La Paz, where the mesa juts like a promontory out into the river bottom, overlooking the vast expanse of country, a gentleman largely interested in mining built an elegant house.[4] The view of the bottom, with its grim cotton-woods, the broad bosom of the Colorado, and the giant outline of the coast range of California beyond, seen as the setting sun lit up the whole with the gorgeous radiance of the Occident, was one not likely to be forgotten. The house was admirably adapted to the climate, built of logs chinked up with mortar, the roof rising sharply above, the inner gables open to secure a free circulation of air, and sloping off into two grand *ramadas*. Between the wings there was an open space always swept by a breeze and never entered by the rays of the sun,

---

[4] Research has not uncovered any information regarding this gentleman or his mansion.

where a hammock slung seemed the perfection of a place for lazy reading and smoking, or for sleeping.

Here he had brought a bride, and was busy surrounding her with the thousand little things so common at home, yet so unwonted here, such as carpets on the floor, mirrors on the walls, center tables covered with books, and the nameless little things that betoken the presence of woman. They arrived from California soon after I did, and it had been a favorite ride of mine, of a moonlight evening, to their house. Once while I was there one of these sand storms came up, sweeping in clouds all around the house, driving my horse under the *ramada* to escape the fierce blast of the sirocco. But inside we laughed at it, although the wind put our light out and we sat in the dark. In an hour it was still and the moon shone peacefully.

The morning after the rain we heard in town that this charming residence was a ruin; the tornado had struck it, and scarce a vestige of it remained. I rode down there with the lady, who had come to town in the evening, escaping from the falling timbers unhurt. The track of the wind was but little wider than the house, and the very arrangements so complete to secure protection from the heat invited the assault of the storm. There were but three persons in the house at the time, the proprietor having gone down the river. The family were gathered in one of the rooms as the wind fairly lifted the house, shaking the timbers apart, to come crashing down around the group. One person in the kitchen was bruised slightly by being crushed between the cooking stove and some timbers.

When we reached there in the morning, what a sight met the eye. Busy hands were at work to secure the most from the wreck; everything was gone above the floor, save the fireplace; the rain had drenched everything, and the mortar used to fill up between the timbers had saturated everything with lime, — carpets, curtains, pretty dresses, tiny gaiters and gloves, brooches and other bridal jewelry all crushed, soaked, and mortared. Some things were carried hundreds of rods away. The reed shed, erected to shelter the animals, was the only thing left; singularly frail, it was strong against the wind, because of the weakness. Under it, out of the sun, we were looking at the dismal debris of this home, when the steamer rounded the bend, and in a few minutes the proprietor of this establishment came galloping up the mesa. What a change. What a welcome. Thank God, no one was hurt. It is such blows as this, that show the wonderful elasticity of the people of new countries; never discouraged, never disheartened, they rise with renewed strength from every such blow of adverse fortune.

The advancing heat of the season and the departure of friends led me very gladly to accept an invitation to spend some days with my friend, Major Hammond, at the Apache Chief mine. Since I came in there, a tired, worn traveller from the desert, Major H. has completed his house and, desolate as are volcanic surroundings of the place, its comparatively pure, cold air and nights, make it a pleasant relief from the sultriness of the river bottom. Our house is not such a building as would be dignified with that appelation at home; yet ·it answers the purpose tolerable well, when it rains, and that event may be counted on safely as likely to occur once or twice a year, on any given space of ground here. But when it does rain, it rains, and no mistake; the water comes down in sheets that hang like trembling drapery over the mountain side. The house is built of split poles, nailed so far apart as to allow ample ventilation, and is divided into three rooms; there are no doors, and a broad ramada on two sides shuts out the sun. Books, we have in abundance, and time slips away very quickly. One gets used to staying in a house, when the sun glows outside, much sooner than you think. Toward sunset, your imprisonment ceases, and, gun in hand, you ramble over the hills, watching the shadows deepening over the mountain sides. Once in the while, you get a chance to shoot a dove, quail or hare; and either forms no mean addition to a table without fresh meat. Nearly every evening, it rains somewhere round us; it seems as though ours was really the driest spot in this dry country.

These showers, with their dark masses of storm clouds, lightning, more vivid, and thunder deeper than any I ever experienced elsewhere, creeping around the crests of the mountains that circle like an ampitheater about us, are often grand at evening. The cool wind fairly bathes you luxuriously; there is no sand here to blind the eyes; perchance the sun shining too, spans the east with the completed arch of a rainbow, thrice reflecting itself on the sky. The storm passes on beyond the farthest mountain to spend itself on the arid expanse of desert, the wonderful radiance of the setting sun lingers till the moon rises, and you lie and watch the stars as they peep out one by one, learning to mark the time by the revolving constellations around the north star, and counting the endless array of meteors that in this climate are exceedingly brilliant, shooting in every quarter of the heavens.

Sometimes the thunder will rouse you from sleep and the whirling wind betoken but too surely that there is little time to lose in preparing for the deluge; thick boots and clothes are hurried on, books, papers, and all destructible things are covered with rubber blankets, and then you wait for the coming rain complacently. It pours, your house is a perfect sieve, the arroyas are filled with the rushing torrents. In an hour it is passed, and the morning scarce shows a sign of the water the thirsty earth, or rather rocks, have drunk up.

Only those who have tired of the cloudless sky of such a country as this know what a delicious thing a cloudy day is; a cloudy day to the sojourner here means all that the clear day the May Queen watches for means; it suggests rambles over the fierce upturned mountains, down into inaccessible arroyas; a chance for a deer or mountain goat;[5] explorations of lodes, visits to your neighbors, in short, out-door life. We have neighbors here; within a couple of miles are several mines that small parties are developing. Within our own limits a tunnel is being driven into the side of one mountain, and an inclined shaft into another by forces of Mexicans working night and day, searching for the true vein that threw up the piles of surface ore that made the Apache Chief famous; the dull reports of the blasting alternate at regular intervals day after day, and night after night.

A trip down the railway into the inclined shaft is one of those things one to whom all mining is novel would not miss, and would never care to repeat. Slowly you are lowered down, until the light of day disappears and somehow an impression steals on you that perhaps you won't get back, your candle burns dimly or most likely won't burn at all, for the air is very impure; you reach the bottom where two or three naked figures are drilling by the pale flicker of two or three candles kept burning by a stream of air forced down the pipe that runs alongside of the track. In the dim light it seems as

---

[5] Allyn expresses himself in the tradition of Thoreau, his fellow New Englander, in his enthusiasm for nature. The judge undoubtedly refers here to the Gaillard or desert varieties of the Big-Horn Mountain sheep, *Ovis canadensis gaillardi,* which ranges the mountains of northwestern Sonora and southwestern Arizona, or possibly *Ovis canadensis nelsoni,* which is found in the mountains of southern California. The mountain goat, *Oreamnos americanus,* on the other hand, is confined to the higher elevations of the Rocky Mountains from Alaska to Montana. (William T. Hornaday, *Camp Fires on Desert and Lava,* pp. 329–46; H. E. Anthony, *Field Book of North American Mammals,* pp. 542–49.)

though you were shut up here without an exit and the figures of the miners flitting about are weird and unnatural. Their cautious salutations destroy that illusion, you strain your eyes, try to see something, all the rocks look alike to you, and grasping a piece freshly knocked off, you scramble back to the car and strike the pipe as a signal to be hoisted out — at least that's about what I did. Mining, everywhere uncertain enough, is preeminently so in this range of mountains; they are upturned and torn into every conceivable shape, fire and water have been at work here perhaps for centuries; I doubt if any other part of the globe can show such evidences of the power of both these elements, miles and miles of rock literally burnt, arroyas worn out of the mesas, until what is left are isolated mountains without a trace, scarcely, of the old table land, leading to washes a half mile wide, and the stone has been ground to gravel by the rivers that sometime swept down them. This term wash is particularly expressive; a wash is apparently the dry bed of a stream where the rocks have been washed down. This whole belt of country is full of gold placers, which only need water to draw a large population; now they are abandoned to Mexicans, who somehow live without water, or very near to it; a single *basso*[6] carrying forty gallons, will supply a whole party for a week. They separate the gold by what is called dry washing, which is nothing but shaking the sands, blowing it off, while the heavy particles of gold fall to the bottom, an operation requiring patience and breath. Perhaps sometime capital will bring the waters of the Colorado through on a canal. It would not be a difficult undertaking compared to many ditches in California.

Out here is a splendid place to study the reptiles of this outcast section of the country; and first the rattlesnake — not the long, proud crested serpent, the terror of your school boy days, but a short, slimy, dirty little snake, whose bite is deadly. It is a strange provision of nature that where these poisonous reptiles are native there is uniformly a weed that is a perfect antidote to its bite, at least this I know to be the case all across the country from the Missouri. The Mexican running the tunnel was bitten the other day in the calf of his leg, and after it had deliberately killed the snake, then

---

[6] "Basso" is doubtless Allyn's phonetic spelling of the Spanish *vaso*, a vessel or container for liquids, or possibly of the Spanish *barro*, a clay drinking vessel. The sounds of the Mexican consonants "b" and "v" are not distinguishable.

picked some of the weed that grows hereabout, chewed some of it, made a poultice around the bite, bound it up with a handkerchief, and went on with his work without suffering any inconvenience. The weed grows all about this part of the country and when you break its stems it discharges a white milky substance. So certain is the efficacy of this and smaller weeds found elsewhere, that it is an easy matter to get an Indian to allow himself to be bitten by a rattlesnake for a quarter of a dollar.[7]

We have, too, the finest specimens of the scorpion, tarantula, and centipede. I do not know that any of these are deadly, but I think I would as lief be bitten by a rattlesnake. The centipede is the worst both in looks and the wound he inflicts; he is a long, dark colored worm, sometimes six inches in length of body, with long yellowish legs projecting like a finger on each side of the body, every one of which makes a wound so that he can't pass across you without stinging you as many times as he has feet. I believe all the others, let alone, will let you alone.[8]

One morning just as we were rising, one of these centipedes deliberately marched in the open door, crawled rapidly up on a pile of clothes, and was apparently making straight for the bed the Major had vacated. A more vicious, ugly sight can scarcely be conceived of in one's bedroom, and your nerves must be well strung if it doesn't make you a little nervous.

[7] Allyn surely refers here to rattlesnake-weed (*Euphorbia albomarginata* and related species) called *golondrina* by the Mexicans. "They are popularly supposed to be efficacious in treating snake bite, and the root of *Euphorbia albomarginata* is said to have been used as an emetic by the Pima Indians." (Thomas H. Kearney and Robert H. Peebles, *Arizona Flora,* p. 511.)

[8] Allyn expresses here the horror of the desert centipede (*Scolopendra heros*) felt by many pioneers. Charles F. Lummis, the renowned publicist of the Southwest in his 1897 stories of New Mexico wrote, "I have seen one Mexican boy whose whole hand and forearm were ruined — withered and wasted to a dreadful sight — by the crawling of a centipede across his hand ... it buried in his skin the tiny fangs with which its scores of feet are tipped. The flesh sloughed away until the hand and arm were only a distorted skeleton; and only a careful doctor saved the lad's life." (*The King of the Broncos,* p. 191.)

Actually the desert centipede, though a formidable looking creature, is, at most, "a painful inconvenience rather than a serious injury." Far more serious is the sting of certain species of the scorpion (*Centuroides sculpturatus* and *C. gertschi*). These species have been responsible for more human deaths in Arizona than rattlesnakes and all other creatures combined. The tarantulas of the Southwest belonging to the genera *Avicularia, Dugesiella,* and *Aphonopelma* are harmless, beneficial spiders. The bite is painful but not serious, and the fangs are rarely used against humans and then only in self-defense. (Natt N. Dodge, *Poisonous Dwellers of the Desert,* pp. 11–21.)

Letter 13

AN ARIZONA OUTFIT — THE NEW CAPITAL — MEETING OF THE LEGISLATURE — OPENING OF THE DISTRICT COURT

Prescott, Arizona, Oct. 12, 1864
[Published December 29, 1864]

It's a good plan not to write when you have nothing to say, and this is about all the reason of my long silence. Fearing I might be entirely forgotten, and in order to add a link in the narrative this series of letters will form, I break the rule now.

I left La Paz in September, to attend the assemblage of the Legislature and the opening of the District Court here, in company with the expressman and a merchant. We were in light marching order, all that we carried hung upon our horses. When we left La Paz we were quite heavily loaded, carrying food for ourselves and our horses, as well as blankets, firearms and a change of clothes. One never knows what can be packed on a horse until he tries it, and it is these little details that will give you the best idea of traveling in Arizona. From the horn, in front of my saddle, were hung, first, a pair of holsters designed for large pistols, but now holding smoking tobacco, brush, comb, towels and soap; then on one side a huge canteen, holding over a gallon of water; on the other my old tried Spencer rifle, and above all my lariat. The horn of the Spanish saddles you see is far from being ornamental alone. Behind were my saddle bags, with clothes, paper, memorandum books, etc., and above that a large sack containing my and my horse's "grub," to use the vernacular of the country. The "grub" consisted of twenty pounds of barley loose in the sack, and my own comissariat was arranged in a smaller bag, which was dropped into the barley sack, and consisted of still smaller bags, holding coffee, sugar, crackers, *pinoly,* and jerked beef, or "jerky," as it is called, and a bottle of whisky. My blankets were all folded under the saddle, the tin cup that answers all the purposes of coffee pot, wash basin, etc., tied on to the bundle behind, and with hunting knife in the belt, with your pistols, you are "outfitted," that is, supposing you have a good horse, for a trip of 150 miles.

I have described so minutely the trip across the desert to Weaver in a former letter, that there is little to be said now, save that there was now an abundance of water, owing to rains, and that we rode straight through the center of the great valley, now carpeted with green grass, thus avoiding the hard road into the canon, to get water, and made Weaver in three days.[1] We rode morning and evening, and rested through the hot midday under the improvised shade of a blanket thrown over a mesquit bush. It was very hot, but when one's blood has been thawed out by a summer on the Colorado, you don't notice that, and there is always a breeze on the desert.

We rode into Weaver quite into the evening and found most of the people asleep in the street, *a la* La Paz; and after supper we soon followed their example. Not intending to start the next morning, an old habit of mine of sleeping late came over me, and I slept on until the little Frenchman, whose guests we were, if to sleep on the street in front of one's house makes you his guest, touched me on the shoulder and presented to me what was very like a toddy, which I drank about half awake. "Now," said he, "sleep away till breakfast is ready." I did. It always seemed to me that a man who couldn't sleep in the morning had something on his conscience. Perhaps that is harsh, but one thing is certain, they don't know what's luxury. I think the height of human enjoyment is to feel that you haven't got to get up in the morning at the first flush of dawn.

At Weaver they had the usual Indian scare, which is getting to be the chronic condition of this country. The next day we rode to Prescott, over the same trail I took last spring up the Hassayampa. You do not experience any perceptible change of climate after leaving the Colorado, until you cross Antelope mountain; then the transition into a different air is most apparent, the sun is shorn of his terrible power, and men and animals feel more lightsome.

---

[1] The "great valley" is doubtless the Aguila Valley west of the present town of Aguila. The "canon" may refer to Cañon Springs. See Letter 11, note 12.

Prescott must be about 6,000 feet higher than La Paz; frosts occur
here in June and September, at least they did this year.[2]

We left Prescott last June, just as the frantic competition for
lots at the first auction was over, and there were one or two straggling houses just crawling up into being. Now there are perhaps
fifty houses, straggled around the Plaza, that looks so large that
it is very difficult to credit the surveyor's testimony that it is but
six hundred feet across it. In the centre of it, on a fine flag staff,
flaunts the starry banner that grimly confronts Richmond and
proudly floats over Atlanta.[3] We rode into town just as the moon
was silvering the valley, and a crowd thronged round us to get the
news, and it was an admirable time to find out the political pro-
clivities of bystanders. Prescott is a western town; just like scores
of them you will find on the railroads in Illinois or Iowa. It is as
different as possible from La Paz, each on the vanguard of their
respective emigrations. La Paz is cosmopolitan, like the Pacific;
Prescott is provincial, like the valley of the Mississippi. The one is
built solid and compact, the other scattered all over an immense
space.[4] The one has neat restaurants, and little tables and white
table-cloths; the other has crowded boarding houses, where just
before meal hours it looks as though a lottery was about to be drawn,
and when the onslaught on the provisions begins, you would think
it was the last meal they ever expected to have.

---

[2] Prescott is exactly a mile (5,280 ft.) above sea level and can experience
frost, even in June or September. In the late nineteenth and early twentieth
century the area became a summer residence for many Arizonans escaping the
110 to 120 degree heat of the desert regions.

[3] By October 1864 Grant's forces were investing the strongly entrenched
Confederate capital. The spires of the city could be seen clearly from the
Union trenches. Atlanta had fallen to Sherman on September 1, 1864. The
flagstaff referred to by Allyn, which had been prepared for the celebrations
of the 4th of July, was a 144-foot Ponderosa pine tree. (Samuel Eliot Morison,
The Oxford History of the American People, pp. 688–90; *Arizona Miner*,
July 6, 1864.)

[4] This is not the first of Allyn's perceptive comments on the character of
the frontier and its establishments. As pointed out in the Background section
of this book, on his trip west the judge noted the conservative settlement pro-
clivities of New Englanders. Now the astute commentator compares the sup-
posedly "stable" frontier town with a new, raw one. Prescott was indeed
founded mainly by Easterners, but apparently their initial efforts did not lend
themselves to eastern or New England order. Curiously, La Paz, started by
Californians only one year before, was relatively compact and orderly in plan.
La Paz's stability proved to be illusory, since it was practically a ghost town
by 1872. Prescott, of course, survived even the loss of the territorial government and retained its strong New England flavor.

The convening of the legislature and the opening of Court had brought an unusual crowd into town. Honorable members of the Council and House, and sedate members of the Bar were sleeping on the floors of the stores and in rows, and the bar rooms were in full blast day and night. The building erected for the legislature was just made tenantable, and resembled a large livery stable; there was no floor, and the partitions dividing it into rooms did not reach the roof, so that the murmur of voices in one could be distinctly heard in all the others. The furniture was of the simplest kind, consisting of pine tables and chairs, unpainted; the respective presiding officers were upon slightly raised platforms, the tables being covered with fancy blankets and the American flag hung up behind them. Ex Gov. Bashford,[5] of Wisconsin, was elected president of the Council, and Wm. Claude Jones,[6] late Attorney General of New Mexico, speaker of the House. The Governor delivered his message in person, and the work of law making began with a zeal that made one fully realize that the *per diem* of members, three dollars in greenbacks, would not pay board bills.

The Court House, hired for the occasion, was even farther from completion than the capitol; rough benches were provided for juries and spectators; the Judge was upon a raised platform with a parapet of rough boards in front, covered with blankets, a table and some

---

[5] Coles Bashford (1816–78) was a founder of the Republican party in Wisconsin and a strong opponent of the extension of slavery. This undoubtedly contributed to his election as governor of that state in 1855. Originally from New York State, Bashford was a graduate of Wesleyan University there and was admitted to the bar in 1842. He enjoyed a successful practice and served as state district attorney before leaving for the Northwest. Bashford returned to private practice following his one term as governor, and was a resident in the nation's capital early in the Civil War. He accompanied the territorial party to Prescott and was the first lawyer admitted to the bar in Arizona. Bashford was elected president of the Legislative Council of the First Territorial Legislature in 1864. Between 1866 and 1868, he served as delegate to Congress and was appointed (1869–76) by U. S. Grant as secretary of state of the territory. He died in 1878 in a house still standing in Prescott, the oldest residence which has survived. (Arizona Historical Society Biographical File; Jay J. Wagoner, *Arizona Territory 1863–1912*, pp. 44–45, 52. See also Gilbert J. Pederson, "The Founding First," pp. 50, 53, 54.)

[6] William Claude Jones was a native of Ohio but by 1856 was a resident of New Mexico and of sufficient prominence to have been elected delegate to Congress. (*Weekly Gazette* (Santa Fe), November 1856.) Jones reportedly sent information concerning Union troop movements to the Confederate secretary of war. (Arizona Historical Society Biographical File.) He became New Mexico's attorney general but by 1864 was a Tucson resident. Letter from Rex W. Strickland to the Arizona Historical Society, January 1962.)

chairs, borrowed from the legislature for the clerk and Bar, completed the outfit. I have rarely seen a more intelligent Grand Jury than the one empanelled here. The Judge's charge was brief and listened to with the closest attention, especially that portion of it devoted to the crime of treason.[7] The utmost decorum prevailed during the entire session. There were no cases tried at the term. An application was made for an injunction to restrain the working of a mine, upon which an order was made for delinquents to appear and show cause before the Judge at Chambers.[8] The hearing upon this subsequently came off in the hall of the House of Representatives. It was argued at length by Gov. Bashford and General Jones, and attracted a very large attendance of miners and others interested. The Judge refused the injunction.[9]

So mining litigation is inaugurated in the young territory. It seems to be the nature of mines to lead to law suits; it is very rare when a mine proves to be valuable that there are not numerous

---

[7]Judge Allyn of the La Paz second district presided at the third district court term in the absence of Chief Justice Turner, who was in the nation's capital. Court opened on September 27, 1864. Allyn's charge to the United States and territorial grand juries was later printed and contained severe criticism of recent election practices and the territorial government. (See *Charge of the Hon. Joseph P. Allyn, Associate Justice of the U.S. Court, to the U.S. and Territorial Grand Juries, September Term, 1864.*) Two of the chairs used in the court sessions are preserved in the governor's mansion, Prescott. (Pauline Henson, *Founding A Wilderness Capital, Prescott, A.T., 1864*, p. 222.) The presence of Southerners and Confederate sympathizers no doubt accounted for the "closest attention" to Allyn's remarks on treason.

[8]The injunction referred to involved the first mining case, *Murray* vs. *Wickenburg, Moore*, et alia, or the Vulture Lode case, in the territorial administration. The mine in question was one of the richest in Arizona history (see Letter 14, note 4). With the assistance of King Woolsey and others, Henry Wickenburg (1820–1905), originally Hemsel or Heintzel, a native of Austria, discovered the fabulous outcroppings about seventeen miles southwest of Wickenburg, on November 1, 1863. The Moore of the court case was James A. Moore, a close friend of Wickenburg. According to Farish he was an election judge in the third district. (*History of Arizona* 3:80.) Several of the original discoverers apparently had not contributed to the development of the lode or registered any claims to it. When Wickenburg and others later confirmed the location of gold-bearing veins and posted their claim, some demanded a share. (United States District Court, Arizona Third Judicial District, *Docket No. 22*, Prescott, 1864; Arizona Historical Society Biographical File; James M. Barney, "Henry Wickenburg: Discoverer of the Vulture Mine," p. 26.)

[9]Allyn's decision, denying the injunction, involved in part the provisions of Spanish-Mexican law requiring the registration of claims to mining properties — a requirement with which the plaintiffs had failed to comply. The judge's ruling concluded that "It is not necessary for the purpose of deter-

claimants to it, who had at sometime or another claimed it, and then abandoned it, so that the truest measure of the mineral wealth of a territory is the prosperity of its lawyers.

The fall climate here is delightful, a little cool for one whose blood has been thinned out by a summer on the Colorado, but healthy and bracing.

---

mining the question raised by this prayer for a writ of injunction, to pass upon the question whether the mining laws of Spain and Mexico, are in force in this Territory. It is sufficient that the complaint itself does not show that those laws have been sufficiently complied with, to vest in the complainants such a right of property in the Vulture lode, as to call for the extraordinary exercise of the chancery powers of this Court in granting a writ of injunction. The prayer for the writ of injunction is therefore denied." (*Arizona Miner,* October 26, 1864.)

Letter 14

TRAVEL IN A NEW COUNTRY —
THE GREAT HASSAYAMPA GOLD MINE

Maricopa Wells,[1] Nov. 28, 1864
[Published March 10, 1865]

After the adjournment of the legislature I left Prescott, in company with two wagons, bound for Tucson.[2] It is pleasant enough to travel on horseback, as we did from La Paz, when the weather is warm; but when the water freezes solid during the night, it is desirable to be able to carry more bedding. One of the wagons in this outfit contained a Mexican family, the other an American, so we had the society of women *ad libitum*. The American lady (I believe all women in the vernacular of the states are ladies) was a bride, hardly turned of sweet sixteen; she was one of the recent arrivals from Texas, and married after a brief courtship a gentleman much her senior.

When I saw the wagons roll out I had some misgivings. The Mexican had a lean, saw-backed mule harnessed in along with a gaunt sorrel mare of Indian stock; one wouldn't pull, and the other couldn't. There were two men with them, one did the driving, walking by the side of the team, while the other did the hallooing and pushing. Our American bridal outfit consisted of a light wagon,

---

[1] By 1858 Maricopa Wells in Pinal County near the Santa Cruz riverbed, a few miles south of Komatke and east of the Sierra Estrella Mountains, was an important coach stop for the Butterfield Overland stages. Before that it was an exchange point on the San Antonio and San Diego mail line. The place had long been known to travelers for its pools of water. It seems likely that Father Kino stopped at this place in 1694. The pools offered the last water for crossing the Forty Mile Desert to the west. They were first enlarged by the Mormon Battalion in 1846, while on its way to Tucson. By 1870 the place had six to eight wells and was graced by adobes, corrals, and sixty-eight people. Seven of the wells are still to be seen. (Byrd H. Granger, *Arizona Place Names*, p. 299. Also consult John A. Carroll, *Pioneering in Arizona: The Reminiscences of Emerson Oliver Stratton and Edith Stratton Kitt*.)

[2] He had left before November 23. The *Arizona Miner* of that date reported, "Judge Allyn has gone to Tucson on a visit."

with a good pair of little mules, tough and hardy-looking enough, the groom driving on the front seat, and an assistant (there are no servants in this country) of African descent walking alongside. Beside these there were three of us mounted; my horse was in admirable condition. I suggested my misgivings as to the capacity of the teams for a journey of three hundred miles before starting, and was silenced by the statement that they had brought extra harnesses along, and when we got to Kirkland's,[3] about fifty miles on, they were going to put on two more horses. Leaving them plodding along, I rode on to the first ranche and stopped for dinner, while the wagons passed by. When I overtook them, toward evening, they were engaged climbing a big hill, by the slow process of doubling, — that is, taking both teams to one wagon and coming back after the other. The madam had got out and walked, the groom lustily pushed behind the wagon. The senora sat as contentedly in the wagon, with two little ones huddled in her lap, as if the wagon was rolling along the Central Park. The perseverance of the Mexican race under the manifold difficulties of traveling in this country is almost as marked as their uniform good temper. Somehow they always get through. I should have as soon thought of flying to Tucson as of getting there with that team. Climbing this hill took so long that it was quite dark before we got into camp. Now getting into camp after dark is one of the things that try good tempers in summer; and in cold weather Job himself might find his stock of this desirable commodity none too large. You are chilled, a fire has to be made, you stumble over all sorts of things, getting the wood, and have no easy time getting to water, which is generally off in some out-of-the-way hole, either among the rocks or in a swamp.

The fire blazing, the animals watered, and the supper has to be got. By this time everybody is hungry. The first night in camp, nobody knows where anything is; the coffee pot or the coffee mill will turn up missing, the flour sack will be under a heavy box, every-

---

[3] Kirkland was a stage station by 1864 in Kirkland Valley and located about twenty-one miles southwest of Prescott. Noted for its good food, the stage station was operated by William H. Kirkland and his family of three, following their settlement in the valley in 1863. Kirkland (born in Virginia, 1832) came to Arizona in 1856, and in 1860 he and his wife were the first Americans to be married in the territory. Kirkland Village was a Santa Fe railroad stop after 1894. The valley had been largely settled by 1869. (Pat Savage, "The Ruby Story," p. 141; Granger, *Arizona Place Names*, p. 348.)

body is in everybody else's way, of course, in the dull uncertain
light of a flickering fire. It is lucky if, as we did, the first night out,
you camp near a party just coming in, for then you can borrow
things. At last, all difficulties surmounted, the blanket is spread and
supper is ready. Our bride and groom dispensed with forks, not like
the Chinese I apprehend, because they preferred sticks, but because
they hadn't them. Still barring these little *contretemps,* food is a
great soother of the little ills of this life and we had really a jolly
meal, and a lively evening over our pipes after it.

Camp life is after all much the same, and as we have been over
this road before, there is very little worth alluding to in the next
few days. Ranches are now established about every day's ride and
trains and wagons are constantly passing over the road. At Kirkland
we waited a day to find those horses, and when they were found at
last, and the extra harnesses got out, bridles proved to be missing.
This would have been remediable, but the collars proved to be mule
collars, and no amount of persuasion could possibly induce them to
stretch enough to fit a horse, so we had to go on without increasing
the team.

Now this want of foresight is not usual in this part of the
world, and I really fear it must be charged in this instance to the
matrimonial account; a young bride turns the head of a man even
in the mountains. For some time there have been no Indian depredations, and now the road is so well settled up, I apprehend there
is really little danger. Still our friend with the young wife was fearfully apprehensive; he heard the stealthy tread of the Apache in
the rustle of every leaf, and fancied every howl of the coyote at
night was only an Indian's mimicry. Nervously, every evening he
would say, "Well, now we must stand guard tonight;" then he
would look to see that all the shot guns were capped, but I noticed
that he never pressed the standing guard business. The inexorable
law of the plains makes every man take his turn, and perhaps he
didn't want to be disturbed at night; at any rate, no guard has yet
been stood. We tied our animals at night by our sides, and took
our chances. Still some of the mischievous members of the party
could not help amusing themselves with this worthy gentleman's
fears. The night we were near Kirkland, they got a couple of tame
Indian boys that were on the ranche, to go out in the bushes near
the wagons, and mimic the coyote, in a way that caused a grasping
of shot guns that was creditable to the alertness of our friend.

We reached Weaver at last safely. Here we were overtaken by a train of empty wagons bound to Maricopa wells. They took our heavy trunks out of the little wagons, and we rolled on with them.

Weaver is the same dull place it was when we were here before. The rich placers on Antelope mountain are not yielding much, and many are moving down to the Vulture lode,[4] sixteen miles below, on the Hassayampa. This is the fabulously rich lode that is in litigation, and concerning which an injunction was denied at the September term of the district court at Prescott. In the afternoon I rode to Dutch Henry's, as Henry Wickenburg, the discoverer of the lode, is called.[5] Some of you may recollect that last March when I came up the Hassayampa with Col. Poston, and an escort of Pima and Maricopa Indians, we camped one day at a point where we met the Governor coming down, and near the camp of a German who was then the only settler there. This was Dutch Henry's. I recollect his telling me of his lead, but it was fifteen miles away from the water and I listened to him, as I had to a thousand similar stories of the enthusiastic prospector, rather pitying his credulity. I saw the rock and the tiny bits of gold got by pounding it in a mortar, but this I had seen many times before, when I knew there was no mine. Still there was something of the sublime in the faith that prompted that patient waiting, in the courage that still held on, when tidings of Indian outrages came on every breeze, and all his partners had left,

---

[4] See Letter 13, note 8. The Vulture Lode of Maricopa County was indeed one of the richest and most famous mines of the Southwest. The name "Vulture" was attributed to either Henry Wickenburg's shooting of a vulture and discovering nuggets where it fell or his observation of vultures circling over the discovery site. The mine was producing about $700 a day in 1865. Judge Allyn's estimates of the Vulture's future were somewhat exaggerated; nevertheless, the Vulture was a richly productive mine. In a ten-month period of 1866–67, it produced over $145,000. Wickenburg sold part of his original claim for $75,000 in 1866, well before the mine's most productive period. He seems to have sold more of the claim in 1875 for $85,000. The Vulture had produced $10,000,000 by the 1880s. The lode was worked out by 1897 with a brief revival taking place in the 1930s. This famous property was sold again as recently as 1970. (Arizona Historical Society Biographical File; Richard J. Hinton, *The Hand-book to Arizona*, p. 144; *Arizona Republic*, June 30, 1970.)

[5] The nickname "Dutch" was commonly applied by Americans to those immigrants such as Wickenburg who were of Teutonic stock. Like many a pioneer he was to die poor. It was said that he had lost his wealth owing to his trusting nature. Though well and hearty as late as 1904, he shot himself the following year. (Arizona Historical Society Biographical File; *Arizona Miner*, December 26, 1868, November 18, 1871; James M. Barney, "Henry Wickenburg: Discoverer of the Vulture Mine.")

when each night he changed his dark and silent camp to elude the watchful eye of the tireless savage.

A mile before I reached the old familiar knoll, where last spring our Indian allies spread their picturesque camp, the grazing herds, the many fires, the groups of tents and wagons in sight, all betokened a wondrous change. There was the old hill, the broad, grassy plain, but how changed! I asked the first man I met for Dutch Henry, and found he still lived in the precise spot where we had camped. I rode up the slope. It was a busy scene. Two *arrastres*[6] were at work on my left, a half dozen men were breaking rock small enough for the *arrastres,* a steer was being butchered under a tree, midway the cook was busy over a huge fire, a long mess table under the trees near by, to the right were piles of flour and wheat in sacks, huge loaded wagons, a dozen horses feeding, and the same little tent of last spring. I was soon at home. Henry wore the quiet look of a satisfied man, the "I told you so" look. There were the *arrastres* proving every day that every ton of this despised rock would crush out one hundred dollars in gold. On the top of the ground is a deposit of the rock that simple figures demonstrate to contain near a million tons of this rock. One hundred millions of dollars in sight! Grant there is no true vein underneath, that some wild freak of the fierce elemental forces that split the crust of the earth and pushed upwards the mineral treasures of the seething laboratory at the centre, has tumbled this magnificent deposit upon the desert, and closed the portals of the vein whence the mineral came, here is still enough to make this take the first rank in the world's scale of mines, here is enough to build up a state. The day's work over, we sat around the fire and waited the coming of the wagons. The bride with us had come from Texas with a party of emigrants that had stopped here, and as the wagons rolled into

---

[6] The use of the *arrastres* (arrastras) indicates not only the primitive nature of mining on the frontier, but that the mine was rich indeed to use such a wasteful method. The *arrastre* was a circular stone-paved track (approximately six to ten feet in diameter), in which large blocks of stone were dragged by mules or other animals, crushing the ore in the trough. Long used by the Mexican miners, much bullion ore was undoubtedly lost in the process. Stamp mills for crushing the ore, including one operated by Jack Swilling, later replaced the *arrastres.* (For descriptions of the *arrastres* see Wallace, *Image of Arizona,* pp. 85, 148ff. Also consult Otis E. Young, *How They Dug the Gold: An Informal History of Frontier Lode-Mining, and Milling in Arizona and the Southwest.*)

camp, every description of fire arms blazed, shot guns, pistols and rifles, all in grand *feu de joie,* much to the terror of the timid gentleman, who fancied the Indians were attacking us.

Next day I rode around among the camps which extend four or five miles on the stream, *arrastres* working at each. One of them cleaned up, that I might see the entire process, which was wholly new to me. The rock is drawn from the lode in ox wagons at a cost of twenty dollars per ton, a team making the trip easily in two days; it is in large pieces which are broken by hand down to a moderate size, say about that of a hen's egg, ready for the *arrastres.* A crushing machine such as you use to crush the stone for your streets is the thing to do this work. One man showed me an ingenious crushing machine he had contrived. It consisted in lifting a heavy force of granite by means of horse power applied to a large cog wheel so contrived that when the weight was raised to a certain height the cog would knock the lever off which held the stone, and it would drop on the quartz underneath and then the revolving wheel would pull it up again until it reached the next cog. An *arrastre* is the simplest and most primitive of the modes of getting gold out of rock.

It is a stone tub, so to speak, about eight or ten feet in diameter, and the sides a couple of feet high built on the ground; from the center rises a post or shaft, from which radiate cross bars or spokes; from these are suspended heavy blocks of granite or some other hard rock, and to the end of these cross bars, or spokes, are attached your horses or mules. The tub is then filled up with the small pieces of rock and water, and the animals begin to draw the heavy weights around that slowly pulverize the quartz.

Into the mass of mud, for the pulverized wet mass is nothing but mud, quicksilver is thrown, ounce for ounce, with the gold you expect. Day and night, animals tread that unceasing round, blindfolded, lest they get dizzy; more rock and more water being thrown in, until the owner wants some money. Then he draws on his mud, quicksilver bank, which is more secure than the latest patent burglar-proof safe with combination lock. It was the honoring one of these drafts I saw. First, the water is drawn off, then the running mud is thrown up in a pile with a shovel, the bottom scraped, a sharp instrument being used to clean out the crevices between the stones. Here you begin to watch the sparkle of little particles of quicksilver. A rawhide is spread out and the dirt cleaned out of the crevices is thrown upon it. When this is all done thoroughly, the rawhide is carried to water, or water to the rawhide, and the dirt is washed by hand in a pan, just as it is in the placers, and all the quicksilver got out of it. The quicksilver is then poured upon a cloth and the ends gathered up and twisted until the quicksilver runs out like water. The little ball thus left, not larger than a hen's egg, is then placed in an iron retort upon the charcoal in a forge, a pipe leading from the retort into a pan of water. Through this pipe the quicksilver passes and settles on the bottom of the pan. When the quicksilver is all off, which can easily be ascertained by watching the bubbles, the retort is opened and the cloth that you wrapped so tightly around a silver ball is found crisped with heat, and as you brush the cinders off, you have a little solid ball of pure gold, in this instance weighing a trifle over eight ounces, worth eighteen dollars and something per ounce at the mint; and this from a ton of the rock.

What a stream of gold will pour from the Hassayampa when the quartz mills arrive, and all this tedious process is done by the power of steam. There is no portion of the mineral region so favorable for the working of a large mine. The climate is perfect;[7] it is several thousand feet above the heat of the Colorado, and several thousand below the cold of Prescott; there is wood, water and grass; it is only eighty miles over a good road to the granary of Arizona, the Pima villages, where wheat costs about one cent a pound, and only one hundred miles from La Paz, on the Colorado river, over a good road. The only drawback is the fifteen miles the rock has to be transported, but the experience of all mining proves that sinking shafts brings water, and I apprehend that when machinery comes, water will be reached on the lead itself.

A new town is laid out,[8] stores are building, and Wickenburg bids fair to be one of the towns of the Pacific. Dutch Henry has

---

[7] The elevation of the Wickenburg area is approximately two thousand feet, that of La Paz approximately three hundred feet, and Prescott five thousand feet. Wickenburg is a favorite tourist area because of its delightful winter climate.

[8] There was a settlement in the valley of the upper Hassayampa River as early as 1863. A village developed on the site of what was later called Wickenburg. Its growth was largely due to the proximity of and the servicing of the Vulture and other gold mines in the region (see Letter 13, note 8 and note 4,

already become Wickenburg; by and by, I suppose, it will be Hon. Mr. W. or Col. or Gen. W.

From the Hassayampa to Maricopa Wells was only the routine of ordinary traveling. Maricopa Wells is the ranch and trading station of Mr. J. B. Allen,[9] one of the most enterprising and successful of the business men of Arizona. It is just outside the Pima and Maricopa reservation, and is about twelve miles from the establishment of Mr. White, where I stopped some time last March. Mr. Allen has only been established here a few months, yet already quite a settlement has grown up around him. He is the principal freighter of this section of the country; his fine mule teams are known at Prescott, Wickenburg, Tucson, and Fort Yuma,[10] as really the only mail we have now, since Uncle Sam has deserted us, and to them this will be trusted. Fortunately his hospitality is only rivaled by his prosperity.

---

this letter). When Henry Wickenburg sold his major interest in the Vulture in 1866, he established a ranch near modern Wickenburg. In letters to Governor John N. Goodwin, Wickenburg's friend, James A. Moore (one-time Vulture Mine Company owner and co-litigant), used the address "Wickenburg Ranch." By 1870 the area and the village were known by the name Wickenburg. (Douglas D. Martin, *An Arizona Chronology, The Territorial Years, 1856–1912;* Helen B. Hawkins, "A History of Wickenburg to 1875.")

[9]James Brackett Allen, or "Pie," (1818–99) was a native of Maine who arrived in Arizona in 1857. The nickname derived from his sale of dollar pies to soldiers. Allen later went to Tucson and was mayor of that city and treasurer of the territory. In his final years, his residence was in Florence (Pinal County), and he served as the sole county representative in the Assembly (House) in 1891. (Arizona Historical Society Biographical File. Frank C. Lockwood, "Tucson: The Old Pueblo," pp. 52–53.)

[10]Fort Yuma was originally called Camp Independence (at that location) and was established below Jaeger's Ferry in 1850 on the California side of the Colorado River to protect emigrant traffic to California. A year before, Camp Calhoun (after John C. Calhoun, secretary of state, 1844–45) had been built at the ferry. It was situated on a granite outcrop near the junction with the Gila and about 180 miles from the mouth of the Colorado. The site was famed for its intense heat. Known as Camp Yuma by 1851, it had been abandoned temporarily in that year owing to fierce Yuma Indian attacks.

Early in 1852 Major (later General) Samuel P. Heintzelman reestablished the post as Fort Yuma with a San Diego detachment. During the Civil War the fort was a strategic point of communication for the California Column and as a key supply center for the territory. Fort Yuma was abandoned by 1889. Following the Gadsden Purchase the city of Yuma had been founded on the Arizona side of the river. In 1864 an army quartermaster's depot was established at Yuma and became the distribution point for all Arizona's army posts to the end of the war. (Wallace W. Elliott, *History of Arizona Territory,* pp. 245–47; Ray Brandes, "A Guide to the History of the U.S. Army Installations in Arizona, 1849–1886," pp. 42–65.)

Letter 15

VISIT TO TUCSON —
PRIMITIVE HOUSEKEEPING — THE ANCIENT
AND SPLENDID CATHEDRAL OF SAN XAVIER

Tubac,[1] Dec. 12, 1864
[Published February 24, 1865]

My last was written from Maricopa Wells. — After resting there a day or two, I rode over to Mr. White's, where you recollect we came in last spring from the Verde. Quite a change was manifest here. The steam flouring mill was running, the Indians were bringing in their wheat, pumpkins and squashes, and altogether the Pima villages were a busy, thriving community. The women pack on their shoulders huge loads, a sort of wicker crate is arranged to fit upon their backs, balanced up above their heads, and on them I have seen, I should think, at least 250 pounds of pumpkins, or melons or squashes, carried off at a brisk walk for two miles. The mill here is a great convenience to the miners above, and the day is near at hand when we cease to import flour from California.

---

[1] Tubac (from a Pima word: the meaning of *Tu* is unknown, *Bac* means house or ruin) had been founded in 1753 by the Spanish on the site of a deserted Pima village. A presidio was built there for fifty soldiers and their families, but it was moved to Tucson in 1776. Tubac was the "mother city" for both San Francisco and Tucson in 1775 and 1776 respectively. Due to Apache raids, Tubac was largely abandoned after the 1820s until Charles Debrille Poston made it the headquarters of his Sonora Exploring and Mining Company in 1856. By 1859 the settlement had thoroughly revived under American influence, and Arizona's first newspaper (*The Arizonian*) and first book (*Pastoral Letter* by Sonora's bishop) were published there. Tubac's fortunes waxed and waned in later periods, according to the presence or absence of garrisons and Apache moods. The presidio had all but vanished by 1908. Modern Tubac is not on the site of the original settlement. Old Tubac's presidio ruins have been preserved in a state park about seven miles south of Amado in Santa Cruz County. (Byrd H. Granger, *Arizona Place Names*, p. 326; Rufus Kay Wyllys, *Arizona: The History of A Frontier State*, p. 189.)

From Pima to Tucson we followed the old overland mail road.[2] It leaves the Gila at the last of the Pima villages, and bears about southeast across grass plains, through the Picacho pass, where the California column met the first picket of Texans.[3] Here are the graves of a lieutenant and some soldiers killed in the skirmish. As matter of fact, four men here absolutely delayed the advance of the column for some weeks, the advance-guard were fired on from the bushes and three men killed, and not knowing the strength of the body opposed to him, the officer commanding fell back to the Gila and waited for more troops. There were nine Texans on the picket there, four of them were out hunting, one asleep, and the remainder playing cards, when the cavalry advance came on them and the skirmish ensued.

The road is an admirable one, level, and after you leave the Gila rarely sandy, the old adobe station houses[4] are still standing at distances of ten or fifteen miles, the wells have many of them fallen in, the ropes and buckets are all gone; no sooner is a thing abandoned in this country than it is stripped by either Mexicans or Indians. At certain seasons of the year these wells are all the

---

[2] "The route traversed by the first Butterfield Overland Mail . . . [followed] the old, old road from Yuma up the Gila to the Pima villages; then by Picacho, Tucson, the *Cienega*, San Pedro Station, Dragoon Springs, Apache Pass, and out of Arizona territory through Doubtful Pass." (Frank C. Lockwood, *Pioneer Days in Arizona*, p. 298.)

[3] The "last of the Pima villages" was probably in the vicinity of modern Bapchule just south of the Gila River. (Raymond A. Muligen, "Down the Old Butterfield Trail," pp. 358–67. Also consult Roscoe and Margaret B. Conkling, *The Butterfield Overland Mail 1857–69*.)

Following the clash at Picacho Pass, the Union force withdrew to the north, perhaps in the belief that a superior Confederate force was in the area. Suitably reinforced, the Federals again advanced and retook Tucson by May 1862. The Confederate forces never returned, and Arizona Territory remained in the Union. (D. C. Mott, "Picacho Pass, a Civil War Key Point," pp. 10–11; 21–22; Ray C. Colton, *The Civil War in the Western Territories: Arizona, Colorado, New Mexico and Utah*, pp. 104–107.)

[4] The stage stations were built under the supervision of contractors William Buckley, Frank de Ruyther, William Brainerd, and Silas St. John for the Butterfield Line (which later joined with the Overland Mail Company). Stations of adobe and stone were constructed and in use by the end of 1858. The line, however, ceased operations in 1860 due largely to Apache attacks and the increasing political power of the northern states, which favored a central overland route through Utah. Some of the Butterfield station ruins have remained, for example the Dragoon Springs station in Cochise County two miles southeast of Dragoon. (Hubert Howe Bancroft, *History of Arizona and New Mexico 1530–1888*, p. 496; Granger, *Arizona Place Names*, p. 36; Thomas E. Farish, *History of Arizona*, 2: 5, 10, 13–14.)

water to be had for long stretches, and one would think there could scarcely be such a wretch as to steal a paltry rope from a well, but sufficient for the day is the evil thereof, is a maxim very strictly followed out here; if one traveler gets what water he wants those who come after must look out for themselves.

The climate at this season of the year is superb; in the daytime, mild and bracing; you ride in your shirt-sleeves in the full enjoyment of simple existence, but the nights are bad, they are not as cold as in the mountains, that is water doesn't freeze as much, but I suffered more from cold in sleeping out since we crossed the Gila than I did above; there seems to be a sharp, damp, penetrating frost that will steal in under your blankets and benumb you, no matter how carefully you wrap them around you. I recollect one night several of the party got so chilled that they got up, built a fire, and made some coffee, just because they couldn't sleep. Once over a road in this country, one ought never to be lost; the country, as it were, is fenced off by ranges of mountains from twenty to fifty miles apart, with openings through them three or four miles wide. All these mountains have the common peculiarity of ragged, broken slopes, that catch the radiance of the sun and glow with the richest purple hues; they are desolation itself near to, the home of the spectre *Seguaro* [Saguaro] and the Apache. From their craggy heights the crafty, cowardly assassin and thief Indian watches passing parties and waylays the careless. These mountains are very deceptive as to distance; all day you ride toward them, still they seem as far away as when you started.

At the point of the mountain range beyond Picacho, you strike the dry bed of the Santa Cruz,[5] a stream that, when it runs, empties into the Gila at the Maricopa wells. It is some two hundred and fifty miles in length, and at times huge volumes of water march majestically its whole extent, sweeping and destroying whatever is in its track. Woe to the unfortunate teamster who happens to be

---

[5] Father Kino named the Santa Cruz River in the 1690s. Rising in Arizona, the now-dry river once flowed from its source in Arizona into Mexico then in reverse north to the Tucson area and northwest to the Gila. Beyond modern Rillito, it went underground and its bed has largely disappeared in the Santa Cruz Cienaga. Old maps show the river's probable underground course beyond Rillito. (Granger, *Arizona Place Names*, p. 275.)

driving across its apparently harmless bed when these come; no warning, save the rushing sounds of water; in an instant his team and freight is all gone; men, even, caught sleeping, have been drowned. This is the way water runs in all the rivers of Arizona; even the little Granite Creek at Prescott, an innocent, harmless shoal of sand, sometimes plays the same trick, and it is reported as a good joke, that upon one occasion the Governor, crossing, was caught mid-way upon a little island. The day after, the bed is as dry as a chip, and you would scarcely believe that there could have been such an unruly mass rioting there the day before. The line of the Santa Cruz is marked by its fringe of luxuriant cottonwoods, just now fading into the sere and yellow leaf.

If there is anything that's a bore, it is being well mounted and yet having to crawl along at the slow pace of loaded wagons. Dick was in splendid condition and quite as restive at the snail's pace as I was; so we concluded that we would take the chances of the Apaches and gallop to Tucson. At sunrise I leisurely saddled up, midway between the Picacho and the point of the mountain,[6] some thirty odd miles from Tucson, and started alone. After crossing the Santa Cruz the road leaves the river to the left, passing through quite a dense growth of mesquit;[7] the valley between the two ranges, now on either hand, is of fair breadth and with a good growth of grass. In all that long ride I did not see a living thing until I met three Mexicans driving a herd of mules out to some wagons left on the Salinas, where the Apaches a few days before had stripped them of their animals. They told me I was very near to Tucson, and I was on the *qui vive* for the first glimpse of this ancient town, the

---

[6]The "point of the mountain" may refer to the pinnacle called Desert Peak at the south end of the Tortolita Mountains. But there was a stage and freight stop farther to the southeast on the road with ample water at "Point of Mountain" in the vicinity of modern Marana. (Granger, *Arizona Place Names*, pp. 324–25.)

[7]Allyn encounters here the "honey mesquite" (*Prosopis juliflora*), which grows chiefly along the desert streams of the Southwest. It is a large shrub or small tree reaching to a height of thirty feet. The beans of the mesquite were a basic food for the Indians, especially in time of drought, and the tree is still the most important honey plant in Arizona. (Thomas H. Kearney and Robert H. Peebles, *Arizona Flora*, p. 402.)

extremest limit of Spanish settlement.[8] At last it opened on the river, apparently built on a slight rise of gently sloping ground; from here it looked about twice the size of La Paz, the buildings were larger and there were no spaces between. No flag was flying, and in the stillness it seemed a deserted city; no murmur of industry or voices disturbed the deception. Suddenly Dick gave a plunge, and I saw we were passing quite a flock of sheep, grazing in the bushes under the charge of a herder, crouching on his *serepe,* under a mesquit tree, motionless, perhaps asleep, at any rate he gave no sound. Stretching off to the right were the cultivated fields, some two hundred acres, perhaps, and closer scrutiny showed here and there men and oxen at work; and you could trace the tiny threads of the *acequias.* Stopping at the first *acequia* to let Dick drink, we entered Tucson. Scarcely a person was stirring, stores looked dark and gloomy. Riding up to an old friend's, I met the cordial welcome of the country and was at home.

Tucson is about half in ruins; there are still many very fine old adobe buildings; the flag staff was taken down when the troops removed to Tubac. There was a fine adobe church begun, but no one was at work on it; quite a number of stores with well assorted stocks of goods, indeed, the best I think in the territory, but they are in Mexican buildings, dark, narrow, and making no display. There is no hotel, boarding house or restaurant in the town, and

---

[8] Tucson was an ancient town indeed, since Hohokam ruins have been discovered there dating back to A.D. 900. Father Kino visited the site in 1694 and referred to the running water along the Santa Cruz River and a large population of Indians.

The name *Tucson* is the Spanish derivation of the Pima term for the dark base of Sentinel Mountain (*chuk son*), beside which lay the earliest Spanish settlement in Arizona. By the mid-eighteenth century, Tucson was a *rancheria visita* of San Xavier del Bac. In 1769 a walled settlement with a church was built for defense on the site of modern Tucson. And in 1776 Don Hugo O'Connor built a presidio there. The name *San Augustín del Tuquison* or *Tucson* was applied to the place, to distinguish it from the Sentinel Peak settlement, called *Augustín de Pueblito de Tucson.*

Tucson was a Mexican outpost from 1822 to 1856. Intermittent U.S. military occupation began in 1856. The Confederates held Tucson briefly in 1862, until General Carleton reoccupied the town for the Union in June. Tucson was declared a municipality in 1864 by Governor Goodwin. Allyn visited there when the population was probably under one thousand, including less than one hundred Americans. By 1880, Tucson had 7,007 people. It was the territorial capital between 1867 and 1877. (Bancroft, *Arizona and New Mexico,* p. 618; Granger, *Arizona Place Names,* pp. 284–85. See also Frank C. Lockwood, *Life in Old Tucson, 1854–64* and Sidney B. Brinckerhoff, "The Last of Spanish Arizona 1786–1821," pp. 5–20.)

From J. Ross Browne's *Adventures in the Apache Country*

When Allyn was in it in 1864, Mexican-influenced Tucson was partially in ruins from Apache raids. "If the people were not hospitable," said the judge, "it would be a sorry place for a stranger."

if the people were not hospitable, it would be a sorry place for the stranger. I staid here several days with a gentleman who had traveled much, and is now in the country as the superintendent of the Maricopa Copper Mining Co.,[9] patiently waiting for currency affairs at the east to become settled so that capital can be transferred here without the ruinous loss of one half or two-thirds, and he can commence operations. From all that I can learn, the mine is very valuable. It is on or near the Gila, about sixty miles above the Pimas.

My friend was *hatching* it, that is, doing his own house work, and a description of our daily life gives a vivid picture of Tucson to-day. You know I am not famous for early rising; before I was up he would usually be out foraging; and we never knew what we were to eat until the time came. There is no market, no regular butcher; and while I was there, the baker was essentially unreliable;

[9] The Maricopa Copper Mining Company (also known as the Maricopa Mining Company and the Maricopa Mine), incorporated in 1859, was a New York-owned mine producing copper and silver. The superintendent, Allyn's host, was the mine's discoverer, A. B. Gray, a former engineer-in-chief of the Pacific Railroad, who had become surveyor of the Mexican boundary under the Treaty of Guadalupe Hidalgo. The mine was located near Ojo Verde, forty miles from the junction of the San Pedro and Aravaipa rivers and three to four miles from the Gila. (Arizona Historical Foundation Name File; Farish, *History of Arizona* 2: 72.)

that is, sometimes he baked, sometimes he didn't. So the bachelor pokes round from one Mexican house to another, getting some eggs at one place, potatoes at another, etc. During the time I was in town the only thing of animal sort killed, was pig; so pork steaks were our only reliance in the meat way; but we had eggs, butter and cheese all the time. When you get the run of a town and the people, you generally get whatever you want, but it is very difficult for the uninitiated. Store-keepers get very independent out here; they shut up when they feel like it, and open at the same time. It is *on dit* that one once was playing some game or other, when a Mexican boy disturbed him by asking for some candles; now it was midday, and candles are supposed to be designed for the night season, so our store keeper brusquely told the boy to come at the proper time and he could have the candles, and resumed his game. Tucson was especially dull because the Mexicans are busy in the fields, and the Americans, perhaps catching the fever from their trip to Prescott, were all out prospecting; "feet," the great leveller of the Pacific, have at last attacked the sober, staid old town and perhaps it will be as crazy as the younger mushroom places that grow up in a single night.

In the old time, when one had a mine, he had something that every body didn't have, perhaps it was a bill of expense, but then he was a mine owner, but feet every body can have. Did I ever explain to you what "feet" are? You go out prospecting, you see croppings of rich looking rock; there may be a vein, so you write a notice claiming so many feet on it, the custom of the district regulating the number of feet you have a right to claim, and stick it up on the rock. Then you get it recorded; it don't even take any money to do this, for the recorder is a clever fellow and you put his name down for some feet, of course he won't ask for his fee, a paltry dollar or so, when perhaps you have given him a million. If this proves to be a vein and the rock is rich and the vein is large enough to pay for working, you have then something valuable.

Generally a long time elapses after the first discovery before industrious men take hold of it and find out whether it is really valuable or worthless, and then generally a law-suit is the result, if it is rich somebody turning up who had located and recorded it before. If this vein were all there was to feet, it would be a harmless lottery enough to take your chances, both of the Indian and of there being a mine, but the curse of a mining country is the men who want to mine in Wall Street, that is post up the little paper notice, knock off a piece of rock, have it assayed, and then sell the "feet" to some company who in turn mean to sell the stock. Sometimes I fancy even the rock doesn't come from the place it is said to, but even if it did it proves nothing, for there is an abundance of rich rock where there is no vein, or properly speaking mine. A true vein is one that goes to the centre of forces, it is where the mineral has been forced out through the primitive rocks and always has well defined walls on either side with casings of different formations. There are, particularly in the country where it has been disturbed by volcanic action, deposits of rich mineral that are not forced outward at the point where they are found, but have in the convulsions been thrown miles away from the vein which perhaps closed again, and they settled as they could into crevices of rocks, forming what are called pockets; of course when they are worked out there is nothing left.

But this is getting away from Tucson. Every body there is a little touched with "feet" on the brain. I do not recollect a day while there that some one did not bring in specimens of rock from some new lead. There were no *baile* while I was there, so I had no opportunity of seeing the women; where the *baile* plays out, the seal of death is on a Mexican town. There was a horse race or two and the monotony was still further broken by the arrival of a train or two from Sonora, bringing some very welcome additions to our commissariat in the shape of butter, potatoes and quinces.

Sometimes we walked up to the Mill,[10] something less than two miles from the town, where the Santa Cruz runs quite a respectable stream of water; the buildings here were all burned at the time of the abandonment of the country by the troops, and are now in a very dilapidated state; the machinery now running was brought down from Tubac. When the troops were here the Government herd was kept near the Mill and the Apaches used to cut the pickets of the corral and steal the animals, while the sentinels were upon

---

[10] The mill in question was very likely the one established in Tucson by R. Jackson or Captain Roulett and brothers in 1858 or 1859. It is described as being stoutly built with cottonwood logs. It processed wheat from Sonora but at very high prices. (Wallace W. Elliott, *Arizona Territory,* p. 255; Farish, *History of Arizona* 4: 255.)

the opposite side. Between the Mill and the town you pass the crumbling remains of the old Mission Dolores.[11] With the advance of the Spanish civilization the soldier and the priest always went hand in hand. The Presidio and the Mission together were in the vanguard of the stream of population and until revolution broke out in Mexico their success in developing the country and catholicising the Indian was marked.

Tucson was the farthest point they ever reached and now for ten years with varied fortunes the American protestant scheme of development has been at work, under such unfavorable surroundings that it is not fair to contrast the two results.

Toward evening one day I rode away from Tucson on the road toward Sonora. Some seven or eight miles of good road skirting a thick growth of mesquit brought the famous church of San Xavier[12] in full view, just as the setting sun was tinging its towers, buttresses and dome. A prettier sight rarely greets the eye; there was the grand old church, the adobe walls of the old mission garden, the Indian town, the broad irrigated fields, the moving herds, all forming a picture that one would not soon forget.

The church of San Xavier del Bac was commenced by the Jesuits in 1694, and was not quite completed at the time of their expulsion. This mission and church is the sole exception to the universal abandonment of the missions of Arizona, with priests or without. The Papagoes or baptized Indians have watched and guarded the fine old pile with rare fidelity. This church is entirely

---

[11] This mission was constructed by the Franciscans on the west bank of the Santa Cruz River "sometime between 1797 and 1810." It was a large, two-story *convento*. (Brinckerhoff, "Last Years of Spanish Arizona," pp. 15–16.)

[12] The foundations of Mission San Xavier del Bac were laid by Father Eusebio Francisco Kino in 1700, at a place the Papagos called *Bac* or "a watering place in an otherwise dry river." This was the first of three churches built on or near the site. A second church was constructed in 1757 by Father Alonso Espinosa, the earlier structure having crumbled following a Pima uprising. In 1783 the present building was begun by Father Juan Bautista Velderrain, slightly to the south of the older structures. It was completed in 1797. Famed as perhaps the finest example of Spanish colonial mission architecture in the United States, the church is known as the White Dove of the Desert. San Xavier was abandoned in 1828, but was protected by Papago Christians. The restored church serves them today. (Augustine J. Donohue, S.J., "The Unlucky Jesuit Mission of Bac," pp. 127–39; Bernard L. Fontana, "Biography of a Desert Church: The Story of Mission San Xavier del Bac," pp. 1–24.)

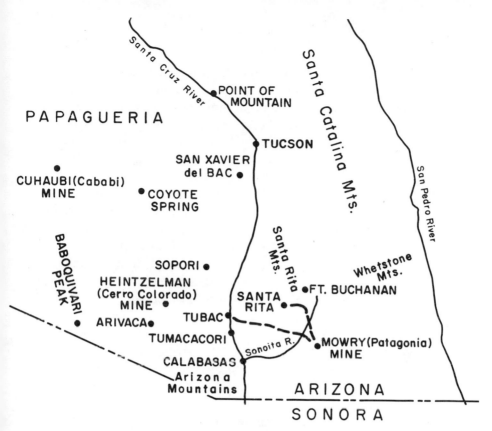

Excursions Around Tubac, Dec. 1864 - Jan. 1865

built of brick covered with a plastering of cement. There is no wood work about it, save where sticks of ironwood are used for want of iron, about which to mould ornaments, columns or statues; where these are broken they disclose now a central rod of wood. The church is in the form of a Latin cross, a large dome rising over the transept, surmounted by a cross and smaller ones forming the remainder of the roof; at the corners of the front are two large towers that above the roof rise into open-worked belfries and pinnacles supported by flying buttresses at the corners. The front is elaborately ornamented with mouldings, statues, etc., all formed of brick covered with cement and probably once colored. One of the towers above the roof has never been plastered, and the whole exterior has been much defaced by exposure and want of repairs. As a whole it is a wonderful architectural success, perfectly proportioned; it seems poised over the surrounding country like a thing of life; all its lines harmonize, it is neither too high, too long, or too broad.

The interior is very dark and it is difficult to criticise the frescoes that ornament it, but the brilliancy of most of the colors is remarkable, and the drawing is certainly equal to most of the more modern churches of Italy. The several altars in the dim light now glitter with the masses of gilding that form their adornment, and it is recorded that at one time forty thousand dollars worth of silver ornaments were stolen from the high altar; whatever was left the Indians take good care to keep out of sight, even Bishop Lamy failed to get a glimpse of them. There have been bad, avaricious priests as well as laymen, as these Indians have found out. The church was in the charge of an Indian Sacristan, who showed you willingly every thing. Bishop Lamy left two padres here,[13] but they were absent when we were there. On the evening of my arrival, however, as I understood them, it was the beginning of the feast of Our Lady of Guadaloupe, and candles were lighted upon the high altar, a Madonna was taken and borne by young Indian girls, bearing candles and chanting, amid the firing of guns, in solemn procession all around the plaza, the whole population uncovering their heads or kneeling, then returned to its place in the church.

The view from the pinnacles is very extensive, sweeping the valley of the Santa Cruz for miles. The staircase that ascends the tower passes in the wall, and is just wide enough for one person; the cement on the sides here, untouched by the weather, is light and hard as stone; a back staircase leads from the roof to the belfry that is concealed from view below by the battlements. The bells form an imperfect chime, and were brought from Spain. Near the church is an enclosed cemetery, with a cross in the center and a little chapel whereon to rest the coffin; it was quite filled with graves.

We camped near the church and had an amusing time buying corn, eggs, butter, etc., around among the Indians and Mexicans.

---

[13] Bishop John B. Lamy had visited Tucson on March 19, 1864, with a Jesuit priest, Reverend J. M. Coudert. There were two Jesuits in the area at the time, Fathers Charles Evasius Mesea and Aloysius María Bosco, the priests of Allyn's reference. In August 1864, before Allyn's visit, these clerics returned to California, leaving Catholics of the region temporarily without spiritual guidance. In 1865 Bishop Lamy headed the bishopric of New Mexico, Arizona, and Colorado. Lamy returned in 1866 to attend to the needs of Tucson in person, with the Reverends Francis Boucard, and Patrick Birmingham and a Mr. Vincent, a young school teacher. (Norman M. Whalen, "The Catholic Church in Arizona, 1820–1870," pp. 61–69.)

There are quite a number of Mexicans living here for security from the Apaches, who never dare invade the domains of San Xavier. We got all that we needed and at very moderate prices, and (let Secretary Fessenden[14] take courage) payable in fractional currency. If paper money is an evidence of civilization, these Indians have the advantage of the people of California. The moon rose clear and almost full, silvering everything, kindly hiding the ravages of time upon the noble old pile that towered so majestically over the little Indian town, and dropping as it were a veil over that cosmopolitan sacrilege of scribbling your name on every such famous old monument, that even this church, in its remote Indian fame, has not escaped.

It would have been very easy to have let the imagination loose and peopled this scene with the men of other days, when the Jesuits were in the plenitude of their power, and these missions rich and powerful; when the fathers worked mines and branded their tens of thousands of horses and cattle; when every soldier of the Presidio had his two horses, one to ride and one to lead, and his pursuit of the Apache was untiring — the missions furnished the horses. But the present was too real and too sad to allow of such *dilettante* luxuries. We have to do with the Arizona of to-day, to bring back if possible the material prosperity of other days, and to add to that the elements of a self-sustaining state, brave, self-reliant, industrious, intelligent and liberty-loving citizens. It is a task in many respects the most difficult the American has ever undertaken, but the prize is worth the struggle. Arizona holds out no inducements to the idle or the cowardly, no sudden fortunes are to be made here without work, but it does offer homes, independence and the chances of fortune to industry.

---

[14]William Pitt Fessenden (1806–69) was appointed secretary of the treasury by President Lincoln in July 1864. The finances of the Union were in a difficult state at the time owing in part to the withdrawal of government bonds from the market. The price of gold soared, and the value of the paper dollar dropped to thirty-four cents. Congress authorized the use of paper notes of fractional currency or "shinplasters," some of which had denominations as low as three cents. Some fifty million dollars of this money contributed to the war income of the government. Fessenden refused to issue further paper money and was successful in stablizing federal currency. (Arthur Cecil Bining and Thomas C. Cochran, *The Rise of American Economic Life,* pp. 319–20; *Dictionary of American Biography* 6: 348–50.)

Letter 16

THE APACHE MENACE —
AMERICAN OCCUPATION —
THE CALIFORNIA COLUMN — TUBAC —
WAR IN SONORA — SANTA RITA

Tubac, Dec. 22, 1864
[Published May 8, 1865]

My last brought this narrative up to San Xavier. The road thence to this place follows the Santa Cruz and is marked by the ruins of deserted ranches, whose crumbling walls, *acequias* filled up and covered with a dense growth of underbush and tall grasses, wells caved in, corrals tenantless, with the graves that line the way, are the too sad monuments of the desperate attempts that have been made in the past to hold this fertile region against the hostile Apache. No stronger evidence could be produced of the reality of the mineral wealth of Arizona than these mute witnesses to the faith of the little band of Americans in its existence, shown in this ten years of grim holding on, seeing, one by one, their old associates die at the hands of the relentless savage.

No such task has before been laid upon the American pioneer as this. It is true there have been bloody Indian wars in the history of our westward march across the continent, but the advance of settlement has been, as it were, the steady, majestic tread of millions. The savage looked down upon the curling smoke of the venturous pioneer cabin, saw its grazing animals and ripening harvests with envious eyes; but he knew that behind that tiny little family, so surely in his power, was a mighty nation, and that vengeance, swift

[176]

and sure, would follow the slightest harm done them. Here all was reversed. A hundred years ago the Spanish immigration was advancing slowly and surely toward the Gila. One by one, Presidio and Mission, the soldier and the priest, hand in hand, had been established at regular distances. The Indian became their bondman, mines were worked, herds of fabulous extent grazed in these valleys; vineyards and fruit trees were planted, rich architectural monuments, like the grand old church at San Xavier, rose. Once in the while an insurrection disturbed the even tenor of their way, but on the whole this civilization was slowly and surely making a garden of the country and advancing northward.

Suddenly all this changed. The Mexican revolution[1] broke out, the soldier was recalled from the frontier, and the cross was left alone to face the Apache in the front. The revolution succeeded, and with it successively came decrees expelling Jesuits and Franciscans. The Apache swept down on the now defenseless missions, and was master of all, save San Xavier which the Papagos protected.

About two years ago[2] the country passed into the hands of the Americans and small ranches took the place of the enormous Mission, and land was divided by acres instead of leagues, houses were in sight of each other almost, in the valleys, instead of the Presidio and the Mission fifty Spanish miles[3] apart; mines began to be worked, emigration to set in, and overland stages swept by daily, crossing the continent. In the twinkling of an eye rebellion did for the American what revolution did for the Spaniard. The posts were abandoned, troops withdrawn; the Texans swept over the country; the Apache laughed and fancied it was he who had done all this; the Mexican shrugged his shoulders, with an "I told you so" air; he was used to revolution; and both concluded that civil war was their harvest season, and rioted in plunder. Again desolation was the order of

---

[1] Mexico's independence from Spain was declared in October 1821, but revolutionary struggles continued intermittently during the century until 1884, when Porfirio Díaz became president.

[2] By "two years ago" (1862) Allyn must refer to the actual settlement of the mission lands by Americans rather than to the Gadsden purchase of 1853. However, Father McCarty of San Xavier del Bac has said the mission records show that Americans actually began settling on these lands as early as 1859. (Interview, November 11, 1971, Tucson.)

[3] The Spanish mile varies between ⅞ and 1¼ English miles. (Charles T. Onions, *The Oxford Universal Dictionary on Historical Principles,* p. 1249.)

the day. Save the Mowry mine[4] and Tucson no settlement was left outside of the Papagaria or country of the Papagoes.[5]

Next comes the march of the California column across to Rio Grande, leaving a garrison at Tucson,[6] and more lately the establishment of a territorial government for all that portion of New Mexico west of the Rocky mountains. The term of service of the California column expired last fall, and instead of making arrangements for their return home, and discharge, a grand campaign was inaugurated against the Apaches, destroying their harvests. The column hurried to the Rio Grande and there mustered out of service, a thousand miles away from home, with most inhospitable deserts to cross, and strict orders given to commanding officers at all posts on the route not to furnish them provisions.

If this was designed to encourage reenlistments, it was a terrible mistake, for I have met hundreds of noble fellows who had given up three years to their country, trudging back through long weary miles of desert; and it is pleasant to bear testimony to the fact

---

[4]The Mowry, previously the Patagonia or Corral Viejo mine, was purchased by Sylvester Mowry (1833–71) from Elias Brevourt and H. T. Titus in 1860. Mowry was a native of Rhode Island, a West Point graduate, and a former lieutenant of artillery. The mine proved to be a rich one, and had produced 1½ million dollars by 1862. Mowry's fortunes shifted, however, and in that year he was arrested and jailed by General Carleton for six months as a Confederate sympathizer. His mine was located in Santa Cruz County approximately fifteen miles south of modern Patagonia. (Bernard L. Fontana, "The Mowry Mine: 1858–1958," pp. 14–16; Pima County, Arizona, *Mortgages,* Book 2; Bert M. Fireman, "What Comprises Treason?" pp. 5–10. Also consult Sylvester Mowry, *Arizona and Sonora.*)

[5]The Papaguería was located in the approximate area of the present-day Papago Indian Reservation, roughly sixty by ninety miles in size. The area stretched between Ajo and Tucson along the .international boundary and north into Pima County.

The Papagos were among the first Indians to be observed by Anglos in Arizona and were generally friendly. An agricultural people, many Papagos lived along the Rio Santa Cruz and frequently made war on the Apache. Considerable numbers became Christians at San Xavier del Bac. (Byrd H. Granger, *Arizona Place Names,* p. 274; Hubert H. Bancroft, *History of Arizona and New Mexico 1530–1888,* pp. 550–51.)

[6]The California Column under Colonel West (see note 15 below) established a camp within the town of Tucson at Scott and Fourteenth streets in May of 1862. This garrison had been removed in September 1864 before Allyn arrived but was reestablished in May of the following year. In 1866 the post became permanent and was named Camp Lowell. In 1873 the garrison was moved seven miles to the eastern side of the town, where it remained until abandoned in 1891. (Granger, *Arizona Place Names,* p. 270; Ray Brandes, *Frontier Military Posts of Arizona,* p. 86.)

that the moment the weary wanderers cross the Colorado river into the department of the Pacific, they receive rations.

At this writing the garrisons in Arizona[7] number altogether, perhaps two hundred men; and thoughtful men, as the cold advances, tremble when they recall the past and think of the starving Apache in his canon home, watching the hegira of blue coats and bayonets.

But this is an inexcusable digression. It was a lonely day, such as you have sometimes in October and November, when I rode into Tubac. The flag floating in the plaza told of soldiers and security. There is a collector of customs[8] here, and under his hospitable roof we were soon at home. Tubac is prettily situated at the foot of an isolated, golden-hued mountain, where the Santa Cruz runs through between the Santa Rita and Arizona ranges of mountains. It has been so long abandoned that its church and buildings were literally in ruins, but with the advent of troops, population is gathering in, building is going on, and there are many evidences of life. Gov. Gandara,[9] for very many years the governor of Sonora, resides, or rather stays, here in exile, the fortunes of cruel war having made him comparatively poor. I say stays here, for the house he occupied had neither doors or windows, scarcely any furniture, and he seemed to prefer walking up and down on the sunny side of the house, to the

---

[7]General John S. Mason, who commanded the District of Arizona succeeding General Carleton (see Background, note 14), from February 20, 1865, had less than three thousand men at his disposal. (Rufus Kay Wyllys, *Arizona: The History of a Frontier State*, p. 189.) Arizona military establishments in operation during 1864 were as follows: Camp Bowie, Fort Canby, Camp Clark, Fort Defiance, Camp Goodwin, Camp Grant, Camp Lincoln (Yuma County), Camp Lincoln (Yavapai County), Fort Lowell, Fort Mohave, Camp Tubac, Fort Whipple, Yuma Quartermaster Depot. For details on these establishments, see Brandes, *Frontier Military Posts*, and Francis P. Prucha, *A Guide to the Military Posts of the United States 1789–1895*.)

[8]The only custom house officer for the area listed in 1864 census (p. 80) is Henry McCormick Ward, age 26. There was a large and lucrative smuggling trade from Arizona into Sonora. Many of Sonora's "dry goods" were obtained from Tucson. (Bancroft, *Arizona and New Mexico*, p. 602.)

[9]Manuel María Gándara was a former governor of Sonora. He resided in the Tubac area with members of his family and made occasional excursions to Tucson. He seems to have been a contractor of supplies for the California Column. According to the San Francisco *Alta* of January 15, 1864, he visited San Francisco in an attempt to arrange for French aid in ousting Governor Pesqueira of Sonora. (Arizona Historical Society Biographical File. Francisco R. Almada, *Diccionario de Historia, Geografía y Biografía Sonorenses*, pp. 288–94; Rudolph F. Acuña, "Ignacio Pesqueira: Sonoran Caudillo," pp. 139–72.)

trouble of having a fire. He is a fine looking old gentleman, of even courtly manners, and amidst these uncomfortable surroundings, bears himself with dignity. I found him a genial, pleasant companion.

The garrison of the post consists of a company of California cavalry. The commanding officer[10] occupies a large comfortable building erected by the Sonora Exploring and Mining Company.[11] He is quite a young man, and in the present disturbed condition of the frontier, occupies a position requiring delicacy, tact and firmness, qualities in which he is not wanting.

Tubac was a presidio, and is just fifty Mexican miles from Tucson. Its attendant mission was the famous one of Tumacacori, about three miles below the town. Quite a party of us rode over there one of those incomparable winter afternoons of this climate, and spent an hour rambling over this wonderful relic of the priestly time.

Tumacacori[12] is a grander old ruin than San Xavier, or rather is a grand old ruin, while San Xavier is a well preserved old church. No body of zealous Papagoes have been camped round this to preserve it from sacrilegious hands, and time and vandalism have both done their full work of destruction. Tumacacori was a grand old monastery like those of Italy and the East, a vast pile, with chapel,

---

[10] The commander at Tubac at this time was Captain John S. Merriam of the First California Cavalry. (Returns from U.S. Military Posts 1800–1916," Tubac, December 1864.)

[11] The Sonora Exploring and Mining Company was organized in 1856 by Charles D. Poston and his San Francisco colleagues. The company eventually controlled some eighty mines and twenty thousand acres from its Tubac headquarters. By 1859 the Sonora Company was in financial straits. Samuel Colt assumed control in New York and ousted Poston as Arizona company representative. By June 1861 the company's Arivaca mine in Arivaca valley near Baboquivari Peak was superintended by Poston's brother John and worked by 250 men. It was producing about one thousand dollars per day. In the same month, however Fort Buchanan was ordered destroyed to prevent its fall into Confederate hands. As a result of the removal of federal protection, Apache depredations increased sharply. Poston and others left the area. Mining became extremely difficult, and Tubac was taken and sacked by the Apaches. (Thomas E. Farish, History of Arizona 2: 6off; Granger, Arizona Place Names, p. 261.)

[12] Tumacacori is Pima for "curved peak" and refers to an adjacent mountain. Father Kino established one of his three missions in Arizona at Tumacacori between 1691 and 1701. Apaches leveled the first Jesuit mission in 1776. A Franciscan edifice was begun in the late eighteenth century but given up after 1828 and was not reoccupied again. In 1908 it was made a national monument to preserve remaining ruins. Tumacacori is just south of Carmen. (Granger, Arizona Place Names, p. 326; Earl Jackson, Tumacacori's Yesterdays.)

cloister, courtyard, watchtower and refectory. Its architecture is of the same general character as San Xavier, but it was a group of buildings, and lacks the completeness and symmetry of the church. The roof of its chapel was supported by timbers, and they have rotted and fallen in. Its dome, light and airy enough for the chapel alone, does not rise grandly over the whole pile. Here is the same unfinished tower that disfigures San Xavier, and among our party two different explanations were suggested as facts: one was that the priests never finished such a work, as it deprived them of their revenue from contributions towards its completion; the other was, that there was a Catholic tax levied upon all finished churches, and consequently they never were allowed to become finished. Either of these would show the fathers to be sharp, shrewd fellows.

It is evident that those priests worked mines, for you can trace now the remains of furnaces and slag lying about. They had extensive gardens, fruit trees and a vineyard, irrigated by *acequias* that can be easily traced, on one of which was arranged a commodious masonry tank for bathing. The buildings here were covered with the same time-defying, hard, shiny plastering that we noticed at San Xavier, and it is said to be made by fermenting the juice of the prickly pear and using it for an outer coating. Some Americans now claim this mission under some sort of a Mexican title, and are at work putting in a crop. The first newspaper[13] ever printed here was set up in the sacristy, and as though this were not enough of a fall to base uses, at the time we were there, donkeys were stabled there.

While we were at Tubac there was a *baile*. No better evidence could be given of the resurrection of the town. It was a *distinqué* affair, of the *gente fina*, or fine people. There were Gov. Gandara's sons,[14] young men who somehow have not inherited their father's manners, but evidently bold riders and good *rancheros;* the American officers, and a half dozen quite pretty Mexican women, some

---

[13] As far as is known, the first newspaper in Arizona was the *Arizonian*, published in Tubac from March through July 1859. William S. Oury and Sylvester Mowry then bought the operation from the Santa Rita Silver Mining Company and moved it to Tucson. Possibly Allyn has confused Tumacacori and Tubac. (Andrew Wallace, *Image of Arizona*, p. 89; Bancroft, *Arizona and New Mexico*, pp. 498, 607.)

[14] Governor Gándara had four sons: Juan, Jesús, José, and Francisco. The only son in politics was Francisco (1837–1903), who served as lieutenant governor of Sonora, 1883–87, and then as governor. (Almada, *Diccionario de Sonorenses*, pp. 287–88.)

of them famous, two having had the honor, I understand, of tripping the light fantastic toe with Gens. Carleton and West[15] at the *baile* in honor of the arrival of the column at Tucson. The affair passed off very pleasantly and the dance continued till late.

Rumors of war and disturbance in Sonora[16] reach us every day, and my trip must be given up. The French are advancing. The governor of Sonora issues funny appeals to his people, orders a draft, proclaims his intention of resisting to the last. The partisans of Gov. Gandara attempt counter-revolution, and to crown all, there is a body of Americans encamped across the line calling themselves Confederates, who are, I suspect, not unjustly suspected of being desirous of possessing themselves of other people's property.

From Tubac I rode out to the hacienda of the Santa Rita Co.[17] It is about ten miles from Tubac, by a good road, most of the way over mesa. The company has resumed possession of it recently, it having been abandoned with the abandonment of the country, and found it a sad wreck, furnaces destroyed, mule power literally carried away, in fact nothing left but adobe walls and roof. There is a small picket of soldiers stationed here forming a chain to old

---

[15] It is doubtful that West or Carleton met socially at Tubac. In neither of Aurora Hunt's books on the subject, *Army of the Pacific* or *Major James Henry Carleton,* is it indicated that such was the case.

[16] At the time of Allyn's writing, the French imperial regime in Mexico, under Maximillian, was approaching its zenith of power. Juárez, who was to become president after the expulsion of the French, had been driven north to Chihuahua, and Sonora was split between pro and anti-French factions. The Maximillian administration was encouraging Confederate refugees to immigrate to Mexico. (Herbert Ingham Priestley, *The Mexican Nation: A History,* pp. 357–58; Acuña, "Ignacio Pesqueira: Sonoran Caudillo," pp. 139–72.)

[17] The Santa Rita Silver Mining Company was a subsidiary of the Sonora Exploring and Mining Company (see note 11 above). The Santa Rita had the honor of having printed the *Arizonian,* the first newspaper and the first book in Arizona in 1859. The editor of the *Arizonian* was Edward E. Cross. He fought a famous rifle duel (no injuries) with Sylvester Mowry and survived only to die as a colonel at Gettysburg. The Santa Rita camp or "hacienda" mentioned by Allyn is described in the Way diary (William A. Duffen, "Overland via 'Jackass Mail' in 1858: The Diary of Phocion R. Way," p. 281. There is an illustration of the hacienda on p. 356.) The Santa Rita mines were at the foot of the Grosvenor Hills (named for H. C. Grosvenor, a company manager killed by Apaches in 1861) about fifteen miles to the east of Tubac. Mine production ceased in 1861 but resumed in the postwar period. (Wallace, *Image of Arizona,* pp. 89, 106, 120 (a facsimile of an *Arizonian* page may be seen on p. 106); Bancroft, *Arizona and New Mexico,* p. 503; Granger, *Arizona Place Names,* p. 317.)

Fort Buchanan.[18] A more beautiful situation can scarcely be imagined. The battlements of a rocky, precipitate mountain literally overhung the houses. Off in the distance the foothills increase in size and height, until they apparently melt into the grand Santa Rita range, its highest peak capped with snow. Whichever way you look you catch glimpses of little valleys nestling among the hills, all well timbered with oak, ash, walnut, cottonwood and mesquit, murmuring streams of water threading the whole. A more deceptive landscape you will rarely meet. Look around you, and you seem to be in a valley a half or three-quarters of a mile across, shut in by the hills all around. Ride straight across and round one of these hills and you find yourself only in another just about the same size, and so on again and again, for six miles at least before you do reach the mountains.

Quite a little colony is being planted here by the Santa Rita Co., represented by Mr. Wrightson,[19] of Cincinnati, under the charge of Dr. John Locke,[20] who is superintending the survey of the land grant and preparing a report upon its various resources. Mr. W. rode over with me and left me for a few days to the hospitality of Dr. Locke. The first day after I arrived we took a ride across the hills, and climbed one of the lower peaks of the range. The day

---

[18] Fort Buchanan's protection against Apache raids, in what is now Santa Cruz County, was essential to productive mining as well as other pursuits. Indeed, when Buchanan was destroyed by army orders (July 23, 1861), mines in the Tubac region virtually ceased to operate. Originally established as Camp Moore, it was renamed Fort Buchanan, for the president, in 1857. Captain Richard Stoddert Ewell, later a famed Confederate officer, commanded U.S. dragoons there. Ewell was popular in Arizona, successfully raided the Apache, and was an occasional silver miner. Fort Buchanan (site of the first Arizona post office), was located on the Sonoita River near the modern town of Patagonia. (Ben Sacks, "The Origin of Fort Buchanan: Myth and Fact," pp. 207–26.)

[19] William Wrightson was manager of the Santa Rita mines, a subsidiary of the Sonora Exploring and Mining Company, in 1858. He had been a newspaper man in Cincinnati and brought to Arizona by wagon via San Antonio, the Washington hand press which printed Arizona's first newspaper (see notes 10, 14 above). The press was later used by the Tucson *Weekly Arizonian*, the *Arizona Star*, the Tombstone *Nugget*, and the Tombstone *Epitaph*. (The press was at last procured by the State Park Museum at Tubac.) Wrightson was subsequently manager of the Salero Mining Company until he was murdered by Apaches in 1864. Mount Wrightson in the Santa Rita Mountains of Santa Cruz County is named for him. (Arizona Historical Society Biographical File; Duffen, "Overland via 'Jackass Mail' in 1858," p. 281.)

[20] Dr. John Locke was not identified in the biographical files of the Arizona Historical Society or in other sources consulted.

Allyn's trip to Tubac was highlighted by striking views of the Santa Rita Mountains, which the young judge compared to "a motionless sea," with hills rolling "in vast waves across the whole."

was cloudy, and it rained around us on several of the mountains, rainbows flashed out, spanning valleys, but not a drop reached us. The rain was extensive, taking in the valley of the Sonoita, once all settled when Fort Buchanan was garrisoned, and stretching off to the distant mountains of Sonora.

The most unique feature, however, was the Santa Rita domain itself. From this point where we overlooked everything, it seemed literally a motionless sea, the hills rolled in vast waves across the whole. Pretty as it looked, it proved hard riding. Underneath the grass were rolling stones and you seemed to cross one hill only to reach another. During our ride we passed several shafts sunk in times past, but they were filled with water, and afforded little opportunity to judge of the mines. Nothing has been done as yet in the way of mining by the present company. When we reached home the clouds had settled down into what threatened a storm.

ADOBE HOUSES IN A STORM —
RECEIVING NEWS FROM THE STATES

Santa Rita,[1] Jan. 3, 1865
[Published April 25, 1865]

Mr. Wrightson left me at the Hacienda to the courteous hospitality of Dr. Locke, and we sat by the blazing fire in the open
chimney in the evening, planning over excursions to make the brief
days of my sojourn at Santa Rita pass swiftly. The doctor's time was
much occupied by the details of organizing his little colony. There
were parties to be sent to the mountains to get out lumber, and to
the quarries to get out stone; parties to make adobes, to cut grass, to
repair the roofs and to work on the roads, beside the regular surveying party. But before retiring we had arranged several little rides,
and I went to sleep, perhaps to dream of future pleasure. During
the night I was awakened by hurried steps to and fro, and the moving
of chairs and beds. I listened, about half awake — drop, drop —
there was no mistaking the sound, our treacherous mud roof was
leaking. I found that a rubber blanket had been thrown over me as
I slept, so that the tiny trickling streams of dirty water glanced off,
and I went to sleep again. Morning came, and I peered out on a
scene of amazing and ludicrous discomfort. One of the men, drowned
out, had tried to make a fire, and the chimney refusing to draw, had
filled our dripping room with smoke. An adobe had fallen into it,

---

[1] The name *Santa Rita* first appears on Mexican maps examined in 1851
by the U.S. Boundary Commission. The mountains east of Tubac were designated "Sierra de las Santa Rita." (Byrd H. Granger, *Arizona Place Names*,
p. 325.) The Santa Rita headquarters from which Allyn writes were on mission lands of Tumacacori which had been bought at public auction April 19,
1844 by Governor Gándara's brother-in-law, Don Francisco Aguilar. From
1865 to 1869, Aguilar deeded the lands to Gándara for $499. Gándara had
been occupying the ranch lands since the 1850s and had thousands of head
of sheep there. (Ray H. Mattison, "Early Spanish and Mexican Settlement in
Arizona," pp. 293–94.)

and there was no way to get it out but to pound it to pieces — by the way, one of the advantages of the adobe over the brick. At last it was broken up, and the fire blazed, the smoke slowly passed away, and one could coolly survey the situation. Out of doors the snow lay four or five inches deep, and it was still snowing; indoors it was raining, for the snow melted on the roof just about fast enough to keep up the regular and unbroken supply of drops. By this time the water had found pretty much all the weak places in the roofs, and we found a dry place for the breakfast table, and by good management after, dry places enough to philosophically pass the day, for we were completely imprisoned. All the old books were hunted up, even mining dictionaries, the driest of reading, came into play to help kill time. But, after all, give an old campaigner his pipe; tobacco may be a luxury in cities, but out in a leaky old adobe house, fenced in by the storm, it really takes rank among the primal necessities of existence; without it, exploration would cease, and immigration be a thing of the imagination. For three days we were shut up in the house, it storming at intervals. Each night was a duplicate of the first, until on the fourth night a bright idea struck us. There was a light umbrella tent, designed for surveying parties, in the house; taking the walls off it, wouldn't it protect our beds, raised in the room? Out it was got, opened and stayed to the four corners of the room. We looked upon it with intense satisfaction; let the storm howl, let the mud roof prove even more treacherous, we were secure.

Just in the moment of exultation, one of our party stepped out the door. When he returned, he wore a most comical look, and at last he burst into a good round laugh. What is up? Still he laughed. Then we went to the door. The storm had passed; every star in the heavens gleamed with unwonted brilliancy. A more striking or ludicrous contrast can scarcely be imagined, than that between outdoors and indoors. It is one of the superlative advantages of a mud roof that it protracts a storm ten or twelve hours after it's done outside and in a country where rain is so infrequent as it is here this is a quality not to be overlooked. Although the sun shone again, our imprisonment was not at an end; the soil here, where it is not rocky, is so porous that rain or snow makes trails and roads almost impassible. Altogether, this is the heaviest fall of snow I have seen in Arizona, and yet there was scarce a vestige left of it seen on the highest peaks, in twenty-four hours after it was over.

Time wore on and Christmas came. Mr. W., returned, a huge Christmas log glowed in the fireplace; green boughs faintly reminded us of the church dressing of home; our dinner if not as elegant as those at Delmonico's was the best the country afforded; oysters and antelope were on the bill of fare and the eggnog of the evening was unexceptional.

Mr. W. brings us the news of the arrival of Col. Davidson[2] of the Cerro Colorado mine at Tubac, after a terrible trip across the mountains from Hermosillo.[3] Col. D. brings the certain news of the re-election of Mr. Lincoln, and also of an encampment of desperadoes over the Sonora line for the purpose of attacking his train, supposed to have a large amount of coin on board. He had mustered some fifty armed men from his own mine to go and escort the train through, and Santa Rita was called on for volunteers. Here was a chance to go to Sonora, and I joined the party. We rolled out from Santa Rita about a dozen strong with the ambulance, when the moon rose, and reached Tubac soon after sunrise. During the morning an express [message] came in from the train that it was safe across the line and would arrive that night; that the party feared had apparently learned of Col. D's safe trip across the mountains; at any rate that they had broken camp and gone toward Texas. After dinner quite a party of us rode down as far as Tumacacori and met his train. I don't now how much coin there was aboard,

---

[2] This was Colonel Mathias Oliver Davidson. When Allyn met him, he was forty-five years old, married, and a director of the Arizona Mining Company. John Ross Browne, in a letter to the San Francisco *Bulletin* (March 18, 1864), described Davidson as an "intelligent and skilful engineer. . . ." The colonel had had considerable experience before coming to Arizona as superintendent of the Cumberland, Maryland, coal mines and as chief engineer of the Havana Railroad in Cuba. Understandably, he spoke fluent Spanish. He had come to Arizona in 1863 to take charge of the Cerro Colorado (or Heintzelman or Colt's) mine near Arivaca. In 1864 he was recommended by C. D. Poston as special agent to the Papagos, whom he found friendly. In November of the same year he warned General Irwin McDowell of the threat of a Confederate invasion from Sonora. In 1864 and 1865 he owned the Catalina, Blanco Blue, and Enriguetta mines, all in Pima County. His title of *colonel* was presumably the result of his command of volunteers guarding the overland mail. Davidson's letter to the secretary of war concerning the need for a volunteer force to protect the mail was published by the U.S. Government Printing Office in 1888. (Arizona Historical Society Biographical File.)

[3] Hermosillo, the capital of the Mexican state of Sonora, was site of a government mint. It had been the center of political power struggles involving Governor Gándara (see Letter 16, note 9) and was captured by the French on July 29, 1865, six months after Allyn's letter. (Hubert H. Bancroft, *History of the North Mexican States and Texas* 2: 656ff, 696.)

but there was some dozen as pretty Concord ambulances with four mules each, as you often see, and it is only valuable freight that they are used for. We took supper in camp with them, got quite a supply of late papers, and at evening returned to Tubac.

The next day I returned to Santa Rita and with Mr. W. arranged for a trip to the Patagonia or Mowry silver mine, distant about thirty miles by the trail. We were delayed in starting until afternoon, and had with us a Mexican boy by the name of Blas to show us the trail. Our road took us across the Santa Rita grant, to the valley of the Sonoita, most of the way upon the old stage road to Fort Buchanan. The afternoon was charming and we reached the Sonoita[4] in good season, but found some difficulty in getting a place to cross owing to the miry character of the soil after the late storms.

We crossed near an abandoned ranch, one of the succession that once occupied the entire valley, and proceeded rapidly down the stream till we came to some very extensive furnaces and other buildings, now in ruins, that were erected to work the ores of the Tinto mines.[5] These works are situated in a most charming little valley; a fine stream of water flowing toward the Sonoita ran through it, the grass was up to the bellies of our horses, and there was a great abundance of wood at hand, while the hills around shut off the fierce winds.

But if we were going to the Patagonia tonight, there was no time to be lost. The sun is already behind the hills, and in the deep grass it is difficult to trace the trail. Blas rides ahead, rapidly following with an instinct, as it were, the faint track, until the sun is fairly down. The valley breaks into arroyos as we near the mountains, and as you looked at the tall, craggy sierra in the uncertain light of the stars, slight misgivings about our seeing the Patagonia that night would creep into one's head. But on went Blas. I saw no trail, but had the most unbounded faith in the mountain instinct of these Mexicans. He turned up an arroyo, and dismounting, began to climb up the side. Still no visible trail. On the top, on a sort of

---

[4] The Sonoita River runs southwestward past the town of Patagonia and drains into the Santa Cruz River between Nogales and Tumacacori.

[5] The Spanish word *tinto* means "deep colored," and is usually applied to red wine, *vino tinto*. The locale of this mine was not found in the sources consulted, including the Arizona Historical Society Files.

bench we all huddled. Blas admitted he had lost the trail, but would find it in a moment. Off went bridles, horses to grazing, out with our pipes, to wait patiently the result of his examination on foot. A half hour passes, he returns and confesses he can't find it, must have taken the wrong arroyo at the head of the valley. We must go back. Down the miserable slope we scrabbled, mounted, rode back to the valley, told Mr. Blas he must be sure and find the trail before we climbed any more hills. He started up the side of the mountain while we stood shivering in the valley, for it was rapidly growing cold. In a very few minutes he came back on the run very much excited, hissing "Apache" and making signs to be still. We gathered on a tree and held council of war. What he had seen amounted to just this: as he was climbing up the trail which he had found, a living object appeared ahead of him, and as he advanced it rolled off into an arroyo out of sight. It might be an Indian or a bear. Blas was sure it was a man. After much discussion, as a measure of prudence and comfort we determined to return to the Tinto works and camp in the houses.

Back we rode, chilly and cross, to the furnaces. There with matches we essayed an inspection of the building. The bats angrily contested our entrance to more than one of them. The house of the superintendent proved to have two rooms in admirable order, so we took possession of one for ourselves and the other for our horses. Inspecting our outfit, we found we had no cup at all; but a felt hat, if it have no ventilating holes in the crown, is an admirable substitute. In one of our saddle bags we found an old lunch of bread and cheese, so we were not to go to bed supperless. A fire was soon blazing, and Blas set to work cutting grass, both for our horses and our beds. This done, the whole place was ransacked for timber to bar the doors so that the Apaches could not steal our horses without noise at least. Blankets were hung up at the doors so that he couldn't see how many of us there were and whether we slept or no. Then we munched our cheese, smoked our pipes and I went to bed. Just as I was falling asleep I recollect hearing someone discuss the necessity of standing guard.

The result of the discussion I do not really know — the only thing I am certain of, is that I wasn't awakened to take my turn. The night passed safely and with the sun we were up and saddled. Breakfast was ahead at the Mowry mine, so there was no useless delay.

We passed rapidly up the valley and found the trail without difficulty. It passes over the highest point of the sierra, winding like a tiny thread along the edge of precipices, whose almost perpendicular walls rise a thousand feet about the valleys below, and presenting a succession of gorgeous and picturesque landscapes; mountain piles of rock were tossed into fantastic shapes and glanced with the radiant hues of the rainbow — you could readily fancy them domes, battlements, castles, crumbling to ruins.

The snow frequently covered the trail and in strange contrast to the dry grasses below, the higher you got the greener the grass became. We passed near the shaft of some mines but none of our party knew anything of them.

Descending into a valley we followed the stream down until suddenly rounding a spur of the mountain we caught our first sight of the Patagonia; acres and acres were stripped of timber, cut off as the Mexicans always do it, as high as they can reach.

At first sight you would have thought the trees were cut down in some fierce snowstorm that had covered the country; wagon roads from one point and another converged toward the distant settlement, the size of which was indicated by the volumes of smoke from furnaces; although the buildings were hid under a swell of ground. As we got nearer you could see herds near by, carefully guarded; hear the ringing of the chopper's ax; see the smouldering pits of charcoal; pass once in the while a stalking Mexican, in gaily colored serape with his inevitable cigarrillo. At last a turn brought us in front of the corral gate opening into a corral encircled by the offices, stores and residences of the officers of the establishment. Then we met Captain Mowry,[6] who bade us alight and come in. Capt. M. had but just arrived from the east and was scarcely more than in camp yet, the wagons with his supplies being daily expected from Guaymas.[7]

---

[6] Captain Charles Mowry, master mariner, was the older brother of Sylvester Mowry. Charles operated the Mowry mine. Sylvester had left the area in November under threat by General Carleton. (Constance Wynn Altshuler, *Latest from Arizona! The Hesperian Letters, 1859–1861*, p. 266.)

[7] Guaymas, the chief port of the state of Sonora, has an excellent natural harbor on the Gulf of California, which made it a natural shipping point for southern Arizona. At the time of Allyn's letter, French warships were outside the port, and it was taken by French troops, accompanied by Governor Gándara, two months later in March 1865. (Bancroft, *North Mexican States and*

Fortunately it was just our host's breakfast hour, and tables are elastic in this country; so a few plates and chairs more and we are all seated at the board. There is a luxury in giving and receiving news out in a wild inaccessible country like this that the quiet denizen of eastern cities never knows, who gets his telegraphic melange served up in the morning, as much a matter of course as his chop, egg or coffee. Here men meet from extremes. After long intervals of time, and great stretches of distance, they exchange the latest gossip of the Fifth or Pennsylvania avenues for the thrilling story of Indian massacre, of adventurous daring and of just discovered mines of wealth in some distant valley of death. Our news is always vivid, lifelike. It may be prejudiced or colored, but it glows with the feelings of the reciter. It isn't tamed down to the laconic, precise, incomprehensible phrases that smack of worn out telegraphic operators and sleepy printers, neither is it contradicted on the morrow. It lasts us to turn over in the kaleidoscope of the imagination for a week or a month at least.

Texas 2: 696.) Guaymas was the preferred port of supply for the Tubac area at this time, except during periods of unrest in Mexico. The other ports were Indianola, Texas, and Yuma, which were avoided because of distance or desert terrain. (William A. Duffen, "Overland via 'Jackass Mail': The Diary of Phocion R. Way," p. 281.)

THE MOWRY MINE —
STEAMSHIPS DIRECT TO NEW YORK —
A SICK HORSE — APACHE TROUBLE

Santa Rita, Jan. 3, 1865
[Published April 29, 1865]

After breakfast we walked over to the mine, distant about a quarter of a mile; the men had not yet returned from their noon rest. The perpendicular working shaft is two hundred feet deep, out of which the ore is hoisted by means of an admirably contrived mule power. It was lying in heaps about, as it is broken up by hand, preparatory to being carried to the furnaces. Much of it seemed almost pure galena, and Capt. M. said that what they were getting out now would pay eighty dollars to the ton in silver, and that it had ranged before from fifteen to one hundred dollars per ton. Meanwhile the workmen are beginning to stray back, and, one by one, to disappear under ground, while others began breaking up the ore on the ground. Capt. M. excused himself from accompanying us underground, leaving us in charge of an accommodating and gentlemanly subordinate officer.

We stripped off our coats and vests, took the loose things out of our pockets, and following our friend, each of us armed with a candle, disappeared in the hole to the right of the main shaft. Down we went by an incomprehensible zigzag and incline, first right, then left, down a slope, then a flight of rude steps, and sometimes a jump of several feet. At times the shaft or gallery was high enough to walk erect in, then you had to stoop, sometimes to crawl, after which you would emerge into a chamber; every little while a gallery led to the hoisting shaft, and you tremblingly peer upward to the tiny speck of sky that showed there was still day above, or down into its apparently fathomless depths, where perhaps the feeble rays of a candle or two showed where a bucket was being filled with ore. About midway down the works we strike into a huge cave, trickling with water, and gleaming with rare crystallizations; above and below it the mineral deposit continues unbroken. Down again, and you begin to hear the dull reverberations of the strokes of the miners; at last a turn discloses in the distance the tiny flicker of their candles, the flitting to and fro of begrimed figures, and a few steps brings us to where work is being done now. I think we saw some twenty men at work here, and they were getting easily a large quantity of ore. One mine underground I suspect is much like all the others; the effect on the imagination is quite as complete two hundred feet down as though by an endless succession of shafts and galleries we had penetrated to the enormous depth of some of the Cornish mines. Works underground never show as works above do; there is no way of getting a *coup d'oeil* view in order to realize their vastness.

The cave in this mine bisecting, as it does, the mineral deposit, is, I believe very unusual, and it leads me, and I speak of such matters with much diffidence, to the opinion that the Patagonia is not a true vein, that is, a vein made by the splitting of the primitive rocks of the earth's crust, and afterwards filled with metal bearing mineral matter, but is rather a grand deposit of mineral or perhaps what is called a contact vein, where the metal bearing mass fills a chasm between different descriptions of rock in the earth's crust.[1] But for the conclusions of the business man in this case, this speculative difference is unimportant. The abundance of the mineral here is patent; there is enough in sight for years and the remaining simple question is, will it pay to work. If the mineral yields eighty dollars to the ton in silver, as Capt. M. told me much of it did, it yields more than most of the celebrated mines of Peru, Mexico, and Washoe do, and the Patagonia is one of the most valuable properties on the Pacific slope.[2] But we are underground and have the journey to

---

[1]Geologically speaking, a "contact" is the boundary surface between different adjacent rock masses. "The so-called 'true fissure veins' are veins that differ sharply in mineral content and structure from their wall rocks and generally break away from them cleanly. Other veins are not sharply separable from their walls; their vein matter blends into the walls. Microscopic study shows that the vein matter has replaced the rock wall without disturbing it, just as in the contact-metamorphic deposits." (James Gilluly and others, *Principles of Geology*, p. 475.)

[2]The Mowry mine produced 1½ million dollars in silver, presumably between 1858 and 1860. Eighty dollars per ton was indeed a respectable yield compared to the Vulture mine's twenty-four dollars a ton in 1868. One of the rich Tombstone veins averaged seventy-three dollars in silver, four dollars in gold per ton in the early 1880s. However, there were richer producers even

daylight before us. It is hard scrabbling and uses up breath, but we go up straighter and quicker than we went down and in a few minutes are in the open air, quite willing to rest.

As we came out a string of thirty wagons hove in sight from Guaymas, bringing supplies from the steamer from San Francisco. The freight paid, I understood, is four cents up and two down, or six cents in coin for the round trip, and then there are the duties to be paid to Mexico. What this country, and in fact the whole of Arizona, and the country above us, east of the Sierra Nevadas want, to insure their rapid development is emancipation from Mexican tariffs and from San Francisco. This last is easily accomplished, if the enterprising New Yorker will look to it, and establish a line of propellers from the Isthmus to the mouth of the Colorado river.[3] It won't pay? Let us see.

I suppose Arizona now consumes monthly, at the lowest estimate, two hundred and fifty tons of New York merchandise, dry goods, hardware, boots and shoes, machinery, tools, etc. How does it reach here? Two thirds of it via San Francisco, thence to Guaymas to reach southern Arizona; and to the mouth of the Colorado for all the rest; the remaining one third is drawn overland either across from the Missouri river or from San Pedro on the Pacific. What freight does it pay now? It pays freight from New York to San Francisco either around the Horn or across the Isthmus, and then by steamer to Guaymas from San Francisco it pays forty dollars a ton; by sailing vessels from San Francisco to the mouth of the river, from one to two months on the way, it pays twenty dollars

---

in Arizona. The Silver King, discovered in 1871, assayed at from one thousand to twenty thousand dollars per ton. The Mowry probably compared well with California mines, though there were many· exceptions. The great Comstock Lode mines of Washoe County, Nevada, were more productive than the Mowry. The Ophir, for example, produced over fifteen million dollars, and the Consolidated Virginia more than one hundred and thirty-three million in silver. (Hubert H. Bancroft, *History of Arizona and New Mexico,* pp. 584, 587 note 6, 588 note 7, 589. See also Otis E. Young, *Western Mining.*)

[3] Sea-going steamers and sailers frequented Libertad on the Mexican northwest coast, Guaymas, and also Puerta Ysabel and Robinson's Landing at the mouth of the Colorado. Ocean vessels did not attempt to sail beyond these last points due to the erratic shifting river channels. Ships unloaded passengers and goods at these tiny ports where they were transferred to lighters or river steamers for transportation to Yuma and points up the Colorado. River steamers usually had only a two-to-three foot draught. (Bancroft, *Arizona and New Mexico,* pp. 500, 602; Leonard J. Arrington, "Inland to Zion: Mormon Trade on the Colorado River, 1864–1867," pp. 239–40; Odie B. Faulk, "The Steamboat War that Opened Arizona," pp. 1–4.)

to the ton. Now Guaymas or the mouth of the river is *nearer* New York than San Francisco is, by about one thousand miles. Suppose we pay a propeller, running monthly, the double freight now paid, that is, the freight to San Francisco from the Isthmus, and from San Francisco to the mouth of the river, and take our goods direct; this would be equivalent to five hundred tons of freight monthly, at usual prices. And it would land goods here at one half what they cost now, for beside saving San Francisco profits, a month of time, port dues, etc., we should save the San Francisco *presto change* by which the San Francisco man pays his bills in greenbacks, and makes us pay ours in coin or dust.[4] In addition to the business of Arizona, there are one hundred thousand people in Utah to be supplied and the whole coasting trade of Mexico below Guaymas. I believe any business man who looks at it will see that there is no flaw in these deductions, and that a line of propellers will pay now, making trips once a month.

In the evening we walked over to the reduction works. These are situated about a quarter of a mile off, in a direction opposite to that of the mine. On the way thither you pass through the village of the mining employees. This is the old site of the camp of Captain, now General, Stone's surveying party, when driven out of Sonora.[5] Here, too, Gov. Gandara lived for some time after his exile; it is a pretty little adobe hamlet, and contains now a population of some three hundred. The works are situated on the banks of a running stream that, dammed, accumulates in an arroyo plenty of water for all purposes, and are substantially built of brick and adobes. An engine of some thirty or forty horse power drives an immense fan which furnishes the blast for the furnaces, which, are, I think, twelve

---

[4] In the summer of 1864, due to a large Union greenback issue (see Letter 15, note 14), the gold dollar enjoyed a seventeen percent premium over paper money. This would explain the desire of San Francisco bankers for gold coin or dust, since in California in 1864 the paper dollar fell in value to as little as thirty-four cents in gold. A contemporary account reported in Thomas E. Farish's *History of Arizona* 3: 35, reports bacon in 1863–64 costing $1.50 a pound in gold, or $3.00 in greenbacks. (See Samuel E. Morison, *The Oxford History of the American People*, p. 649, and Arthur C. Bining and Thomas C. Cochran, *The Rise of American Economic Life*, pp. 319–20.)

[5] This is, no doubt, noted surveyor Charles Pomeroy Stone (1824–87), who constructed a road from El Paso to Yuma and built Camp Jecker close to the Mowry mine. (Andrew Wallace, *Image of Arizona*, p. 119.) He was the author of *Notes on the State of Sonora* (Washington, D.C., 1861). (Arizona Historical Society Biographical File.)

in number, which will consume two tons of ore each in twenty-four hours; beside these smelting furnaces, there were two refining furnaces completed, and two building, to separate the silver from the lead. Only some half dozen of the smelting furnaces were at work, as complete arrangements for the proper proportionate supply of charcoal and ore had not yet been completed since Capt. M.'s arrival. The scene here was a busy and picturesque one. The glow of the flames, the seething metal, the half-naked laborers, the ore going into one furnace and the metal ladled out of another, and the cooling bars; all suggested the busy haunts of men, rather than the isolated little mining camp in the midst of hostile Apaches.

At present they are not separating the silver from the lead, but shipping the bars at once. At present prices for lead, Capt. M. said the lead would pay all the expenses of mining and reduction.[6] That so much has been accomplished in setting this establishment at work, reflects great credit on Capt. M., when one reflects that the mine has just passed out of the hands of a military receiver and the lessee of the marshal of New Mexico, who had been holding the property since the arrival of the California column under Gen. Carleton. As is usual with such occupants the place had been stripped, even the shade trees on the little plaza were cut down for fire wood, it is said.

It was quite into the evening when we returned to Capt. M.'s quarters, and the watchful system of the establishment struck me at once. All the animals were now gathered in the corral; a guard paced there all the night, and the hours were struck as regularly as on shipboard. Every mining establishment here is from necessity, as

---

[6] It is common for silver to be found in association with lead and copper in Arizona ores. The Castle Dome mines in Yuma, for example, had a high lead content of from fifty to seventy percent per ton. They still produced $23 to $190 per ton of silver. The most common "reduction" method used to reduce the ore to metallic form in early Arizona mining was by smelting, as in Allyn's description. It was a cheap process and accomplished the reduction with the minimal equipment available in the remote wilds. However, it denuded most of the mining areas of vegetation. Other processes were used in more sophisticated mining centers and in later periods in Arizona. Principal alternatives to smelting were the dry crush and wet crush amalgamation process. In both of these, mercury was used following the roasting of the ore. The various metals were then isolated in separating pans. The demands of the ongoing Civil War, of course, contributed to the high price of lead. (Young, *Western Mining*, p. 244ff.)

it were, a military post, indeed, sometimes they are the outer pickets, while the military post is in a much less exposed position.

In the morning, it was reported that something was the matter of my horse, he was lying down, wouldn't eat; we went out and looked at Dick; he did not seem to be in pain, yet if forced to get up, would lie down again at once; he was all gaunted up, and you would scarcely have known him for the ambitious animal that took the lead in scaling yonder mountains only a day or two before. What ailed him? What could be done for him? The experts assembled, and pronounced the horse tired, nothing else the matter. This was rather funny, considering he hadn't been used since we arrived. Blas asserted that it was very bad hay, and that if he could ride him and whip him with a hair rope, soaked in water, a sort of cat-o-nine tails improvised, he would be well. Another recommended bleeding at the mouth, pouring whisky and ginger down his throat.

So we tried the last and set a boy to leading him up and down in the sun. All of this proved of no avail and at last Mr. Dick was handed over to the tender mercies of Blas and his improvised whip. If sweating would cure an animal Blas' plan had merit, for he certainly produced a profuse perspiration. Reader, this alluding to a sick brute may seem puerile, but if it ever falls to your lot to ride the same animal over deserts, and across mountains, for more than a thousand miles, and never have his strength or his spirits flag, to have slept by his side night after night, to have been awakened by his neigh in the morning, to measure out to him his miserable pittance of grain, or patiently learn him to eat flour when grain was not to be had, and my word for it you will be vastly interested when he is sick.

Next morning Dick took to his grain with a good appetite and although he looked as though he hadn't slept for a week, we began to think of our return. Just then in comes a Mexican with the news that the Apaches had run off four or five head of cattle belonging to one of the contractors, and that the trail was plain right up the valley our road lay. The saddled horses were ready and at the disposal of the Mexicans for pursuit. They talked and gesticulated violently for an hour before they started off to get ready to pursue. Capt. M. thought we had better wait till they had started, as it would be safer. It was literally another hour before they made their appearance, armed with long spears, short swords, and each with a little sack of *pinole* tied on his saddle as though he was going out for several days. Capt. M. tried to persuade part of them to take another road where there was a chance of cutting off the Indians, but they were unwilling, seeming decidedly to prefer a stern chase. We were all ready, good-by said, yet somehow these fellows didn't start, but went back and got some more arms out of the Captain, and one careless fellow managed to break the stock off from a Colt's revolving rifle in riding through the corral gate and then coolly proposed to go on with the barrel and loaded chambers. This we demurred to so strongly, that he took the shattered weapon back.

While we were at the Patagonia we rode over the hills, by the cemetery, where seventeen American victims to the Apaches lie buried. These simple burial grounds are the saddest feature in these little isolated colonies. Too often they are the only memorial left of the gallant men who died here, far away from home, kindred and the smile of woman; to be placed in the silent grave, no prayer uttered and no tiny flower planted to tell of affectionate remembrances. It is worse than to be thrust into the ocean, for then the eternal requiem of the waves makes the vast mausoleum of the deep, the solemn and fitting portal to the mysterious hereafter. As we crossed the hills we came upon picket guards over the herds, mounted and armed. In addition to all this care one or more horses always stand saddled in the corral ready for instant and hot pursuit of the Indian.

Meanwhile our Blas was missing and there was a pretext for more delay. We said no, leave him, if he don't come along. So we finally got started, Blas appearing on the side of the road, making his last embraces with a dark skinned senorita, which, as I had always understood he was a married man, seemed improper, until he explained that it was his cousin, and took his place demurely in the *rear* of the cavalcade. The Mexicans, save Blas, rode on ahead, all talking at once, and every little while stopping to try to kill quails with stones. At this Blas proved quite expert and killed two. If they had not been the owners of the stock stolen, I should have suspected they were not unwilling to have it got away. Suddenly there was a stop and they all gathered, looking at the trail, and had a grand confab. Mr. Wrightson sent Blas to see what was the matter. When he returned, his face was alarm itself, "Muchos, Indios, Muchos, Senor." We advanced and looked at the trail. Before, it had been plainly the stock, driven by four Indians, now it was evident that three other men walking in the same tracks as the four, had cunningly been several times over the same ground, in order to create the impression of greater numbers in order to turn back pursuers.

Whatever may have been the disposition of the Mexicans before, it was now evident they did not care to go on; however they did not quite like to turn back here, so they went on to the point of the road, where Capt. M. had desired them to send part of their force, and then they turned homeward. The Indian trail led our road still, for we were going round the Sierra, instead of crossing it. Blas was very eloquent in pointing out the tracks, constantly reiterating "Muchos Indios," etc. We told him to go on and proceeded alone. The trail of Indians and cattle left our road about a mile on, turning to the right in order probably to avoid passing the picket at old Fort Buchanan. We reached the valley of Sonoita some miles above where we left it before, crossed and camped to rest our animals and graze them. Here we broiled Blas' quails and they were very good, although it is not unlikely a little salt would have improved them. The rest of the ride home was over the old trail and without incident.

MORE APACHE TROUBLE —
AN INVITATION TO TRAVEL —
CERRO COLORADO HACIENDA —
A NEW TELEGRAPH — MEXICAN COAL

Cerro Colorado,[1] Jan. 15, 1865
[Published May 26, 1865]

From Santa Rita I returned to Tubac. The day we left, the lumber party was driven in from the Santa Rita mountains by the Indians, and but a few days before the military mail for the Rio Grande had been waylaid by some forty Indians, who succeeded in capturing the horses of the two expressmen and the mail, but dared not attack the men with their Sharps' carbines. A heavy scouting party was sent out to the place, "Whetstone Springs,"[2] where the mail was taken, and found the mail, every letter opened — none destroyed except those in large envelopes, and it was our misfortune to have one such, some two score pages, closely written foolscap;[3] there it was hopelessly in pieces, and nothing left but to write it all over again. All the greenbacks in the mail were gone. A first exchange of draft was missing,[4] while a second remained untouched. These were intelligent Indians for Apaches, weren't they?

---

[1] The Cerro Colorado mine was located about ten miles northwest of Arivaca in Pima County. The mine ruins remain there. (Byrd H. Granger, *Arizona Place Names,* p. 261.)

[2] "Whetstone Springs" was probably on the Butterfield road in the Whetstone Mountains of Cochise and Pima counties, west of the San Pedro River. (Granger, *Arizona Place Names,* pp. 56–57.) The name *Whetstone* refers to the presence of novaculite, which makes excellent whetstones. (Will C. Barnes, *Arizona Place Names,* p. 481.)

[3] Allyn's foolscap was very likely long sheets of folio writing paper thirteen by sixteen or seventeen inches in size. The name originated in the use of a fool's cap as a watermark in eighteenth century England. (*Oxford Universal Dictionary,* p. 728.)

[4] Allyn is probably referring to a draft for the withdrawal of money from his bank in Connecticut.

One evening we were a number of us sitting in Capt. Merriam's[5] quarters, the door open, the moonlight streaming in. Col. Powell[6] and Capt. Smith[7] had just arrived from the Rio Grande, and we were exchanging news, when a Mexican, very much excited, came running across the Plaza and, breathless, stammered out to Capt. M., "Los Apaches — one American killed — small wagon — four horses." None of us were experts at Spanish, and while one was being sent for, the ambulance of the Santa Rita company, for it proved to be that, came in sight; its four horses not yet calm from excitement, the driver bareheaded, an arrow yet sticking in his ear. He was naturally round shouldered, and he crouched a little more, involuntarily, not to have this arrow, a full cloth yard in length, touch anything. Of course quite a crowd gathered around, as this comical looking "outfit" drew up; but the sense of the ludicrous was quickly gone when we looked in the bottom and saw a man weltering in his own blood. Where was it? About a mile up the arroyo. How many? Perhaps twenty. These were the brief questions and answers, and in an incredibly short time two squadrons of cavalry made the ground tremble as they galloped off.

The ambulance drove to the hospital; the wounded man proved a pale-faced German boy, one of the discharged soldiers from the Rio Grande, who had just gone to work for Mr. Wrightson. He had served three years without a scratch, only to meet this fearful wound within a month after he was out of it. He was carried in, placed on a bed and Dr. Kunkler,[8] one of the very best of the army surgeons I have met, began an examination of the wound or wounds. I held the poor fellow's head, for even the brief acquaintance of the few days at Santa Rita made me less a stranger to him than the surrounding soldiery. Dr. K. found a terrible wound an inch or more in breadth near the breast bone and another near the shoulder blade;

---

[5] This was John S. Merriam, commander of the Tubac post.

[6] Colonel Powell (1825–1902) is mentioned in the Peter Brady Collection at the Arizona Historical Society as having been a member of a railroad exploration party in 1853–54.

[7] Captain Smith has not been identified.

[8] John E. Kunkler was an assistant surgeon who served at Tubac and Revanton, forty miles south of Tucson, in 1864. He was a graduate of the University of the Pacific, class of 1853. He joined the California Volunteers, served with them in Arizona, and returned to private practice in San Francisco in 1864. (Francis E. Quebbeman, *Medicine in Territorial Arizona*, pp. 49, 352.)

I said another, but in truth it was one and the same one. The doctor's face showed but too plainly that the poor fellow's chance was desperate. He was too weak to talk to, so we looked round for the driver and found him, the arrow still in his ear, though the doctor cut that out for him, and he told us the details of the affair. They were driving along the arroyo, which is well wooded with mesquit, when suddenly the Indians surrounded them with a terrible deafening yell and a cloud of arrows. This was the time the one took the ear, the others took his hat and literally bruised his head without seriously hurting him. The horses fortunately were under control. Although they ran, the driver was enabled to keep them in the road. As the team was running the other man stooped down to get his rifle to shoot at the Indians who were still pursuing, and in this position an arrow passed completely through his body leaving no trace of itself. These arrows are no trifling things. As they got nearer the town the Indians drew off. Next day the poor German boy was dead. Towards midnight the cavalry returned. They had lost the trail and had not seen the Indians.

Col. Bowie[9] and Capt. Smith were desirous of going to Yuma by the way of Cerro Colorado and Cuhuabi,[10] through the Papago

---

[9] This was probably Colonel George Washington Bowie. In 1861 he was a colonel of the Fifth California Infantry and later commander under General Carleton of the Arizona Military District. Bowie carried out the Carleton order for Sylvester Mowry's arrest. Colonel Bowie had various mining interests and in 1864 purchased a copper mine in Pima County. He reported to a Congressional special committee on the Arizona Indian problem in 1865 and was promoted to brevet brigadier general of the volunteers and mustered out the same year. (Francis B. Heitman, *Historical Register and Dictionary of the United States Army, from Its Organization, September 29, 1789, to March 2, 1903*, 1: 234; Arizona Historical Society Biographical File; Hubert H. Bancroft, *History of Arizona and New Mexico*, p. 514.)

[10] Traveler Raphael Pumpelly reported seeing a deserted mine at a place called Cahuabi in 1863, which was probably Allyn's Cuhuabi. In the following year F. Biertu, a noted metallurgist, observed that the Cahuabi Mining Company had been operating a silver-copper mine since 1859 in the Papago region. Herman Ehrenberg was its head at the time, and the ore was evidently quite rich. The original Papago name for Cahuabi was *Ko Vaya* ("badger well"), which the Spanish incorrectly expressed as *Cobabi*. Ko Vaya, Cahuai, or Cobabi was very likely the Cuhuabi of the Allyn party. Modern Ko Vaya (eighteen miles southeast of Quijotoa) is probably the same as the nineteenth century village of that name. There was, however, a Cababi rancheria and mine site a short distance to the west of Ko Vaya. Seven miles to the east there is a modern Papago town of Comobavi. (See Raphael Pumpelly, *Across America and Asia: Notes of a Five Years Journey Around the World and of Residence in Arizona, Japan and China*, p. 38. See also Byrd H. Granger, *Arizona Place Names*, pp. 260, 263, 269.)

country, and extended to me an invitation to join them. We made inquiries as to water on the road, the want of which is in fact its only drawback, and found there was plenty now, and determined to start after a day's rest for the animals. That day we rode over to Tumacacori to take our last look at the wonderful pile, and on the morrow started on our journey for Yuma. We had a squad of cavalry, a wagon, and ambulance, beside our horses. I could not help smiling at the strange way things happen in this country. Here I had been traveling for a couple of months, through a really dangerous Indian country, without other protection than my own good rifle and a kind Providence afforded; now, when we start on a journey that is the very safest in the country, where an Apache dare not cross, we are surrounded with all the pomp and circumstance of war.

The road from Tubac to Cerro Colorado makes a wide detour[11] to turn a mountain that lies right between the two places, so that it takes all day for a government wagon to make the trip, and most freighters would not do it in one. The road is in admirable order now, for more than ninety wagons, eight or ten mules each, have been over it since the ambulance train I spoke of in my last, carrying the machinery, goods and supplies Col. D.[avidson] brought with him to Guaymas. This immense train paid duties on all its Sonora produce to the United States at the collector's office in Tubac, and the arrival and departure of these wagons has made Tubac a busy place for several weeks. We passed quite a number of them returning.

There is but one settlement on the road now: that is at Sopori,[12] where in the old time a Rhode Island company commenced opening

---

[11] The "detour" route from Tubac to the Cerro Colorado mine very likely followed close to the route of State Highway 89 to a road opposite modern Amado which proceeds west to the mine area about sixteen miles from 89.

[12] The name *Sopori* (or *Sepori* in an old Spanish record) was probably a Spanish derivation of *Sobaipuri*, the name of a Piman tribe brought to the Tucson area by Spanish troops. Father Kino had founded a visita (mission station) for them in the San Pedro valley in earlier times. The Indians were later driven from the valley by the Apaches and eventually disappeared from history, although the name has survived. By 1854 a small settlement of Anglo miners was situated at Sopori (about ten miles northeast of Arivaca) when C. D. Poston and Herman Ehrenberg stopped there. Colonel James Douglass of New York was operating a silver mine at the same place (about twelve miles northwest of Tubac) as early as 1851. Douglass was a one-time part-owner of the Patagonia mine before Mowry's purchase of it. In 1861 the Sopori mining company owned 21,000 acres, including the Sopori mine. Mowry was a significant stockholder. (Rufus Kay Wyllys, *Arizona: The History of a Frontier State*, p. 118; Granger, *Arizona Place Names*, p. 325; Thomas E. Farish, *History of Arizona*, 2:68; 4:165.)

some lodes. All I saw left of their Hacienda was the remains of an *arrastra* and some small buildings. I understood the lodes were in the mountains to the left. Whether they are valuable or not, it will take money to determine. Mr. Pennington, one of the old residents of the country, lives here with a family of some half dozen daughters, one or two of them married, and a number of grandchildren.[13]

The young women were pleasant and good looking, and it was quite agreeable to be under a roof where pure and undefiled English greeted the ear with feminine accents. Mr. P. is a fine looking old gentleman, wearing his years lightly, and at present engaged in freighting for the Cerro Colorado, having managed somehow to keep some teams in spite of the Apaches. Mrs. Paige,[14] widowed daughter, being at home, is the heroine of that terrible story of suffering and escape, when, pierced with lances, thrust down a precipice, stripped, she was left by the Indians for dead, and wandered over two weeks after she came to, living on what she could find, before she was picked up by her friends. Ross Browne has detailed it in *Harper's*. It was very difficult to realize that that fragile, dark haired, girlish looking woman could be the one that had endured

---

[13]James Pennington was a native of Tennessee and had journeyed overland to Arizona by way of Texas in 1857 or 1858. He had at least three daughters, if not quite the half dozen of Allyn's counting. Perhaps there was a confusion at Sopori of daughters and grandaughters. Pennington had lived at the old Calabasas ranch on the Santa Cruz River until about 1864. It was abandoned, however, as a result of Apache raids. Apparently he had been forced to move to Sopori by the time of Allyn's visit in order to develop an income for his family. Tragically, in 1869 the Apaches ambushed and killed Pennington and his son Green; another son seems to have died in the same fashion. The remaining family members either moved to Tucson, married locally, or returned eventually to Texas. (John Ross Browne, "A Tour Through Arizona," p. 31; Arizona Historical Society Biographical File; Constance Wynn Altshuler, *Latest from Arizona! The Hesperian Letters, 1859–1861*, p. 271.)

[14]Born Larcena Ann Pennington (1837–1913), she married John Hempstead Paige in 1858. They apparently had one daughter. Several years before the visit of Judge Allyn, Mrs. Paige was traveling with her husband and a young Mexican girl in the company of a larger group. The party was attacked by Apaches, and her husband was killed. When she could not keep up with her Apache captors, she was clubbed, lanced, thrown over a cliff or bluff, battered with rocks and finally left for dead. Maimed and bleeding, she stole away in the darkness and escaped. She survived in the desert for sixteen days and was finally rescued in the Santa Ritas. Browne, "A Tour Through Arizona," p. 31; Robert H. Forbes, *The Penningtons: Pioneers of Early Arizona, A Historical Sketch*, pp. 14–21.)

so much and so bravely. She has one little child, and a casual remark of the mother's shows one of the immunities of Arizona little ones, viz,. from switching. "For," said madam, "if you go out to get a switch the trees are all mesquit and so covered with thorns that you will get over being vexed before you can break one off." An hour slipped away chatting with the family and we mounted our horses to go on to Cerro Colorado.

You ride into the plaza of the Cerro Colorado Hacienda and a scene of apparently chaotic confusion, bustle and work meets you. It was toward sundown. There was the last of this long string of huge Sonora wagons unloading, herds being driven in by Papago herders; little Mexican carts discharging corn into the granary; team animals, tied to a picket rope, being fed with nose-bags, making the air hideous with their noise as their food came down, the noise of hammers and iron in the blacksmith shop; the creaking of the mule power hoisting out of the old perpendicular shaft of the Heintzelman vein;[15] busy men almost run against each other; lazy Mexicans loafed about, as it were in a sort of dream, not knowing what this all meant.

We met Col. D., and he promptly assigned a place for our escort to camp, took us to his room, all he has finished; it is a circular looped hotel tower at the corner of the great wall that is designed to enclose the whole Hacienda. A tame Apache boy, his body servant, soon brought us our dinner, and, after it, by the blazing fire we sat into the wee small hours, the triangle outside striking the hours, showing the guards were on post.

Col. D. is one of those agreeable men that have the faculty of, at evening, throwing off business entirely. The vexatious cares, the weighty responsibilities of managing this gigantic undertaking, do not stalk like grim ghosts into the fireside circle to mar its genial serenity. It is the rare habit of successfully throwing off care that enables men to accomplish great things; it enables the brain to rest itself and prepare for the morrow's work.

I do not remember to have passed a more agreeable evening. Col. D.'s conversational powers are of a remarkable order, and one

---

[15] The Heintzelman or Cerro Colorado silver mine is discussed in note 1, this letter. A contemporary plate of the mine will be found in Andrew Wallace, *Image of Arizona*, p. 119.

notices in his talk, gleams of that same exquisite taste and subtle spiritual preception, that flashed meteor-like, across the field of American poetry, in the transcendant genius of his two sisters,[16] whose untimely death gave Washington Irving an opportunity to garner up with tender and affectionate care, the fragmentary lines they had tossed away in girlhood's hours, that are only too sadly suggestive of what might have been.

With the morning came business. A cup of coffee at sunrise, and Col. D. was at work. The opportunity of Col. D.'s going directly to California, made letter-writing necessary, and duplicates of those the Indians destroyed had to be made.

The works contemplated are of the most extensive character, and are all to be enclosed in one wall, to protect against external enemies, the danger of thieving, and so arranged are the towers as to guard against a peon insurrection, such as has occurred once before under the old management. A large reservoir has been made to hold the rains of the rainy season. A large engine is being put up in place of the small one used before. The mouth of the shaft is inside of a high inclosure, and some thirty-five tons of superb silver rock, said by the assayer to average some eight or nine hundred dollars a ton, was being sacked up for shipment.

One of the grave difficulties of working the mine before has been the stealing of the ores, the amount of this ore received at the mint at Humasilla, Sonora, would show that many thousands, perhaps one hundred thousand, had been stolen and carried off. It is an exceedingly difficult thing to prevent. Mexicans are good judges of ore, and know the good pieces; these are very easily concealed about the person. The Heintzelman mine has, I suppose, produced the richest rock in Arizona, and probably more dollars have been taken out of the old shaft than from any other mine. But the vein is very narrow, at times dividing into threads, and not always bearing

---

[16] The young poetesses, Lucretia Maria (1808–25) and Margaret Miller (1823–38) Davidson, influenced Robert Southey, Samuel F. B. Morse, Washington Irving, and others of the Romantic generation. Both Morse and Southey published memoirs of Lucretia following her death by consumption at age seventeen. Margaret's poems were arranged in an edition by Irving. (Van Wyck Brooks, *The World of Washington Irving,* pp. 451–53. For Lucretia Davidson's works see Samuel F. B. Morse, *Amir Khan and Other Poems.* For Margaret Davidson's works see Washington Irving, *A Biographical and Poetical Remains of the Late Margaret Miller Davidson.*)

From J. Ross Browne's *Adventures in the Apache Country*

Allyn felt that his host at the Silver-rich Heintzelman Mine, M. O. Davidson, managed the mine and works with unusual foresight and efficiency.

mineral. All the experts, however, I believe, pronounce it a true vein; so that it was very problematical whether enough rock to justify extensive reduction works, could be got here in this single shaft.

But Col. D.'s plans do not rely at all on that shaft alone; it is his design to sink at short intervals on the whole extent of the vein (it has been traced over two miles), in fact to rely upon *a hundred working shafts* on this and other veins for the rock, to keep his work employed. If it should happen that three or four hundred feet down the vein should widen, even if the quality of the ore should become poorer, this would become a property such as are very few mines in the world. Col. Colt wished, I have heard, to test this question, but the shaft commenced by his direction is now less than two hundred and fifty feet under ground, and it is estimated that it would strike the vein at four hundred feet.[17]

As you move about here you see what is apparent disorder is really order, and that the appearance of confusion is because the buildings are not finished; not half the things lately arrived are unpacked, and, as will always be the case, those you get unpacked are useless until you get something that hasn't come yet. Among the things unique for Arizona that have arrived is a telegraphic apparatus, to enable the officer here to communicate with the Enregulita Mining Co.'s[18] works, about seven miles away, which is likewise under Col. D.'s direction. I did not go there, but I understand the vein there to be goldbearing quartz, and in such quantities that the company feels justified in getting out a fifty stamp mill, which will make those works quite as extensive as these here. And a photographing apparatus to enable reports to be made to stockholders, showing just how the works look. There are some hundred Americans employed here, beside the Mexicans and Indians, making a large settlement.

---

[17] Hard rock silver mining techniques underwent considerable development on the Comstock Lode in Virginia City, Nevada, in the 1860s. Normally this involved the sinking of a vertical or inclined shaft in order to reach, follow, or find the principal ore veins or body. Drifts, galleries, or tunnels were then blasted and dug out perpendicular to the shaft pursuing likely ore seams. Usually, hard-rock mining necessitated little or no timbering supports which, when used, increased costs enormously. If, however, the rock was soft or was fragmented, the area was stablized with log cribs or square-set timbering and then packed with rubble collected from the blasting. (For illustrations of these techniques, see Wallace, *Image of Arizona,* pp. 153–54.) Much of the returns from a mine could be and were spent on exploration and development by these means. Four hundred feet was not an unusual shaft depth later, but impressive for the period. Mowry (see Letter 17, note 6; Letter 18, note 2) was down to about eight hundred feet. The Silver King (Pinal County) was worked past eight hundred feet by 1884. The Virginia City (Nevada) mines in the late 1860s had reached the seven hundred foot level. Mining at these depths often proved prohibitively expensive because of the need for costly machinery, heavy timbering, the presence of boiling water, and oppressive temperatures. However, if the richness of the ore warranted it, mines were deepened as technology became more sophisticated. By the twentieth century mine shafts in the United States, South Africa, and Mexico sank to five thousand feet and more. (Bancroft, *Arizona and New Mexico,* p. 588; Otis E. Young, *Western Mining,* pp. 244ff.)

[18] This is probably the Enriguetta mine, which the Pima County Book of Records lists as owned by M. O. Davidson, Allyn's host at the Heintzelman. The dates of ownership given were from May 17, 1864, to December 28, 1865. The mine apparently was not being worked by 1878 according to Richard J. Hinton in *Hand-book to Arizona,* p. 130.

In time the question of fuel would be a serious one; but before the wood on the hills within a few miles is used up, there is every reason to believe that the extensive anthracite coal veins,[19] discovered near Humasilla in Sonora, by some of Col. D.'s party, will be worked. The veins are situated about a dozen miles from the Yaqui river, upon which near half the year, coal barges could float to the gulf of California, and with a lock or two, navigation could be obtained all the year around. I saw specimens of this coal, and it is certainly of a fine quality, yielding by assay ninety per cent of combustible matter. There is about forty-five feet working vein matter in the lodes discovered, and the title to them has been confirmed to the American discoverers by the Sonora courts. The successful working of these mines would almost work a revolution in the steam navigation of the Mexican and Gulf coast, and their existence is an important element in the calculation of the capitalist who examines into the practicability of steam communication with the mouth of the Colorado river from New York.

I am almost afraid to write as I really feel about these grand schemes, for I know they will look large and chimerical to many who will, perhaps, read these papers. To those who know him, Col. Davidson's connection with such schemes would go far to secure their careful examination. He has never been associated with failure, and he has been on grand things all his life, from the Erie railroad as a boy, to the present time, like the Croton aqueduct, the Cumberland coal mines and railways, and the Cuban system of railroads. His experience of nine years in Cuba gives him a knowledge of Spanish character and peculiarities that is of immense service in this country, especially where business connections take you through Sonora. Upon the success of this enterprise, or rather these enterprises, depends much of the future of southern Arizona.

------

[19] These coal deposits are found near Ures, northeast of Hermosillo on the Yaqui River. Bancroft reported them to be thirty-six square kilometers in extent. *History of the North Mexican States and Texas* 2: 757.)

BABOQUIVARI —
THROUGH THE PAPAGO COUNTRY —
A PORT ON THE GULF

Fort Yuma, Feb. 1, 1865
[Published May 31, 1865]

A couple of days spent at Cerro Colorado, and we started for Cuhuabi. All the way up the valley from Sopori, there rose above the mountains west, a tiny, pyramidal peak that marks the vast distance off of a mountain. Once in a while a bend in the road would hide it, but it soon again reappeared, in its isolated majesty; this was Baboquivari peak,[1] one of the grand landmarks of the country, which towers way above the range of that name. Cuhuabi lies way on the west side of it, and our first day's journey was directly towards it. We passed the curtain of hills over which it had loomed in its lone individual symmetry and beauty, and unmasked the chain stretching from the Sonora line off toward the Gila, which stripped our peak of much of its beauty. It now seemed only a rugged tower, tossed up above the rest of its associates, and by contrast was dwarfed in size. There was scarcely any road across the valley that skirted the base of this range of mountains, although there was no difficulty in getting a wagon along, except that the soft soil yielded easily to the horses' feet. We bore north and struck the main road from Tucson, thence through a pass of easy grade into another valley. Both of these valleys are without permanent water. But for this they would be wonderfully fertile, as the soil is very rich. In the

---

[1] Baboquivari Peak (7,730 feet) lies in the mountain range of the same name and was sacred to the Papagos. The eastern limit of the main Papago reservation is marked by this unusual crest. The Papago name for it means "neck between two heads," which fits its description when viewed from the south. One of Father Kino's companions thought it resembled a lofty castle. Pools of water were situated on the peaks in the 1850s. (Andrew Wallace, *Image of Arizona*, p. 41; Byrd H. Granger, *Arizona Place Names*, p. 259.) The Bowie-Allyn caravan headed straight for Baboquivari, then turned northwest up the Altar valley, paralleling the Baboquivari range.

mountains on the west side there is a spring called Coyote,[2] which affords water always. We didn't go there, however, as we found enough on the road, owing to recent rains.

The pass through the next range was not as easy as the first, for it crossed a moderately high hill. At this point our escort met with a serious accident; one of the soldiers in mounting his horse, with his carbine thrown over his shoulder and fastened by the sling, managed somehow to strike it against the saddle and fire it, the ball passing through one horse and wounding another in the shoulder. We stopped and grazed our animals, to see if there was any chance to get these horses on, but there was no help for the first one hit, and he had to be killed; the other was led on. They were among the finest animals of the outfit, and it seemed too bad to lose them this way.

A little farther on we passed through an abandoned village of the Papagoes,[3] every hut facing with open hospitable door toward the east, to catch the first glimpse of the coming Montezuma; thus the old religion holds its mystic power, after a hundred years of Christianity and monkish teachings. We are now fairly in both the Papago and Cuhuabi country; the view presents a succession of rolling hills and more distant mountains; there is no grass in sight, and the twining saguaro, with its attendant cacti were strewn over the hill-sides, apparently the sole production of the inhospitable region; seams of quartz could be traced across the hills and other favorable indications of a mineral country were to be seen. The road was good, although over a hilly country.

Toward sundown we passed an abandoned shaft near a pool of very dirty water, and a short distance farther on we came to two or three adobe buildings, the remains of furnaces and mule power. Here we found two or three Mexicans and a Papago. We asked them how far it was to Cuhuabi? "This is Cuhuabi" — where is the

---

[2] Making their way up the Altar valley, the Allyn party, bearing to the northwest, reached modern Pan Tak, which is the Papago term for "coyote sits." It has been known simply as Coyote, and there was a spring there in earlier times. Pan Tak is thirty-eight miles southwest of Tucson. (Granger, *Arizona Place Names*, p. 274.)

[3] Allyn probably passed through the Quinlan Mountains beyond Coyote, or Pan Tak. The abandoned village was possibly near the modern Papago settlement of San Vincente, or Havana Nakya.

camping place, water, grass, wood. "Here the grass is the other side
of the mountain, wood there wasn't any, water back at the hole."
Here was a dismal fix; dirt, saguaros, and stones. Col. B. [Bowie]
sent back to the wagon to take in a supply of wood. Meanwhile the
Mexicans got through some work or other they were doing at one
of the furnaces, with a little fire, and bundling up the result in a
handkerchief two of them disappeared. I suppose they were *Gambusinos*[4] or a class on the frontier who make a precarious living by
stealing ores from old mines and smelting or selling them. Continu-
ing our inquiries, we asked, "Where do Major Stickney,[5] Mr. Tangur,
and some other Americans we expected to find in Cuhuabi, live?"
"They live at the Picacho." This word literally means a peak or
point, and there are Picachos enough in Arizona to confuse the best
memory. "Well, where is the Picacho?" "It's about four miles on."
"Is there a good camping place there?" "No, there is neither water,
wood, or grass."

Col. B. said we would go on, it couldn't be worse, so word was
sent back to the wagon to water all the animals and to follow us on.
By this time it was dark, and for a mile or more the road was gloomy
enough; then on a distant hill the flashing of lights cheered both
ourselves and our animals, and we went gaily on. I rode into the
center of the lights by a shorter route than the ambulance could
take, and found myself in the midst of a sort of a Papago *rancheria*.
The lights were all from fires on the ground, inside the huts, but
the walls were so much on the open work order, that it afforded

---

[4] Sylvester Mowry describes the *"Gambusinos"* as follows: "There is a
numerous body of poor Mexican miners, the 'gambussinos,' who, though
originally a very deserving class of people, have done much harm to the mining interest, and, although their ill-directed industry has contributed momen-
tarily to augment the productiveness of mining, and, indeed, has solely sus-
tained many mining towns, they have nevertheless proved themselves a bane
to the country." (*Arizona and Sonora*, p. 128.)

[5] Major Daniel Hodges Stickney (born May 11, 1815) was a native of
Massachusetts but went to Mobile, Alabama, as a young man and became a
planter there. He came to Arizona in 1857 and was a Tucson merchant in
1860. In 1862, General Carleton had him arrested and imprisoned for three
months on the charge that he had been Confederate customs collector and
flour-purchasing agent. Governor Goodwin appointed him Cababi justice of
the peace in December 1864. Stickney was a member of the first district in the
House of the First Territorial Legislature (1864). He was reelected in 1865
and became a regent of the proposed University of Arizona. (Arizona Historical Society Biographical File.) Mr. Tangur or the lode by that name, have not
been identified.

quite light enough outside to confuse a spirited horse, so that I found myself careering round amidst huts and mining shafts, saguaros, and other things unpleasant to touch or fall into. At last I charged, as it were, almost into a house, and demanded in, I am afraid, a somewhat peremptory manner, where Major Stickney was to be found. The major I knew as a member of the legislature. All the reply I got was a sort of an Indian growl, not a soul stirring. My horse kept plunging about, and reflecting that possibly their education had been neglected, and that they did not understand the king's English, or rather that of the republic, my next essay was in my blandest Castillian, to make the same inquiry. This brought forth a trimly-formed Mexican woman, so wrapped up, however, that in the flickering light it was difficult to say with entire certainty that she was either young or pretty, who said Maj. S's house was *muy circo,*[6] that she would show it to me.

On she went, I after in blind confidence. We crossed the plaza, left the lights behind us, and entered what in the dim uncertain lights of the twinkling stars seemed a grand avenue of saguaros. The *muy circo* seemed a good ways off, and again I asked how far I had to go, and got the same *muy circo* for an answer. At last we passed a little undulation and came among other lights; my conductress here said she was going to her own house and that that was Major Stickney's, pointing to about the only house where there wasn't a particle of light. I rather demurred at being left that way, and she proceeded to knock at the door of the dark house until she roused somebody who did speak English at least as near as I could catch the discordant grumbling of a man half wakened. It was English; it wasn't S's voice, but still it was somebody, and I thanked the Senora and she glided off into the dark.

At last, rubbing his eyes, not more than half awake, out came our friend. "Where is Major Stickney?" "Don't know; he lives here; went down to Picacho (the place I first struck), some time ago; think he will be back soon; won't you come in?" "No, I must see my friends; where are we to camp?" "O, anywhere, there's no difference; there's no water within a mile, and very little there; no wood save cactus, and no grass." This did make all places much alike. "Where does Mr. Tangur live?" "Over there," pointing to a house looking quite a distance off. I turned back to find Col. B.,

---

[6] *Muy circo* is Allyn's misspelling of the Spanish *muy cerca,* very near.

and met him and Capt. Smith on foot, walking up the saguaro avenue having left the ambulance behind.[7] Their investigations had been about as successful as mine, and we started for Mr. Tangur's. We met this gentleman on the way to meet us, and went to his house, where we met his wife, a fine looking woman, a native of California, and two fine looking boys. Mrs. Tangur said there were no candles, coffee nor meat then in the place, which was literally true, they living on *tortillas* and *frijoles,* or their Mexican bread and beans. For candles, the dried cactus make an excellent substitute, burning long and brilliantly.

When our ambulance and wagon came up we camped on the open space between the houses; altogether I think the most perfectly disagreeable and uncomfortable camp I ever made. It was dark — always bad for camping — the wind had risen, whirling the dust everywhere, blowing your fires every which way, beside making it chilly; then when we came to make our beds, the sharp-pointed stones, scattered all about, were exceedingly obstinate about getting out of the way, and our poor animals stamped and fretted for want of hay or grass. Notwithstanding all this, after supper, which we had camp appetites for, we sat on the leeward side of the ambulance and received visitors. Major Stickney came back, the young masters Tangur were around, telling us graphic stories of their adventures since they came to this out of the way country; of a lode one of them had found when out looking for the *burro;* how his mother told him it was no account, the first time he brought in some of the rock; that he went and got more; that it was assayed and proved rich, and was then recorded as the Tangur lode, in honor of its young discoverer. Papagoes stalked about, curious but silent. The wind did not go down, and our supply of cactus was about burned out as the last of our friends departed and we retired to our stony couches. In the morning the sun came out warm and we had a chance to look at the scene of our night's annoyances. There were about us a few stone houses, and the shafts of a mine or two where considerable work had been done. The Papago huts that in the night were so prominent with their blazing fires, were scarcely to be distinguished in the broad light of day from the bushes about them.

Our first business was to see the chief of the Papagoes, or rather

---

[7]As noted earlier, research has turned up no clues to the identity of this Captain Smith. See Letter 19, note 9, for information regarding Colonel B(owie).

the captain here, for the great chieftan lives at San Xavier, and procure a guide for our trip to the Pima villages, distant north about one hundred miles, right through Papagonia, and to arrange with him to take charge of our wounded horse, who was too lame to go on or be sent back. These arrangements were quickly made, a boy leading off the horse with a sack of corn to feed him, and another detailed to go with us for four dollars in silver. All this done, the escort and wagons were put on the march to reach water and grass and wait for us. Then we started with the Americans here to look at some of the mines. Col. B. and Capt. Smith had some interest in the Picacho. Thither we went first; the shaft was full of water that was rather brackish and we had to be content with what we saw on top, where there were very favorable indications of a vein. The rock from this shaft has much of it, they said, averaged eight or nine hundred dollars in silver per ton.

One Padre, a Sonoran,[8] was then making arrangements to go to work here; he was erecting *arrastras,* and from his former experience in working here was confident of making money. The specimens of rock I saw were certainly rich looking. We visited a number of shafts, where considerable work had been done; although there was none now being done except what the Padre was doing. From what little I saw here, it struck me that the veins were very valuable and that some time or other capitalists would find their way hither and smite these rocks with a blow that will be followed by a stream of silver. Meanwhile our little American colony here waits, waits. I never knew what waiting meant until I came here among prospectors. Denying himself, literally, everything that makes life life, and not mere existence, the prospector who has found what he believes is a mine spends years waiting for somebody to come and buy it or work it. Think of this waiting for years, you who are impatient if the cars are ten minutes behind time, and if dinner isn't ready at six o'clock precisely. These men who worship the mineral god in his plutonic home show a faith that those who have been trained within sound of cathedral organ may well envy.

With a port on the Gulf of California this mineral region becomes at once accessible, only a little over 100 miles from tide water.

---

[8] The name of the "Sonoran Padre" was doubtless Father Bartólome Suastegui, a Basque priest at the Altar mission in northern Sonora. The mission records there indicate that he was away engaged in mining activity in southern Arizona about half of his time. (Interview, Father Kiernan McCarty, San Xavier Mission, Tucson, November 11, 1971.)

Letter 21

PAPAGO RANCHERIAS —
PIMA VILLAGES AGAIN —
THE OATMAN MASSACRE —
MURDER ON THE DESERT —FORT YUMA

Fort Yuma, Feb. 1, 1865
[Published June 5, 1865]

One ought never to ride anything but a *burro* in such a country as this. Taking the word of old residents for it, there is grass within three or four miles in one direction and permanent water about the same distance off in another, and this where, altogether, two or three hundred people manage to live. The Papagonia is the poorest watered portion of Arizona, there is hardly any permanent water anywhere, and the Papagoes literally move from one water hole to another as the one gets dry, and frequently you will find a rancheria five miles away from water, the water being carried that distance upon the women's heads. Yet notwithstanding all the disadvantages, the Papagoes are one of the finest bodies of Indians I have yet met. They are good natured, accommodating, brave and industrious, and when in any large numbers they find employment, as at the Cerro Colorado, I found it very difficult to distinguish them from Mexicans.

Toward noon we bid goodbye to our hospitable friends in this inhospitable country, and started after the soldiers. About a mile from town we came upon an *arroya* where they got water. The hole was about six feet deep, and but a small quantity of water was to be got in it at a time. There were several women waiting their turns to get enough to wash little bundles of clothes, all good natured and patient, giving us their pails to water our animals and waiting for the water to run in again after we had drank it dry. We overtook the escort lazily stretched out near a Papago tank about nine miles on. There was an abundance of grass there and our animals evidently enjoyed it. We were now fairly on a vast plain stretching as far as the eye could reach to the north, and for some distance at least

[216]

carpeted with grass and well timbered, or rather wooded. The tank here at which it was evident the stock for miles around was watered was an artificial one, made to hold rain water.

On the whole road from Cuhuabi to Pima, one hundred miles, I did not see anything like permanent water. To be sure we found enough in ravines and the two or three tanks like the one here, but with hot weather and the glare of a summer sun, I should be afraid that there would not be much left. But fortunately, the summer is the rainy season, and the largest quantity of water falls at the time when the largest amount of evaporation takes place. We passed close to two Papago *rancherias* on our way, but did not go to either. We sent over to one, foraging for milk, eggs, chickens, etc., but all our agent made out was that they were *muy pobre,* and that he didn't get the provisions. Most of the way on this road there was grass; but as you neared the Gila it grew scarcer and scarcer.

When we got well in sight of a range of hills lying northward, which we thought were near the Gila, Capt. Smith and myself determined to ride into Mr. White's[1] at Pima, and see if there was any news. Our Papago guide said it was a very long distance, but we felt inclined to rely on our own judgment. It was about 4 o'clock in the afternoon when we started, and we fully calculated on reaching Casa Blanca before dark. We rode very rapidly till sundown, and had not then made the mountain, but we were near to it, and supposed by that we should certainly see the lights of the Pimas. On we rode, till we rode the mountain down and opened another just like it. This was pleasant; not a blanket with us, not a bite to eat or a thimble full of water. We dismounted, lighted our pipes, took a philosophical look at things, and came to the conclusion that news was a good thing, but in this case it was likely to cause us a devil of a ride. The road was not very easy to follow in the dark, wagon tracks every little while radiating from it for wood or grass. But the north star twinkled right ahead of us, with all its circling constellations marching round it to mark the hours, and toward it we rode four mortal hours at a good jolting trot before we saw a light and these gleamed fitfully off to our left. A moment's reflection prevented this from annoying us; for we knew the Pimas went to bed early, and it was a chance if we saw a soul of them; that Casa

---

[1] For identification of White and his home, "Casa Blanca," see Letter 7, note 11.

Blanca had a high adobe wall all around it through which no candle
light would show. We therefore concluded the fires were watchfires
of parties out watching for Apaches. Next, in the dark, we ran into
quite a little lot of oxen and cows, very much to their surprise too,
and in a minute or two more we were nearly unhorsed by the swerv-
ing of our animals to avoid running into an old wagon right in front
of the corral gate at White's. The north star served us well; straight
as the crow flies we had ridden some thirty miles, and struck a dusky
adobe pile you couldn't see a rod away from it.

We banged away at the gate, the dogs howled and dog after
dog took up the chorus until the night fairly barked. Everybody's
asleep. At last comes a sleepy "Who's there?" "It's I — don't you
know me?" Rubbing eyes again, "O, it's you. Come in." Wide
swings open the gate and closes again on us. "Where's Mr. White?"
"He's sick and in bed." Before the horses had done drinking, Mr. W's
familiar voice showed that, sick or well, the old instinct of hospitality
had got the better of his rheumatism. "What's the news?" "Bully;
Sherman's in Savannah! Half Georgia holding Union meetings!"
Now there may have been louder cheers before on the reception of
that news, but I doubt if there were heartier ones. Fatigue disappeared; it seemed as though it was a mistake that we had been riding
some forty miles. The corral was full of discharged soldiers on their
way home to California, and one by one they took up the joyful
shout. They would have given, then, anything to have been with the
army of the Cumberland.

We went in the house and read again and again the worn out
newspaper that recorded the military wonder of the 19th century.
Near by lay Kinglake's graphic three hundred pages, painting how
daringly some paltry thousands of Britons broke from their base
of supplies for twenty-four hours.[2] What a contrast!

Mr. W. went out to get some wheat for our horses and I
noticed there were no animals of his in the corral. "Where are your
mules?" "All gone. The Apaches attacked my wagons in broad day-

---

[2]Alexander William Kinglake (1809–91) was a brilliant nineteenth century English historian who wrote a *History of the Crimean War,* based on
Lord Raglan's private papers. Eight separate volumes appeared between 1863
and 1887. Allyn appears to have found the first volume, describing the siege of
Sevastopol. It was entitled *The Invasion of the Crimea,* (London, 1863). The
history has been described as "one of the most picturesque, most vivid and
most actual pieces of historical narrative in the English language." (*Encyclo-
paedia Britannica,* 11th edition, 25: 809.)

light on the desert, between the Hassayampa and Salt rivers, killed two men, ran off the animals and destroyed everything, even ripping open sacks of flour, they couldn't carry away." This attacking teams in the daytime shows the desperation of the Indians, for it has been a thing unheard of for a long time before.

Next morning we rode over to Maricopa Wells, where we joined our escort again. From the Wells to the first point you strike on the Gila is some forty miles, and I think the worst desert I have yet seen; there is no grass or water. From this point our road follows the Gila all the way to Fort Yuma. The Gila was unusually high and I could understand how some of the enthusiastic early explorers thought it could be made navigable. The road to Yuma, saving that it has water in abundance, is dreary, monotonous, dusty, heavy and disagreeable. I do not recollect seeing a blade of grass during a distance of one hundred miles, although there is grass to be found at considerable distances off the road. All along the road are the ruined stations of the old overland mail. We passed the remains of one or two ranches and quite an extensive earthwork, which showed the industry and prudence of the California column; the graves of the Oatman family, whose tragic story Ross Browne has given you at length in *Harper's*.[3] There were stretches of water fringed with cottonwood and willows that made exceedingly pretty views. The

---

[3] The article referred to is "A Tour Through Arizona," in *Harper's New Monthly Magazine*. All but three of the nine members of the Royse Oatman family were murdered, probably by Yavapai Indians in 1851. In February, the Oatmans had detached themselves from a larger emigrant party (which refitted and rested in Tucson and the Pima villages) in order to reach California before their supplies were exhausted. By February 18 they had reached Oatman Flat, north of the Gila River and just southwest of its big bend, about eighteen miles east of Agua Caliente. Major Heintzelman, commander at Fort Yuma, had received a plea from Oatman for supplies, which were sent, but the supply party did not reach the family before the massacre.

Olive, age sixteen; Mary Ann, ten; and Lorenzo, fourteen, survived the tragedy. The son was left for dead but was only stunned. He escaped and eventually made his way to Fort Yuma. The girls were taken captive by the Indians and carried north into the mountains. Olive and Mary Ann were later sold as slaves to the Mohaves, by whom they were treated rather well, although the youngest "died of starvation." In 1857, as the result of the efforts of Lorenzo and others, Olive was purchased from the Mohaves and returned to Fort Yuma. She went to New York with Lorenzo, attended college, married J. B. Fairchild, and eventually settled in Sherman, Texas. She died in 1903. (R. B. Stratton, *Captivity of the Oatman Girls;* John R. Browne, *A Tour Through Arizona*, pp. 696–97; Edward J. Pettid, S.J., "The Oatman Story," pp. 4–9.)

nights grew warmer, and the cottonwoods seemed almost ready to
bud out.

Soon after we passed the flat where the Oatman massacre took
place, one morning we met two men pushing rapidly along, one an
American and the other a Mexican. They stopped and questioned
us as to whether we had seen aught of a cart with two horses and
two men. We had not. The American was the stepson of an old man
who had been then over twenty days out from the Agua Calliente
ranche,[4] bound for Fort Yuma, and had not arrived at the latter
place or been seen on the road. He was known to have quite a sum
in gold with him, that he was taking out of the country to pay off
a mortgage upon a little place he had in California. That he had
been murdered the young man had little doubt, and his melancholy
errand now was to follow the cart trail to where the deed was done
and see what sort of a story there was traced in characters that
never lie, on the grasses and bushes of that camp of death.

At Fort Yuma afterwards we got the whole story. The old man
had sent his gold ahead to the Agua Calliente bunched in small
parcels. When he arrived there himself he was accompanied by a
young man who likewise had quite a sum in gold, they drove a pair
of roan horses in a sort of cart. While they were at the ranche two
men, quite run down, came in, likewise bound to Fort Yuma. Their
animals were tired, and for the sake of company the old man waited
for them a day or two, and when they did start, carried in his wagon
their forage and food. The cart tracks were easily traced one day's
drive toward Yuma, thence to a secluded camp about two hundred
yards off the road, where the ashes and debris of the camp showed
they had stayed all night. In the morning they had harnessed up to
go on, when the murder was done. The old man was shot as he was
raising the reins, the shot passing under his arms, and the young man

---

[4] Agua Caliente's warm water spring was near the site of an Indian ran-
chería and a mission, Santa María de Agua, founded by Padre Jacobo Sedel-
mayr in 1744. In the 1850s a ranch at the place was stocked with Texas
cattle. Around 1865, King S. Woolsey developed the first American ranch
near the spring jointly with George Martin. It had been noted by Padre Sedel-
mayr that the Indians used the warm spring medicinally for various ailments.
Agua Caliente ranch was located one and one-half miles from the spring,
which was three miles north of the Gila and northeast of the modern town of
Agua Caliente. (Will C. Barnes, *Place Names*, pp. 11–12; for an illustration
which may possibly be the ranch see Andrew Wallace, *Image of Arizona*,
p. 212.)

with him was killed at the same moment. The horses were cut from the cart, part of the harness remaining. There were the two dead bodies, the trail away of the four animals. Meanwhile a party of discharged soldiers arrived who passed two men with four animals at the point of the mountain near Tucson, whose description corresponded exactly with the two men who started from the ranche. These men told the soldiers that they were bound for Mexico.

Our last camp before arriving at Yuma was at Gila city, Ross Browne's city with chimney and coyote.[5] Here some years ago there were thousands of people working in placers. When we were there, there were just two, thin, poverty-stricken, half starved Sonorans. I went over to watch their dry washings. It is a process requiring a great deal more manual dexterity than the "wet washing." All the outfit necessary to the dry washing out of gold from mother earth is a piece of cloth and a wooden *battea,* as the Mexicans call it, a shallow flaring pan.[6] The dirt supposed to contain gold is first got out in a pile. Frequently a shaft or well is sunk clear down the bed rock and the pay dirt hoisted up from the bottom in buckets with a windlass; so you see we have dry wells as well as dry washing. The cloth is spread out on the ground, the *battea* is filled with dirt, and the washer balances it on the ends of his fingers, giving the dirt a rapid rotary motion until the bits of stone are separated and much of the fine dust has blown away. If there is no wind the washer blows it away himself. He picks out the large pieces of stone and throws them away. At last, with a graceful swing of the *battea,* up as high as he can reach, he slowly pours out the dirt upon the cloth at his

---

[5] This is a reference to Browne's well-known remark about Gila City — that in 1864 it had "three chimneys and a coyote." (Browne, *A Tour Through Arizona,* p. 693.) Placer gold mining had been carried on there in 1858, mostly by frustrated California goldrushers. There were a thousand miners on the site shortly after the discovery. Few permanent buildings were erected, which would account for Browne's remark. A terrific Gila flood in 1862 reduced the prospects and the prospectors and, coupled with the exhaustion of the gold, hastened the end of the rush by 1865. Gila City lies a mile and one-half from the modern town of Dome and about twenty-four miles northeast of Yuma. (Wallace, *Image of Arizona,* p. 148 [contemporary illustration of Gila City, p. 151]; Byrd H. Granger, *Arizona Place Names,* p. 373.)

[6] The Mexicans were the first to use the gold pan or *battea.* Americans generally used one of metal rather than of wood (for an illustration of this type of pan, see Wallace, *Image of Arizona,* p. 148.) Placer gold normally originated in upstream or mountain deposits. Over the millenia, the soft, heavy gold flakes and nuggets were released from the mother rock and washed down to the placer or sandy, gravel detritus in the stream or riverbed.

feet, thus giving a gentle wind a chance to blow away more of the dirt. This he continues until he gets the results of eight or ten *batteas* on his cloth, then he cleans up, that is, takes a *battea* full of this earth. Now you will see he handles it more carefully. The particles whirl round and round, he gently blows the earth off, tips it up by a dexterous twist, catches the earth again and at last has left as the result just the least color of gold. I saw eight *batteas* cleaned up and I should think about five cents in gold obtained. This is carefully placed in a quill which they wear tied to a string about their necks. These two men, the sole occupants of Gila City, declared that they made on an average twenty-five cents a day. But I suspect they did not tell the truth, for this gold washing, wet or dry, is gambling; every once in the while a piece is found weighing an ounce, or even more, and it is the hope of getting these chances that buoys up these gold hunters.

If there is any large quantity of gold in these hills at Gila city, capital will some day get it out, for there is an abundance of water within less than a quarter of a mile. There was camped near us here a family on their way from California to Hermosillo in Sonora; they had poor animals, any quantity of children, and were making that trip just to see relatives. They said they liked California, and were coming back. They have at least one stretch to make of sixty miles without water, and nobody but Mexicans would dare try it with their outfit. But they are as cheerful and as far from apprehension as though they were on a pleasure trip; in fact, I suspect that's what they would have called it.

We reached Fort Yuma before noon the day we left Gila city. Here Col. Bowie and Capt. Smith left me, they proceeding on to California, and I waiting for a steamboat to get to La Paz. It seems as though my journey was at an end to get where I can go on a boat.

Letter 22

STEAMBOATING UP THE COLORADO RIVER

La Paz, May 20, 1865
[Published July 19, 1865]

For many years attempts have been made, with greater or less earnestness, to make the Colorado river the channel of supply for the vast country that lies between the Rocky Mountains and the Sierra Nevada. As long ago as the Mormon war, propositions were made to supply the troops in Utah at less rate than by the overland route, which Floyd then adopted for obvious political reasons, viz: that the war he waged was against the rising antislavery sentiment of Missouri, and the end he proposed was the preparing the way for the destruction of the republic when the present war should break out.[1]

In 1850, Capt. George A. Johnson,[2] with the steamer *General Jessup,* started to explore the upper river, then *terra incognita* above Fort Yuma. He succeeded in reaching the deep rapids below El Dorado canon,[3] and being out of provisions turned back to Fort

---

[1] The "Mormon war" refers to hostilities between the Mormon immigrants in Utah and non-Mormon settlers and travelers. It was highlighted by the Mountain Meadows massacre, some 350 miles south of Salt Lake City in September, 1857, when Indians and Mormons attacked a California-bound party accused of seizing Mormon supplies. John Buchanan Floyd was appointed secretary of war by President Buchanan in 1856. He became a commander of one of Lee's brigades during the Civil War and was the object of much hatred by Northerners. (Howard R. Lamar, *The Far Southwest, 1846–1912,* pp. 340–53; *The National Cyclopaedia of American Biography* 5: 7.) For the Colorado River as "the channel of supply" see Leonard J. Arrington, "Inland to Zion: Mormon Trade on the Colorado River, 1864–1867," pp. 239–50.

[2] According to Hubert H. Bancroft (*History of Arizona and New Mexico,* p. 490), George A. Johnson arrived at the mouth of the Colorado in the spring of 1851. He did not command the *General Jesup* until January 1854. That steamer exploded the following August. Johnson organized the Colorado Steam Navigation Company in 1852. (Rufus Kay Wyllys, *Arizona: The History of A Frontier State,* p. 271.) The steamer was named after General Thomas S. Jesup. Allyn misspells it "Jessup."

[3] El Dorado Canyon drains into the Black Canyon of the Colorado below Hoover Dam on the Nevada side of the river. Some of the earliest placer gold workings were located there. (Byrd H. Granger, *Arizona Place Names,* p. 208.)

Yuma, having demonstrated the navigability of three hundred miles of the river above Yuma. This was the first steamboat that ever penetrated the valleys of the Chemehuevis[4] and Mohaves,[5] or threaded their canoned portals.

Shortly after this trip of the *Jessup,* Lieut. Ives[6] explored the river to the head of Black canon, where there is now a town building at the Vegas wash, which he mistook for the mouth of the Virgin river.[7] All who are familiar with the report of Lieut. Ives will readily attest the sublimity of the canons he has engraved, and bear witness to the rare beauty of the language he employed in portraying this unique and picturesque grandeur.

He proceeded up the river at the lowest stage of water, in a small iron steamboat admirably adapted for the purposes of exploration but for an unfortunate blunder in attempting to strengthen her frame, by bolting timbers outside of her bottom instead of inside, which added to the water she drew and made it more difficult to work through the shifting sand bars.

Last summer a company of soldiers marched from Salt Lake

---

[4]Chemehuevi Valley and Indian Reservation lie north of Parker Dam on the California side. The Chemehuevi were a Shoshonean tribe, a branch of the Paiute. Whipple's party met them in February 1854 and found them friendly, although these Indians later clashed with Anglo immigrants. (Frederick Hodge, *Handbook of American Indians North of Mexico* 1: 242; Grant Foreman, *A Pathfinder in the Southwest,* pp. 227–31.)

[5]The Mojave Valley and Indian Reservation are in Arizona north of Topock. The Mohaves were a Yuman tribe living to the north of the Chemehuevi. They were noted for their warlike ways. Whipple spent time with the Mohaves when he met Lieutenant Ives. (Foreman, *A Pathfinder in the Southwest,* pp. 232–62.)

[6]Joseph Christmas Ives first came to Arizona in 1853 with the survey party of Amiel Weeks Whipple, who was searching for railroad routes to the Pacific. He navigated the Colorado on the steamer *Explorer.* Ives' report was entitled *Report upon the Colorado River of the West, Explored in 1857 and 1858.* It was published in 1861. (Foreman, *A Pathfinder in the Southwest,* p. 116, n. 12; Godfrey Sykes, *The Colorado Delta,* p. 20.)

[7]The head of Black Canyon became the site of Hoover Dam; the Vegas Wash is a few miles northwest of the dam. The Virgin River mouth was above Boulder Canyon to the east, but it has been submerged by Lake Mead.

The town being built at Vegas Wash was Callville, or Mormon Landing. At the time of Allyn's visit in 1865, lumber, agricultural machinery, and other merchandise were shipped to Utah from this site. The town itself boasted 150 lots, stone corrals, and a large warehouse. Unfortunately the roads from the landing to Mormon communities along the Muddy and the Virgin rivers were at times impassable due to floods and quicksand. Callville was abandoned well before the completion in 1869 of the Union Pacific railroad. (Arrington, "Inland to Zion," pp. 246–50; map, p. 247.)

to Fort Mohave[8] to examine the overland route as to the practicability of supplying government posts in Utah this way. The officer in command reported warmly in favor of it.

During the past winter, the steamer *Esmeralda*[9] with a barge in tow, started for the Mormon landing,[10] but learning as she reached Black canon, that the Mormons had then left, turned back to El Dorado canon, where she tied up while her captain proceeded to Salt Lake. During the last year the Mormons have been examining the question of using the Colorado river both for their supplies and emigration. Four hundred families are already ordered into Arizona to form settlements on the Big Muddy[11] and Virgin rivers, and at the Vegas wash, thus completing a continuous chain of settlements from the river to Salt Lake. It is said a railroad[12] is likewise ordered to begin at Salt Lake, to follow this route, which should it be completed would revolutionize the supplying of the region north clear to the head waters of the Columbia river, and even there during the winter months.

---

[8] Fort Mohave was established by Major L. S. Armistead in 1859 as a base for military operations against the Mohave Indians. It was located at a ford known as Beale's Crossing, where Lieutenant Edward F. Beale had projected a wagon route to California across northern Arizona in 1857. The fort had been abandoned in May 1861 and reoccupied in May 1863. From then until 1865, when nearby tribes "accepted civilization," the post was used to control lawless Mohaves, Chemehuevis, and Paiutes. The crossing was a few miles above the present town of Needles, California. (Arizona Historical Society Place File; Philip J. Avillo, "Fort Mohave: Outpost on the Upper Colorado," pp. 82–99.)

[9] The captain of the *Esmeralda* was Thomas E. Trueworthy, who brought the ship under her own power from San Francisco to the Colorado. He hoped to break the river monopoly held by Captain George A. Johnson's company, but in 1867 Johnson ended competition by buying the *Esmeralda*. (Hazel E. Mills, "The Arizona Fleet," p. 261; Odie B. Faulk, "The Steamboat War that Opened Arizona," pp. 4–5.)

[10] Mormon Landing, or Callville, at Vegas Wash, was the first county seat of Mohave County, but it became a part of Nevada when that portion of the county west of the Colorado River was transferred to Nevada. The town lay above the head of Black Canyon. (Granger, *Arizona Place Names,* p. 200.) For additional information, see above note 7.

[11] The Big Muddy (now called the Muddy) in southeastern Nevada. In Allyn's time it entered the Virgin River, but now it flows into Lake Mead. (Department of the Interior Geological Survey map, Overton Quadrangle, Clark County, Nevada.)

[12] The Union Pacific Railroad on May 10, 1869, was connected with the Pacific Coast near Ogden, Utah, and in 1889 a line was run from Salt Lake City southwest through Las Vegas along the route described by Allyn. (David F. Myrick, *Railroads of Nevada and Eastern California,* pp. 454, 623.)

The first freight actually sent by this route was shipped from San Francisco in March or April,[13] arrived at the mouth of the river about the 1st of May, was placed on board the *Cocopah,* Capt. Robinson,[14] that arrived at La Paz on the third of May, when I went aboard of her, and on the morning of the fourth we started for the head of navigation.

We were loaded light, having no freight except for the extreme up river, still I could not help wishing that we had the *Mohave,* the new boat of the line, instead of the *Cocopah.* The *Mohave* has engines of much greater power, and I foresaw that we might need all the force we could get before we got back. By way of compensation, however, we had Captain Robinson, who was the navigator of Ives' boat, and beyond question the most skillful pilot on the upper river. There was a moderate stage of water, the river having been rising and falling as the little freshets from Williams Fork[15] and the Little Colorado came down for some weeks, and the *Cocopah* had made a very quick trip from tide water to La Paz.

We got away soon after sunrise, on one of the loveliest days of this almost tropical climate. It had been very warm in La Paz for nearly a week — thermometer rising to 110 degrees, suggesting many misgivings as to an early and unprecedented overflow from the melting of the snows of the Rocky mountains, but a gentle

[13] Allyn made his river trip at a time of great activity. Johnson and the Colorado Steam Navigation Company ran a fleet consisting of the *Cocopah* (one hundred tons), the *Colorado,* and the *Mohave* (seventy tons each). They also owned three one-hundred-ton barges. During the late sixties and early seventies, the company prospered on the river trade. Most of this resulted from the transport of passengers and freight unloaded at the head of the Gulf of California by steamers and sailing ships from San Francisco or San Diego. The complete passage from San Francisco around Cape San Lucas to Yuma, including transfer time at the river's mouth, took from twelve days to two weeks and cost passengers sixty dollars cabin or forty dollars steerage. When the Southern Pacific Railway tracks reached Yuma from the California coast in 1877, the Colorado River shipping business ended. (Sykes, *The Colorado Delta,* pp. 28–29, 34.) For the story of steam navigation on the river consult Arthur Woodward, *Feud on the Colorado.*

[14] Allyn's *Cocopah* was evidently the first boat of that name on the Colorado, having been assembled in the estuary in 1859 from parts made in San Francisco. (Mills, "The Arizona Fleet," p. 261; Sykes, *The Colorado Delta,* p. 27; Woodward, *Feud on the Colorado,* p. 144; Allyn, pp. 258, 275.) *Cocopah I* was replaced in 1865 by the second boat of that name, which continued service until 1877. (Woodward, *Feud on the Colorado,* p. 144.)

[15] "Williams Fork" was the Bill Williams River, draining an area west and north of Prescott. Allyn was unaware of the distant sources of the Colorado in the Rockies, and it is probable that the rise of the river was due to more than the "little freshets from Williams Fork and the Little Colorado."

It took Allyn about two weeks to reach Yuma on the *Cocopah I,* which tied up along the banks at night due to the unknown conditions of the Colorado.

breeze sweeping from the north, was so delightfully cool that it at once dispelled any such gloomy ideas, and we watched the rising sun bathe in crimson the frowning, desolate mountain range[16] that stretches off toward California. Steadily the old *Cocopah* worked on all that day, only once touching bottom slightly on a bar that occasioned no detention. On one side of us stretched the broad bottoms of the great Colorado valley, bounded by the bastioned mesas that sweep off to the first mountain range, and green with a dense growth of willows, cottonwood and mesquite; on the other we successfully passed two barren mountain ranges, the first called . . . half way from Yuma to Mohave, and the second Riverside, both so utterly sterile that even the cactus would not grow on their rugged, broken slopes.[17]

All day the foam floating on the muddy water vividly sug-

---

[16] The "desolate mountain range" was probably the McCoy Mountains, northwest of modern Blythe, California.

[17] The name of the first mountain range was omitted from Allyn's dispatch, apparently by typographical error. The reference was probably to the Big María Mountains. The Riverside Range is in California, west of Poston, Arizona. (U.S. Geological Survey map, Salton Sea, California, Arizona.)

gested the rising of the river, and every now and then the rumble
of a falling bit of bank made us still more thoughful. At night, when
we tied up to the bank, for the river is not well enough known to
navigate after dark, a water gauge was set to determine the important question of the rise. We had a moon in full tropic brilliancy,
and there was an inexpressible charm in the blandness of the climate, as we spread our bedding on the deck, and with the ripple of
the river to lull us to sleep, lay down without having to stand guard.
Long before sunrise we were under way with the too certain knowledge that the river was steadily rising. Still there was the hope that
cooler weather would intervene above, and that we should not en-
counter the great annual overflow which last year came in June.
Today another range of similar character to those passed yesterday
swept along the California side of the river, called the Monument
range, from a single isolated point that stands boldly out, as though
it were a monument erected as a land mark.[18] On the other bank
the Colorado valley continued until we reached the Williams Fork
range of mountains, through which the river winds its serpentine
way; this canon is a rapid succession of broken mountains, huge
boulders and massive peaks.[19] Nowhere has it perpendicular walls.
A sharp turn around a mountain, brings you to the mouth of Williams Fork, quite a stream of water, flowing from the mountain
region near Prescott, down which the Whipple Pacific railroad
exploring party managed to reach the Colorado.[20] On the Mesa at
this junction a town is laid out; although still without inhabitants,
it is rapidly becoming the principal exporting point on the river.[21]
There were twenty-five hundred sacks of copper ore piled up on
the bank waiting shipment when we passed, all from the Planet,
Eliza and Hacuvar mines.[22] Arrangements are rapidly being made

---

[18] The Monument Range lies directly west of Parker Dam. Monument
Peak has an elevation of 2,602 feet.

[19] Allyn probably refers here to the Buckskin Mountains.

[20] Amiel W. Whipple descended the Big Sandy Wash (which he called
the Williams River) to its junction with the Bill Williams and from thence
proceeded west in 1853. (Foreman, *A Pathfinder in the Southwest,* pp.
198–231.)

[21] No permanent settlement developed here. The local mines became less
productive, and the river lost its importance as a commercial artery.

[22] The Planet Mine was discovered in 1864 by Richard Ryland, and the
town of Planet was established there. The post office was closed in 1921. It
was located a few miles up the Williams River in Yuma County and was the
only one of the three mines of major importance. (*Arizona Miner,* September, 7, 1864; Granger, *Arizona Place Names,* p. 383.)

to secure the working of other mines in the vicinity, and there is little doubt that before fall, the monthly shipments of copper ores from this point will reach many hundred tons. The Planet mine is already delivering one hundred tons monthly. The ores are all forty per cent ores as far as heard from.

These enterprises are the work of men without means, save their own labor, and a small stock of provisions. When the attention of bona fide capitalists is attracted to this country, and the mines are worked with the economy of ample means, this country will become one of the principal copper producing points of the world. Then the poorer ores that will not bear transportation will be made available by reduction works here; then vessels will receive the ores at the mouth of the Colorado and sail directly for New York *at a less freight than it now costs to San Francisco;* then a railroad over an easy and practical grade for thirty miles will enable the mines, now too far away from the rivers to be profitably worked, to become productive.[23] The time will come, sooner or later, when the region within forty miles of Williams Fork, will turn out, daily, hundreds, perhaps thousands, of tons of copper ore, averaging from fifteen to fifty per cent.[24]

In the afternoon we ran on for three or four hours and tied up at a wood yard. On Saturday we started early and made Chemehuevis valley, where we found no wood cut and had to tie up while the boat hands cut enough to take us to the Mohave valley. The Chemehuevis valley is a small one. In the distance you could see the grim barrier of the Mohave range.[25] When we neared it, the Needles, as some slender pointed peaks were named by Ives, became prominent and seemed as though they were quite at this end of the canon, although in point of fact they are very near the upper end.

We entered the canon[26] about four o'clock in the afternoon. For several miles it ran through broken mountains sloping towards the shore, until at last, as the sun was getting low, we passed the portals of the canon proper. Huge perpendicular walls of rock rose an hundred feet, unbroken on either hand; now and then a craggy

---

[23] A Santa Fe Railway branch line now cuts through this area from Salome to Parker.

[24] In 1972, the only major producer remaining in this area is the Bagdad Copper Mine west of Prescott.

[25] The Mohave Range lies between Topock and Lake Havasu City.

[26] The "canon" is Mohave Canyon between the present Lake Havasu City and Topock.

projection was piled like battlement or tower above the wall; the shadow of the rock wall on the one side was darkening the gorge, while in the clear rushing waters was mirrored the face of the other. Ever and anon the river would turn a sharp corner in the midst of its rocky surroundings, and here and there a giant boulder would stand sullen sentinel over the route of the disappearing stream.

It is these corners that are the terror of the steam boatmen. With power enough you can stem any current, but the river forms eddies that make a boat unmanageable at these angles in its course. We encountered one right at the grandest turn in the canon. It caught our bow, and despite steam and rudder tossed us like a chip right upon the inhospitable rock wall; the signal rung to back, and the sharp tramp of many feet showed that the crew was mustered to fend off; we touched the rock as light as a feather bed. We got another start and next time made the riffle, yet it was nearer destruction than one likes to go. There are few prettier effects than the shadows as they creep over canons or mountains in this country. We did not get out into the valley, but camped among the hills into which the canon degenerates at either end, when the last tints of the setting sun and the paler rays of emerging moonbeams, commingled in as it were a grand kaleidoscope, were shifting light and shadowy in wavy forms of unique beauty.

Next morning we entered Mohave valley and were steaming through it all day. It is an exact reproduction of the larger Colorado valley, in which La Paz is situated. It looked green, being covered with a dense growth of willows, cottonwood and mesquite. Just at dark we reached Fort Mohave, a small post erected years ago to overawe the then hostile Mohave.[27] It is situated at the Beal crossing[28] of the river, where at one time many immigrants were attacked,[29] and is now the military depot to supply Fort Whipple, and probably will become the one to supply Utah, unless still another should be established further up the river. Fort Mohave is situated

---

[27] When Allyn reached the post, it was officially known as "Camp" Mohave. It had been abandoned at the start of the Civil War and then reopened in May 1863 with the new designation. (Granger, *Arizona Place Names,* p. 216.)

[28] See above note 8.

[29] The "hostile Mohave" attacked the J. L. Rose immigrants in 1859. They were on their way to California when they were massacred by Indians at the Colorado River. Few survived. (*Alta California,* May 7, 1859, June 11, 1859.)

on a mesa overlooking a beautiful cottonwood bosque. At present it is garrisoned by a company of Californians under Capt. Coolidge.[30] In the early days of Fort Mohave, the regulars had a fierce fight here with the Mohaves, and whipped them so soundly that since then there has been no disturbance. Adjoining the fort is Mohave city[31] — every new settlement is a city by way of discounting its future greatness — the county seat of Mohave county. There are some twenty or more houses here, the county offices and a couple of stores. As at La Paz, the Mohave Indians swarm about here, docile, trustworthy, and tolerably industrious; models, both men and women, of the human form divine.[32] You may search the galleries of Italy for models, the Venus de Medici thrown in, and anywhere here I will match you an Indian girl, with prouder step, more delicately turned foot and ankle, exquisite hands, and the bust of a Cleopatra, who walks in her native costume of stripped bark, utterly unconscious, in her innocence, of the lavish display she is making of her charms.

The river still continues to rise, sweeping by Mohave in magnificent volume. Capt. R. shakes his head, and it is easy to see he has little faith in our getting to Callville,[33] as the Mormon landing is called, or indeed of our getting much further up the river.

---

[30] This was a company of the Seventh California Infantry. Captain Walter Scott Coolidge, a native of New Hampshire, was a California druggist until commissioned in 1864 by the governor of California. He marched with 101 men from the port of San Pedro across the desert to Fort Mohave, where he was in command from April 15, 1865, to February 17, 1866. (R. H. Orton, *Records of California Men in the War of the Rebellion*, pp. 763, 773; E. D. Coolidge, *The Descendants of John and Mary Coolidge of Watertown, Mass.*, pp. 247, 251 55.)

[31] Mohave City was a settlement just outside the Fort Mohave reservation boundaries. It became the Mohave county seat with a post office in 1866. In 1869 the reservation was enlarged to embrace Mohave City, and residents were notified to leave but, because of protests, a population of 159 residents remained to be included in the 1870 census. No traces remain of Mohave City. (Granger, *Arizona Place Names*, p. 217.)

[32] Paintings of these Mohaves by Balduin Möllhausen, a German artist who accompanied Ives in 1857–58, can be found in Ives' *Report upon the Colorado River*. It shows the men in breechclouts and the women with short bark skirts, naked above the waist. Möllhausen had served as cartographer and artist on both the 1853 Whipple and the 1858 Ives expeditions. He published an illustrated account at Leipzig in 1858. (See Balduin Möllhausen, *Diary of a Journey from the Mississippi to the Coasts of the Pacific, with a United States Government Expedition*.) For the sad fate of these Mohaves in the next decade or so, see Bancroft, *Arizona and New Mexico*, pp. 545–46.

[33] For information regarding Callville, see above notes 7 and 10.

Letter 23

EXPLORATION OF THE COLORADO —
THE PAINTED CANON
THE MYSTERIES OF THE BLACK CANON —
EXCITING ADVENTURES

La Paz, May 20, 1865
[Published July 22, 1865]

On Monday we steamed on to Hardyville,[1] a landing some six miles above Mohave and a rival to that place. This is all the work of an enterprising business man, such as the frontier develops; he is retailer of everything one can want, jobber to the interior, freighter on either river or land; yonder are his mule teams; there are his fleet of barges; hotel keeper, with adjuncts of bar and billiard room; blacksmith shop and a five stamp quartz crushing mill, are connected with the establishment; everything is Hardy's[2] There is a block of adobe houses, what are they? Hardy's — put up to rent. There is a ferry, and so on to the end of the list of necessaries and luxuries in a new country.

Back of these landings is reported to be one of the richest mineral regions in Arizona, but as I did not visit the lodes or learn

[1] Until 1864, Hardyville was known as "Colorado River Ferry." It was located nine miles above Fort Mohave. (John L. Riggs, "William H. Hardy: Merchant of the Upper Colorado," pp. 179–80, 186–87.)

[2] Hardyville was purchased by William H. Hardy of New York in 1864. He established a trading post on the east side of the Colorado crossing nine miles above Fort Mohave. Hardyville quickly became a key supply and shipping point for the Cerbat Mountain mines. For several years the "city" (thirty-two people in 1864, twenty persons in 1870) was also important not only for Mohave County freighting, but for Prescott as well. By the early seventies, however, the settlement of Ehrenberg had been established on the Colorado, eighty miles north of Yuma. Since this new landing was closer and more convenient to Prescott, it soon usurped Hardyville's commerce and significance. Then, in 1883, the final blow came when the Atlantic and Pacific Railroad (later the Atchison, Topeka, and Santa Fe) crossed the Colorado below the town. Today nothing remains of Hardyville. (John L. Riggs, "William H. Hardy: Merchant of the Upper Colorado," pp. 179–80, 186–87.)

of many being sufficiently developed to enable one to judge whether they are mines or not, I shall not particularize. The somewhat famous Moss Lode[3] is in this district, and is still being worked. This mine has yielded some of the richest gold bearing quartz ever seen on the Pacific. I saw the returns of the gold extracted from some silver rock out of the Michigan Lode,[4] by an *arrastre,* and it was eminently satisfactory. This lode is worked by its owners, and it is to such enterprises Arizona looks for her sure development. It has been our misfortune that those who have played the role of capitalist out here, have almost uniformly been those who preferred to mine in Montgomery[5] or Wall Street, or, to speak more plainly, to specu-late, not to mine. These men, for there is no use in mincing words, are the bane of every legitimate enterprise, and the blighting curse of every country they touch. Mines are sold from samples of ore (taken from some other place) that the purchaser never finds; stock-holders are induced to build steamboats to transport ore that is not in *esse,* experts are brought out to testify to anything or every-thing the peculiar condition of the stock market may require; the ore from a large deposit is shipped and the shares of the mine are sold when the venders know there is no mine, and that every pound of ore in the deposit has been shipped; if it so happens, as it will sometimes, that the speculator gets a really good thing, then com-mences the game of freezing out, the mine is incorporated, a board of trustees is elected, an assessment ordered on the shares, to com-mence work, and those in the ring or the freezers, pay up with a memorandum check or borrow the money back again, while those out in the cold, or the to-be-frozen, are driven to sell part of their shares to pay assessments on the other, which of course the freezers buy; if they commence work the superintendent is interested to work so as to get the mine in a saleable condition not to develop it so that its real quality can be known, or so that it can be economically

---

[3]Captain John Moss established the Moss mine in 1863–64 after being shown surface gold by a friendly Mohave Indian chief. He is said to have taken a quarter million dollars in gold from one small shaft. But as frequently happened with these early miners, he died a poor man. (Hubert H. Bancroft, *Arizona and New Mexico,* p. 548; Byrd H. Granger, *Arizona Place Names,* p. 217; Otis E. Young, *Western Mining,* p. 145.)

[4]The nearby Michigan lode was never as rich as the Moss.

[5]Then, as in modern times, Montgomery Street in San Francisco was the most important financial center in the West.

worked, but always so that it will look well; if he strikes a rich pocket, he mustn't move a step further for fear that it may play out. In this way many mines pass into the hands of those who neither do anything with them themselves or let anyone else.

Real, *bona fide* capitalists are actually needed here, before the real wealth of the country can be known; and if there is anything in surface indications, in general geological deductions, and the results of the work already done, a richer return awaits the employment of capital, than in any other mineral region on the globe. "It takes a mine to work a mine," is the Mexican proverb, and there is no use in attempting mining operations without means enough to await patiently returns. Mines cannot be opened in a day, or made to pay the first day they are opened.

There are two elements in the calculations of the capitalist, pertaining to the mineral region on the Colorado river, that ought not to be overlooked. First, the cheap transportation the river affords to tide water; *no other mineral region in the United States has this*. Look at the canals and railroads that have been built East to transport coal, which only yields five or ten dollars per ton, while here the copper ore alone will average from seventy-five to one hundred dollars. The last shipped from the Planet, brought one hundred and forty in San Francisco. With capital, the lead mines on the river would pay at present prices of lead. Cheap transportation is no mean item for gold and silver mines; it brings you cheap machinery and provisions. Secondly, the absolute security of the river country. Here there is no Apache to steal animals or murder men, and the Indians that do surround you are available for cheap labor. They cut all the hay and wood used on the river, they make adobes, and can be taught almost any kind of rough work. Hardy's buildings were almost entirely built by them. The gold and silver bearing quartz lodes may be first developed, for a less amount of capital is required to work them. The present season will probably see many around Fort Mohave and Prescott, shipping bullion enough to demonstrate their value; but in the long run I fancy the baser and more useful metals will prove the true source of prosperity of the country.

Our freight for the Mormons was consigned to Mr. Hardy and he came aboard here, as well as a number of gentlemen interested in mines and mills at El Dorado Canon.

There was little hope of getting to Callville, but we were still sanguine of getting to El Dorado canon, which was as far as Lieut. Ives took his steamboat. We had on board some amalgamating pans for a quartz mill there, and Capt. R.[obinson] determined to make every effort to get up; besides, from El Dorado there was a wagon road to the Mormon road.

We made a good run in the afternoon, constantly working through rapids, occasionally using a line either to keep her head on or with the capstan to aid in pulling her through. Towards evening we reached Deep Rapids,[6] and in attempting the passage we pulled up a tree, tried another which held, and then we snapped our cables as though they were pipe stems, swung on some rocks and made a hole in our bottom that required attention. So thorough was the discipline of the boat that I never knew the last until days after. We tied up for the night in the rapid, still hopeful of reaching El Dorado, for if we got through this, they said there was but one more rapid to be surmounted. It was about this point in the river that the *Jessup,* under Captain Johnson turned back. The river now swept by in such majestic body that most of the rapids and rocks that delayed Ives so long, were all buried several feet under water. With power enough to stem the current a more magnificent stream to navigate could not be imagined; but a river during a flood is not in the best condition to enable one to judge of its general navigability.

Tuesday morning we got through the rapids by dint of two cables and sharp work at the capstan, swept slowly up the grand old river, encountering no difficulty save the steady drag of the current, stopped at Cottonwood and Round Islands[7] for wood, and passed the Painted canon,[8] a break through a low range of mountains, whose slopes are mosaiced with different hued mineral and vegetable matter. It was literally painted by the hand of nature, with strongly contrasted and blended colors; sometimes it was almost checked with distinct red, white and blue; then again crimson, pur-

---

[6] Deep Rapids has been covered by Lake Havasu.

[7] Cottonwood and Round Islands are now within Lake Havasu.

[8] Painted Canyon, about fifteen miles above Davis Dam, was so named by Ives in 1857. He considered it "the most picturesque and striking" of all the river canyons. (Joseph C. Ives, *Report upon the Colorado River of the West, Explored in 1857 and 1858,* p. 79.)

ple, blue, and drab gently blended or faded into each other. Over it all the sunlight played, adding the fitful shading of shadow. All day Mounts Nunburg[9] and Davis[10] were in sight on either side of the river, both huge black masses, and in the distance the flat top of a high table mountain pointed out the entrance to the famous Black canon, the site of Explorer's Rock,[11] now some feet under water, where Ives' steamer stopped. We tied up at night at an Indian rancheria, and were about forty miles above Hardy's. At night the river was closely watched, a fall of a foot might save us yet, and in the morning it seemed to have stood still; still the most vivid imagination could not figure out that it had fallen, the foam still swept by and once in a while you heard the rumble of a falling bit of bank. The river was master of the situation.

Next morning we got under way, passed one of Hardy's barges, met a current we could scarcely stem, got out a line, worked on till a strong wind compelled us to tie up for the rest of the day about eight miles below El Dorado. Capt. Robinson pronounced this the head of navigation for the *Cocopah* in flood time, but determined to wait one day and see if the rise might not slack so that we could get to El Dorado.

A party of us started on foot, and four hours hard walking, under a sun blazing up in the hundreds, brought us, myself at least, exhausted and used up,[12] to the brush houses[13] at the canon landing. The trail is one of the roughest I ever saw; it crosses a succession of low mountains or high hills, I hardly know which you would call

---

[9] Mount Nunburg was on the California side of the river.

[10] Mount Davis was named by explorer Ives in honor of the U.S. Secretary of War, Jefferson Davis. Later, as president of the Confederate states, Davis was to issue a proclamation on February 14, 1862, declaring Arizona a territory of the Confederacy. (Thomas E. Farish, *History of Arizona* 2: 96; Granger, *Arizona Place Names*, p. 207.)

[11] The rock was under water because of the spring flood. It was named after Ives' boat, the *Explorer*. (War Department Explorations and Surveys map no. 1, Rio Colorado of the West, 1858.) For the modern Black Canyon area see Department of the Interior Geological Survey map of Kingman, Arizona, Nevada, California.)

[12] It is likely that at this time Allyn was suffering from a recurrence of the pulmonary tuberculosis that had plagued his youth.

[13] The "brush houses" were probably those of the Mohave Indians described by Lorenzo Sitgreaves as ". . . rectangular, formed of upright posts imbedded in the ground, and rudely thatched on the top and three sides." *Report of an Expedition Down the Zuni and Colorado Rivers in 1851*, p. 18.

them, but I think if you walked over them you would be perfectly satisfied that they were mountains. The trail is faint and at many places almost dangerous. I learned afterward that it is not much used now, a longer and easier one being preferred; fortunately for me the torrid rays of the sun were tempered by a fresh, bracing mountain breeze, that swept over the mountain tops like the elixir of life. From the summits which the trail crossed, there was a magnificent view of the table mountain. It is one of the grandest piles of this home of desert grandeur; like a Titanic fortress it domineers over all its surroundings; it does not look like a mountain, but like some vast work of the gods, reared perhaps as an outlying post to guard the dark, stern mysteries of the yet unexplored canon, through which the Colorado winds for one hundred miles, where the sun never gleams on its ripples and no mortal eye has scanned the story of the earth's stratification, written on its thousands of feet of perpendicular wall; the vast treasure house, perhaps, of nature's laboratory, where the adventurous will find piled the diamonds[14] and precious stones that have baffled the avarice and the daring of the Hidalgoes.

For a mile or so, before reaching El Dorado, the trail creeps along the river bank, almost under the overhanging rock of the mountains, in some places the high water was actually over it, and one had to creep along narrow steps in the rock; a roaring torrent below and overarching rock overhead. If you never have realized what a luxury water, even muddy water is, just walk over these burnt hills two or three hours in the sun and come to the muddy Colorado, where you can easily reach it, and if you don't drink a gallon with as much gusto as you ever sipped champagne, you are more fastidious or less thirsty than the writer was.

At El Dorado canon there was lying the steamer *Esmeralda*, waiting the return of her captain from Salt Lake. There are two ten stamp-quartz mills, for one of which we had the pans, the other was in running order, and had been crushing rock. The mines are four or five miles off up the canon; there were no animals to be had,

---

[14]While diamond deposits have not been discovered in Arizona, "tiny black diamonds" were found in the cavities of a meteor in the vicinity of Canyon Diablo in 1891. (Frederic W. Galbraith & Daniel J. Brennan, *Minerals of Arizona*, p. 8.)

it was mid-day, I had to walk back, would anybody have footed it up to see those mines? I wouldn't for an interest in the Ophir.[15] Much work has been done in the way of development and there are fine indications of silver mines, but for some reason or other, there have always been obstacles, apparently unsurmountable, in the way of washing; the owners were many of them non-residents, and it is not unlikely something of the "freeze out"[16] has been going on. That word "freeze out" is a particularly refreshing one in this climate, and I sometimes have wished in a very hot day that I might be "froze out," just to experience the cooling sensation.

The officers of the *Esmeralda* hospitably asked us to dinner on board. I saw Lieut. Ives' book and glanced over the plates and text for the first time since I left the states. The *Esmeralda* had been further into Black canon than any steamboat, and her officers declared that they had never seen such walls as are engraved there. It was evident my trip into, or through, as I had fondly hoped, Black canon, was indefinitely postponed. To be sure it was only a few miles off, but a few miles here are sometimes as insurmountable as Niagara. All there was to be done was to look at the range of mountains and imagine the height of the walls. It evidently is twice as high as Mohave canon, perhaps more. Those who have been through it all speak of its deceptive character. You keep turning, whither you cannot see, and at last, round an apparently impenetrable rock wall, you in an instant emerge into daylight again and the canon is passed.

After dinner the mate of the *Esmeralda* offered his skiff to take us back; as it would take near two days hard work to get her up again, this was hospitality of the genuine sort. It only took an hour or so to fly back. At the six-miles rapid, we passengers got out, while the oarsmen shot the boat through the surf, and walked round. Just

---

[15] Allyn may be referring here to the Comstock Lode in Nevada, in which the Ophir mine was an early development, or possibly to the source of King Solomon's gold mentioned in Kings 9:28, Job 22:24 and elsewhere in the Old Testament. (See Young, *Western Mining,* pp. 238ff.)

[16] This is a humorous reference to the freeze-out tactics of the mining speculators. "Freeze-out" is a form of the game of poker in which all players start with equal capital. As each loses his stake, he must drop out of the game, thus leaving everything to the last remaining player. With reference to mining, the term refers to the tactics of big speculators who forced smaller stockholders to relinquish their holdings by imposing large assessments on mining shares held, or by other dubious methods. (*Oxford English Dictionary* 4: 528–29.)

about sundown we hauled along side of the *Cocopah*. Hardy's barge was moored just below us. A council of war of those interested determined that the pans, etc., for El Dorado were to be landed here and taken to their destination on the barge as soon as it was possible; the Mormon freight be taken back to Hardyville, where wagons could get for it, and a messenger started for Callville to inform them of the facts. Here was the end of a trip, a failure, like Bunker Hill, in not accomplishing all that was designed to be accomplished, but a noble success in the obstacles overcome, the patient perseverance shown, and the actual results obtained. With an old boat of not remarkable power, the flood of the Colorado has been stemmed *for the first time;* with a boat like the *Mohave* and a steam capstan, you could even go above Callville, I believe.

THE WONDERFUL "GREAT CANON" — STEAM BOATING DOWN THE COLORADO — SPLENDID SCENERY — INDIAN TROUBLES — THE FUTURE OF ARIZONA

La Paz, May 20th, 1865
[Published August 21, 1865]

One ought not to turn his face southward without saying some-thing about the Great Canon,[1] the sole remaining unexplored geo-graphical wonder of the world; the myth as it were around which clusters all the wild traditions and stories of the mountain men and the Indian. I have seen men who said they had been through it, and told how their hair stood on end as the mid-day darkness closed around them and the terrible roar of rushing waters, echoed and re-echoed in the dizzy heights of the *six thousand* feet of mountain wall that closed in the cavernous recesses of the mysterious gorge. I have seen Indians who talk of crossing it at this height on cotton-wood logs. You may believe them if you will, I can't. Lieut. Ives saw the great canon at the mouth of the Diamond creek,[2] or rather he saw a canon into which Diamond creek enters, and has given a geological sketch of the stratification of the walls there. I have seen persons recently who have followed Yampa creek,[3] a branch parallel to Diamond river, to a canon. At both these points the walls are

---

[1]The "Great Canon" was, of course, the Grand Canyon, which John Wesley Powell was yet to explore in the summer of 1869. It was also called "Big Canyon." (Will C. Barnes, *Arizona Place Names,* pp. 185–86.)

[2]Ives made this trip in the spring of 1858. After ascending the Colorado River, he traversed northern Arizona from the Mohave villages to Fort Defiance. (See Joseph C. Ives, *Colorado River of the West,* pp. 103–31.) Dia-mond Canyon and Creek are located at the extreme southward loop of the Colorado River which lies directly north of Peach Springs. Although the canyon walls of the Colorado are only about two thousand feet high here, it was the usual tourist viewpoint for the Grand Canyon before the Santa Fe railroad ran its branch line north from Williams in 1907. For an early print of the Canyon at Diamond Creek see Wallace W. Elliot, *History of Arizona Territory,* (frontispiece).

[3]"Yampa" creek is apparently Allyn's spelling for Yampai Creek, the name given by Lieutenant Lorenzo Sitgreaves to the canyon now known as Truxton Wash. In 1851, he found a party of Yavapai Indians camped there and the name "Yampai" was his own version of Yavapai. This creek runs

thousands of feet high, and so near perpendicular that the sky seems a thread overhead.

What is the great canon? It is the bursting through the great table land south of the Salt Lake basin of the waters imprisoned there for long centuries in a large lake.[4] Probably for two hundred miles the Colorado cuts this vast mesa with canon walls averaging from three to four thousand feet high. It may not be continuous canon — indeed it isn't, if by continuous one means unbroken walls — but if we use canon in the sense it is used elsewhere on the river, as the whole passage of a range of hills or mountains, then the great canon may be two hundred miles long. It has only been seen by following down the seams made in this vast table land by some of its tributaries. It cannot be followed on the bank, for these seams are impassable; it cannot be followed on account of the current, up the river. Other tributaries may yet be followed down to it, and more thorough knowledge obtained of the canon. It was the opinion of Dr. Newberry[5] of the Ives expedition, that there was a strong probability of finding diamonds here, and Gov. Gilpin of Colorado arrived at the same conclusion from geographical and geological deductions, without having been here.

On Friday, having landed our El Dorado freight on the bank, about noon, we turned our head towards the gulf and in two hours and a half were moored at Hardyville. Talk about sliding down hill, talk about racing horses, talk about locomotives, but if you want the most exciting and grandest sensation of all, sweep down the great Colorado of the West on a freshet like this. Twenty miles an hour on any river is fast enough to be remembered, but twenty miles an hour, with the most unique canon and mountain scenery unfolding on either hand like the unrolling of a great panorama, is one of

---

west of Diamond Canyon and empties into Red Dry Lake. (Lorenzo Sitgreaves, *Zuni and Colorado Rivers*, p. 15. See also Byrd H. Granger, *Arizona Place Names*, p. 225; Hubert H. Bancroft, *History of Arizona and New Mexico*, pp. 481–82.)

[4]Allyn is in error here. The Great Salt Lake basin is landlocked. High ranges cut it off from the Colorado drainage to the east.

[5]Dr. John Strong Newberry was the first geologist to investigate and describe with accuracy the Grand Canyon. He was a surgeon with the 1857–58 Ives expedition. (Ives, *Colorado River of the West*, pp. 100–101.) For an account of the great Arizona diamond swindle, which ensued in the seventies, see Bancroft, *Arizona and New Mexico*, pp. 591–92 and Rufus Kay Wyllys, *Arizona: The History of a Frontier State*, pp. 292–93.

the few experiences that the most blase travelers will never forget. Going up the river slowly the eye tires of watching the scenery, it seems so long between the gaps; but coming down, the variety is unceasing, and you watch the changes of color and shape with exquisite pleasure. Paradoxical as it may seem, you see more beauties and get a more vivid idea of the scenery going down than in coming up. You are wearied by excitement, and every nerve and sense is on the *qui vive* — nothing escapes you. Cottonwood and Round islands, Painted and Pyramid canon,[6] all seemed a gorgeous picture in that brief two hours; but in the four days spent going up, they are so many isolated facts, that, if you didn't keep a notebook you could scarcely tell which came first.

On Saturday we landed our Mormon freight opposite Hardy's and dropped down to Fort Mohave, where we lay an hour, and then got under way, and reached Williams Fork that night. The Mohave canon was glorious as we swept through. The Needles seen coming down are really needles, so slender and threadlike do the points arise. In the old turn of the canon where the eddy caught us going up, we caught it again, and for a few minutes the staid old *Cocopah* took a waltz with the Colorado of the West. In the grandest salon, the hand of Nature has fashioned for such unique dances, round we whirled, down we swept, rocks on the right, rocks on the left, not into the jaws of death, but into the stately swelling current of the straight river. Other mountains and smaller canons were passed, but looking at them now was like looking at the citizens on horseback, or the boys on foot that make up the tail end of a procession in the States; the great man or the crack corps had gone by.

At Williams Fork we found that the *Mohave* and barge had cleared off all the ore but fifty-five sacks which we took on board that night.

Next morning we reached La Paz before ten o'clock and walked into town,[7] only to learn the sad story that the Indians had actually cut us off from Prescott and the upper country, that several

---

[6] Pyramid Canyon, named by Ives in 1857, featured a natural pyramid about thirty feet high. It lay below Painted Canyon. These canyons, together with the islands mentioned, were submerged by manmade Lake Mohave. (Granger, *Arizona Place Names*, pp. 219–20.)

[7] La Paz was a short distance from its landing on the Colorado. By this time (May 1865) the placer gold boom was over. The landing was washed away in a river flood in 1870, which marked the end of the city's life. (Barnes, *Arizona Place Names*, p. 238; Nell Murbarger, *Ghosts of the Adobe Walls*, p. 22.)

most valued citizens and dear personal friends had been killed; that there was a small body of cavalry from Fort Whipple in town, and that an express on horseback had been sent to Fort Yuma to ask military assistance.[8] At the request of many citizens I at once agreed to accompany a committee down to Fort Yuma and make such arrangements as were possible for the protection of the upper country. Capt. R. worked while the brief arrangements were made, letters read, etc., and about four o'clock we were en route for Fort Yuma, and were nearly half way there when we tied up for the night.

Monday morning opened magnificently. The air was clear, the rich purple crimson of the coming day was spread like a mantle over the mountains. We are just above the canon or pass into the great Yuma valley; like a race horse the *Cocopah* started. A few miles opened a grand view of the Chimney Peak or Rock,[9] a grand isolated land mark that can be seen for a hundred miles on the desert. From above it seems some massive gothic tower to a huge hidden cathedral, its corners fretted with the armature of the sculptor's art.

This fancy of mine has sometimes caught someone else, for Capt. R. remarked that the bend near the rock was called Monastery bend. Nearer, this illusion vanished, and the rock seemed to me like two leaning towers, like that at Pisa, the fretted corners of the gothic now resembling the tracery of the collonades, one above the other, of the Pisa towers. Here we are at Light-House Rock,[10] the sturdy

---

[8] No record of this Indian uprising has been found in the *Arizona Miner.* Most issues of that paper for 1865 have been lost, and no such Indian raids are mentioned in those available. Dan L. Thrapp, an authority on Apache warfare, states that he has been unable to find material on this incident and believes that Allyn may have exaggerated. (Letter of December 6, 1971.) It is possible that Allyn's account is a rumored version of the engagement reported as follows in the *Returns from U.S. Military Posts 1800–1916,* Whipple Post, March 1865: "Scout against the Apache Indians on the 24th of March 1865 and Returned in the evening of the Same Day at 8 A.M. and Reported an Engagement with said Indians at the Point of Rocks and having two of his Men Wounded and one killed but killing 10 of the Indians and wounding several of them."

[9] "Chimney Peak" is Picacho Peak in California. It has an elevation of 1,947 feet and stands a little over four miles southwest of Picacho, Imperial County, California. (Department of the Interior Geological Survey map of California, southern half.)

[10] Lighthouse Rock was about ten miles above the present California town of Picacho. It was so named by Ives in 1857 because it marked the center of the river where channels divided to either side. River silting has since caused the river to flow entirely to the west of this pinnacle. (Granger, *Arizona Place Names,* p. 379.)

boulder that marshals the way into the passage. Just below here we passed the barge, with the Fork ore[11] in, and if the volume of profanity its master shouted at us as we swept by was any indication of the trouble he had had getting thus far safely in this fierce current, his position was not an enviable one. Below Light-House rock we came to Red Rock gate; most felicitously named. Two giant red rocks like pillars of Hercules, imprison the whole current of the river, as it were a gateway. Next, we are confronted by the Barriers, a line of rocks like huge stepping stones that stretch clear across the river, but the water is so high that we sweep through them in an instant. Chimney Peak disappears, hidden by the hills closer to the shore, and we begin watching for Castle Dome,[12] another landmark on the Arizona side of the river. It is some twenty miles away from the river, and is one of the peaks of the Castle Dome range that rises like a dome above the range; it, too, can be seen for miles across the desert and up the Gila. Soon it comes in view, and in a few minutes more we are passing Castle Dome city, which was to be the landing for the mines believed to be rich in silver and lead; none are now worked, and there seemed to be but one family living there now. Emerging from the canons we sweep by the Purple Hills of Ives and the little settlement at Laguna,[13] and are in the great valley of the Yumas. With a good glass the old flag can be seen gleaming in the morning sun at the post. At a little before 11 o'clock we were safely moored at the steamboat landing at Yuma, having made a tolerable trip from the *head* of high water navigation, twenty-two hours steaming in all!

The express had not arrived. Fortunately, we found General Mason,[14] the commanding officer of the district here, and he promptly acceded to our request for troops, ordering a company to embark

---

[11] The "Fork ore" was the copper from the Planet and other mines which the steamer *Mohave* had loaded at Williams Fork.

[12] Castle Dome peak is approximately 3,800 feet in elevation. Castle Dome City was later known as Castle Dome Landing. The post office was discontinued in 1884. (Granger, *Arizona Place Names*, p. 370.)

[13] Laguna was established in 1864 by gold placer miners. It is now the site of the dam of that name. (Granger, *Arizona Place Names*, p. 378.)

[14] General John S. Mason was sent by General McDowell of the military department of California to supress the Indian depredations in Arizona. His campaign did not get under way until November and was not very effective. He was relieved of his command the following spring. (Bancroft, *Arizona and New Mexico*, pp. 555–56.)

the next morning. Fort Yuma has changed since I arrived there last
February; all is haste and confusion, the new troops are passing,
steamboats are all busy, piles of freight line the banks, and the presence of General Mason, staff and escort, gives all a gay appearance.
My old host Commodore Johnson,[15] was down at the mouth of the
river, but his wife, a charming woman, did the honors of the house
with a grace and hospitality that made one feel at home. That afternoon the *Mohave* came up from below and was at once ordered to
prepare to transport troops to La Paz. Next morning she hauled
over to the fort side and by noon everything was on board — a company of veterans, two six mule teams, and rations for ninety days —
and off we started. The great power of the *Mohave's* engines began
to be manifest; she breasted the terrible current as easily and as
rapidly as though it were an ordinary stage of water. We camped that
night at Castle Dome. It was a lively and animated scene as the
soldiers began getting supper on the bank; the bivouac fires lit up
the tenantless houses of this embryo city, blessed that night with a
larger population than ever before.

Long before sunrise we were off. Today was the trying day;
Scylla and Carybdis[16] were ahead, the canon to be passed, the river
was still rising. With many misgivings I watched the boat as she
struck the narrowed channel and accelerated current; how much
depended on that machinery then; speed and strength now might
prevent the abandonment of the upper country. Bravo! the current
didn't seem any more to affect the speed of the Mohave, than mos-
quitoes or horseflies that once in a while came out from the bottom
to attack us. Never a fast boat, she seemed to go equally as fast no
matter what was ahead or underneath. Without once using a line,
a pole or a capstan we marched right through the canon; eddies had
no power to swerve us from our course; we passed the most famous
without a remonstrance from the subdued whirl of water; the terrors
all melted away before the power of that engine and the master hand
at the wheel; Red Rock gate, Third Point bend, the Barriers and
Light House rock, were all simply pleasant little points to indicate
progress by.

---

[15] For background on George A. Johnson, see Letter 22, note 2.
[16] "Scylla and Carybdis" refers to Red Rock Gate, previously described
by Allyn, behind Laguna Dam above Yuma.

That night we camped in the Colorado valley. Next day we reached La Paz at 10 o'clock in the morning. The current was running a mill race by Olive and Mineral cities[17] (two defunct towns below La Paz that I ought to have mentioned before when we went down, but forgot, as one often does those things which are every day present to him; these two abandoned cities are our Pompeii and Herculaneum), and for a minute or two it seemed as though the Mohave had met her master; but no, she was only gathering herself, then the waters parted, the trees on the bank began to move down the stream, and we are at La Paz. Thus ended two weeks on the Colorado. The time will come when upon the broad bosom of this Mississippi of the Pacific will float the wealth of giant states; when upon its mountain banks there will be teeming thousands engaged in extracting mineral wealth, and its broad bottoms shall wave with fields of cotton and sugar. It may be longer and it may be shorter, no one can predict the sudden change in the flow of capital and population on the Pacific.

There are vast difficulties in the way of utilizing the facilities of a country as rich as this, that only capital can overcome. I cannot believe that forever will the enterprise of the American people overlook a copper region vaster than almost any other known; a river with a delta enriched as never was the like, and a gulf that to the Pacific slope is what the Chesapeake is to the Atlantic.[18] Soldiers were keen enough to see that Fortress Monroe[19] was the key to the

---

[17] Charles B. Genung wrote in his 1863 diary: "We ferried across [the Colorado] that evening and landed at Olive City in Arizona. The city consisted of one house about 12x10x10 feet high, covered with brush and sided up with willow poles stuck in the ground...." (Thomas E. Farish, *History of Arizona* 4: 34.) Mineral City was so designated in March 1863, and it was surveyed in that year by Herman Ehrenberg. In 1867 an adjacent site was named Ehrenberg in memory of the surveyor, who had been murdered the previous year. (Farish, *History of Arizona* 3: 153–54; Granger, *Arizona Place Names*, p. 374.)

[18] Allyn's predictions on the future of Arizona copper mines were more than fulfilled. The Gulf of California obviously never became another Chesapeake Bay: among other factors, Mexican control of the river's mouth precluded this. In any case, upstream dams have made the lower Colorado River bed dry.

[19] "Fortress Monroe" is on the peninsula between the James River and Chesapeake Bay. It is a key defensive position, since it dominates the entrance to Hampton Roads Naval Base in Virginia. It was held throughout the Civil War by Union forces. (*Encyclopedia Americana* 2: 613; Allan Nevins, *The War for the Union,* 2: 41, 50.)

southern Atlantic states, but a strange fatuity blinds them to the fact that a similar situation in Lower California is the key to the vast mineral empire of the republic.

It remains yet to be determined how is the best way to water these vast rich bottoms. I do not believe that *acequias* will hold water without, at any rate, being lined with boards, and there is no lumber here; even if they would, the constant changes of the river and the fierce annual overflow, would make it very expensive to take care of them. My own judgment inclines to the practicability of irrigation by means of windmills and tanks; water is found anywhere in ten or twelve feet, and a single windmill will irrigate an acre certainly, and the cost is much less than that of an *acequia*.[20] A recent discovery of a secure harbor[21] at the mouth of the river removes the last difficulty in the way of direct trade with New York or Europe, exchanging our ores for their manufactures without the intervention of port charges at San Francisco, the profits of one transfer and three or four thousand miles of extra transportation. We are a thousand miles nearer New York than is San Francisco. All the copper ores now produced on the Pacific go to Boston for a market, and the tax of taking ours to San Francisco is one the intelligent miner or merchant will not endure longer than he is compelled to for want of capital to do otherwise.[22]

---

[20] Again, Allyn could not foresee the amazing development of these *acequias,* or irrigation canals, lined where necessary with concrete. The Wellton-Mohawk Canal in Yuma County is an example of such development in the area of which he speaks. Windmills and the modern submersible pump have indeed revolutionized Arizona agriculture — irrigated acreage increased from 2,000 in 1854 to 755,000 in 1947. However, falling water tables have resulted. (Stephen C. Shadegg, *Arizona: An Adventure in Irrigation,* pp. 4, 7; R. H. Forbes, *Irrigation and Agricultural Practice in Arizona.*)

[21] The harbor referred to by Allyn was named Puerto Isabel. It was actually a shipyard, formed by excavating a tidal slough on the Sonoran shore of the river's mouth. It provided warehouses for storage and supply and operated as a drydock for the repair of hulls. (Godfrey Sykes, *The Colorado Delta,* pp. 27, 30, 34.)

[22] When the Southern Pacific Railway bought out the Colorado Steam Navigation Company, the Puerto Isabel shipyard was demolished in 1878. (Sykes, *Colorado Delta,* pp. 27–28.) Thus ended Allyn's and other's dreams of the Gulf of California as Arizona's "Chesapeake Bay." As early as December 1865, Richard C. McCormick, the acting governor, had urged upon the territorial legislature the urgent need for acquiring Puerto Libertad on the gulf in the state of Sonora, with intervening land, for an Arizona seaport, but there were to be no more "Gadsden Purchases." (Jay J. Wagoner, *Arizona Territory 1863–1912,* p. 65.)

III. Epilogue

A PUBLIC LOSS

Joseph Pratt Allyn presided over the second district court of Arizona for the last time in April 1866. Despite the political disappointments he had recently suffered, his description of his departure from the territory preserves his characteristic enthusiasm: "The iron chain of circumstances that heretofore limited our wanderings westward to the waters of the great Colorado of the West, was at last broken, and, toward evening, on a genial sunshiny day of February, we were at the ferry waiting the tardy movements of the ferryman preparing to put us across the river — for yonder bank is California."[1] Allyn rode west from Yuma.

California Impressions

After the harshness of the desert crossing, Allyn was greatly impressed with the lush beauty of the almond orchards and vineyards and ploughed fields of the San Bernardino valley and spent two days at a ranch there, remarking that "it is worth a little privation to sharpen up ones faculty of perceiving the beautiful." Long starved for female companionship, he took note of the "charms of sundry young ladies composing the [rancher's] family, right pretty blonds, too."[2] In the town of San Bernardino, he observed the spacious grounds surrounding each of the old Mormon homes, "a plan especially desirable where one man was expected to live with a number of women."[3]

---

[1] *Hartford Evening Press,* May 25, 1866. The date of Allyn's departure is uncertain. He probably left around the middle of February on the "La Paz Express and Saddle Train," which made semimonthly trips between La Paz and Los Angeles via San Bernardino. (See advertisement in the *Arizona Miner,* November 23, 1864.) He arrived at the Bella Union in Los Angeles on March 22, 1866. (*Los Angeles Semi-Weekly News,* March 27, 1866.)

[2] *Hartford Evening Press,* June 1, 1866.

[3] *Hartford Evening Press,* June 8, 1866. Quotations and descriptions in the following paragraph are from this same source. San Bernardino, though originally founded under Spanish rule in 1810, was given its present city plan and was developed by Mormon settlers beginning in 1851. (Hubert H. Bancroft, *History of California,* 7: 520–21.)

Arriving in Los Angeles early in March, he was pleased with its setting amid orange groves and green hills and thought it "had charms for a residence that are rarely equaled." Marring this pastoral beauty, he found the community in the midst of oil fever with many wells in process of drilling. He saw springs "slimy with oil and bubbling with escaping gas."[4] He quickly sympathized with the native Californians dispossessed of their lands and herds by the occupying Americans. The legal requirements for proof of ownership of the ranchos were so unfamiliar and confusing to these old California families that many lost their fortunes before the onslaught of squatters and schemers. To the Arizona judge's mind, the court procedures were nothing short of legalized injustice.[5]

Allyn went on to San Francisco.[6] The first thing that struck him about the city on the Golden Gate was its cosmopolitanism. "Its vices and labor are oriental, its luxuries French, its religion liberal, its politics conservative; its commerce joins the orient and the occident; its board sidewalks remind you of Chicago, its hills with hanging houses suggest Milwaukee, its little houses with a garden about them look like New England; the rapid walk of a broker on Montgomery street is as fast as that of a New York bear."[7]

He was impressed by the city's fair inhabitants. "Take an equal number of women at random here, on Chestnut Street, or on Broadway, and it is my impression that any fair judge will concede the palm of beauty to the Occident."

Despite the attractiveness of San Francisco, Allyn observed that almost all who came there arrived with the idea of returning home rather than remaining. "Men come out here to make fortunes, leaving families behind them, and stay away for years in the pursuit . . . until they are too proud to return and acknowledge that

---

[4] The modern petroleum industry had only just begun with the drilling of a producing oil well at Titusville, Pennsylvania, in 1859. Although known from early times, the oil deposits in Los Angeles were first worked in 1865. (Bancroft, *California* 7: 661.)

[5] For the background of these disputes see Bancroft, *California* 6: 328–35.)

[6] Allyn gives no hint in his March 15 letter, datelined San Francisco, as to how he reached the city. It would seem, however, that he traveled from Los Angeles by steamship, since in a later trip from Los Angeles by stage, which he describes in detail in a July letter, he gives the impression of seeing Santa Barbara and San Jose for the first time.

[7] *Hartford Evening Press*, July 27, 1866. Quotations and descriptions in the following two paragraphs are from the same source.

they have failed and are still poor. May be they make money, but are harnessed to it and cannot go home, so send for their absent wives, only to wake to terrible disappointment, as some pallid woman, grown old, that they would scarcely recognize, comes off the steamer, instead of the young and lovely person whose image they had been worshiping these long weary years, forgetting that we all grow old."

Judge Allyn took the river steamer to Sacramento to observe legislative politics in action. He watched a protracted debate over the raising of rail fares in San Francisco and was surprised that although all the debaters agreed that fares should not be raised, when the vote came they were raised from five to six cents. A day or so later the same issue was raised again, with precisely the same arguments, and the same body voted not to raise fares.[8]

It puzzled the Connecticut visitor that gunplay was so frequent in the public life of such a "civilized" state. "Strange commentary," he wrote, "on the new life of the Pacific, that those whom men honor most dead should have all died by the bullet.[9] There is James King of William,[10] the journalist, whose death was the birth of the vigilance committee; Broderick,[11] the New York rough, who grew to fill (not unworthily) the Senatorial toga, and had tried to oppose the committee in the interest of organized law, who died by the hand of the then Chief Justice of the Supreme Court in a duel; and lastly

---

[8] *Hartford Evening Press,* August 3, 1866.

[9] *Hartford Evening Press,* June 22, 1866.

[10] James King of William was the editor of the San Francisco *Daily Evening Bulletin.* He was a fearless reformer, and when he exposed the criminal record of an influential politician, James Casey, he was murdered by the latter on May 14, 1856. Aroused citizens met the following day to form a new vigilance committee of eight thousand armed men. Casey was forcibly removed from jail, tried "with all fairness," and condemned to death. On May 22, while James King of William's body was being solemnly paraded to the cemetery in a procession two miles long, Casey was executed. (Bancroft, *California* 6: 746–54; Ralph J. Roske, *Everyman's Eden: A History of California,* pp. 286–88.)

[11] David Colbert Broderick (1820–58) came to California "penniless and sick" in 1849. A Democrat, though not a supporter of slavery, he became head of the majority faction of the party and won the 1857 contest for U.S. senator. Two years later, over a fancied insult, Broderick was challenged to a duel by Judge D. S. Terry, whom Broderick had defended against the vigilantes two years earlier. Terry resigned from the supreme bench to duel with Broderick, whom he coolly shot through the chest when the senator's pistol discharged prematurely. (Bancroft, *California* 7: 659, 661, 731–33; John Walton Caughey, *California,* pp. 282–83.)

Ned Baker,[12] as Californians delight to call him, senator, soldier, and orator."

Allyn was later to become keenly aware of the hold that monopoly capital had on California life. He was appalled at the same time that he could not help admiring the cool and ruthless sophistication of the banking and railroad cliques. "California is a monopoly ridden state; the telegraph is a monopoly; the news is a monopoly; the express is a monopoly; the teaming is a monopoly; the California Steam Navigation Company is a monopoly; the stage lines are monopolies; banking, no, there isn't any — money lending is a monopoly."[13] He was critical of the founder-to-be of Stanford University and his control of the Pacific Railroad. "The truth is Mr. Leland Stanford and Associates have the biggest thing in the United States, and unless there is some reserved right in the federal government to secure the people the mineral regions . . . and if they [Stanford, etc.] live twenty-five years, their fortunes will be grander than those of your Eastern money princes."[14]

An End to the Travels

The young judge was now determined to go home. But before undertaking his journey to Connecticut, Allyn made a brief excursion by stage to Yosemite and one by steamer to Portland, Oregon.

---

[12]Colonel Ned (Edward D.) Baker was actually a senator from Oregon but always considered himself a Californian. He was a close friend of Lincoln and, when the Civil War broke out, gave up his U.S. Senate seat to serve in the army. The transcontinental telegraph line was completed shortly thereafter, and the first through telegram to California announced Baker's death on the battlefield at Ball's Bluff in October 1861. (Bancroft, *California* 7: 292–93; Caughey, *California,* p. 287.)

[13]*Hartford Evening Press,* July 11, 1866.

[14]*Hartford Evening* Press, November 2, 1866. Leland Stanford (1824–93) came to California in 1852 and was elected Republican governor of the state in 1861. He was a founder and president of the Central Pacific Railroad and later U.S. senator from California from 1885 to 1893. His association with such financial geniuses as C. P. Huntington, Mark Hopkins, and Charles Crocker was to be an extremely profitable one. Stanford had previously acquired familiarity with railroad construction while working for his contractor father. This practical background combined with legal experience in the Wisconsin courts gave him distinct advantages in the struggle for control of railroad and other enterprises in the burgeoning California economy. In memory of his son, Leland Stanford, Jr., he founded Stanford University in 1885 with an enormous endowment. (Bancroft, *California* 7: 544–81; Caughey, *California,* pp. 367–71.)

After his return from Oregon in September, Allyn again took the river steamer from San Francisco to Sacramento to begin his arduous trip to Hartford via Salt Lake City.[15]

The boat was crowded with passengers going to the California state fair, a spectacular occasion even in that early day. Arriving at the state capital, he could not resist the temptation to stay overnight and take in the parades and horse races and the displays in the gay pavilions. He was astounded at the arrays of California fruits and vegetables. "Such cabbages, why you have to cut them up to get them into the house; one will last a whole winter. . . . Then such fruit. . . . The capabilities of California horticulture are exhaustless. When the climate comes to be thoroughly understood and the choicest varieties of the world's productions are domesticated and acclimated, this will be the fruit paradise of the world."[16]

He took the new Central Pacific Railroad from Sacramento to a station named Alta, which was at that time the end of the line eastward. The train of three crowded passenger coaches traversed a total of seventy miles to its terminus high in the Sierras, and from there a six-horse stage completed the trip to Virginia City, Nevada.[17] Along the route Allyn observed the labor gangs working on the roadbed at a rate calculated to reach Salt Lake City in fifteen years. "Chinamen were literally swarming over the granite where it begins; but when we passed they had not yet made enough of an impression upon the face of the rock for one to have suspected it was a tunnel that they were at work on; and I was told its estimated length was to be 1700 feet.[18]

---

[15] Two letters describing Allyn's side trips appeared in the *Hartford Evening Press.* "A Trip to the Yosemite" was written in August 1866, published October 5; "A Trip to Oregon," was written in September, published October 12. Allyn's letters describing his journey home, all written in Salt Lake City between September 24 and 30, are as follows: "From Sacramento to Salt Lake, November 2; "San Francisco to Salt Lake — the Stage Ride Continued," October 19; "Crossing the Sierras — Tragedy at Donner Lake," November 9; "Sacramento to Salt Lake — Common Sense View of Mining — Austin: A Humbug City."

[16] *Hartford Evening Press,* October 26, 1866.

[17] *Hartford Evening Press,* November 2, 1866.

[18] Ibid. Allyn's estimate of fifteen years was based on the rate of construction at that time. He was aware that easier terrain east of the Sierras would accelerate the laying of track. The Central Pacific actually reached the Union Pacific line at Promontory Point northwest of Ogden on May 10, 1869. (John M. Blum, et al., *The National Experience: A History of the United States,* p. 358.)

Judge Allyn reached Virginia City at a time when the silver fever over the discovery and development of the Comstock lode seemed to have run its course, and the early speculative bubble involving that "second city of the Pacific Coast" had burst.[19] With his Arizona experience and perspective on mining enterprise, he risked comment on the fate of the Comstock. "The army of speculators is gone, the day of wild and feverish gambling in feet is over, the mammoth fortunes of a few years ago have dissipated into thin air, the American has come to learn by sad experience something of silver mining."[20] He entered and inspected the great Gould and Curry Mine and marveled at the amazing system of drains, pumps, hoisting machinery, and other mechanisms that enabled the work of extraction to proceed so efficiently.[21]

After a brief stay, he resumed his coach journey across Nevada, making the twenty-four-hour journey across the Humboldt Basin to Austin, a flourishing mining town on the Reese River. But Allyn called Austin a "Humbug City," for much of its activity and "prosperity" were due to the sale of mining locations of dubious value to Eastern suckers. He described the boom town thusly: "Austin has one straggling business street with banks, brick stores, bar-rooms, gambling hells, restaurants, etc. . . . The rest of Austin is dropped along the side of the hill, mixed up with the mouths of tunnels and piles of debris. I . . . saw some very pretty and distingué looking women. Eastern investments have, I think, secured to Austin some nice Eastern society, but unfortunately I did not penetrate its mysteries or enjoy its pleasures."[22]

After a day or so of rest in the mining town, Allyn was fortunate in the offer of a ride to Salt Lake City in a through stagecoach which had been reserved by two telegraph company officials. Relieved of the necessity of frequent stops, waits, and change of coaches, he saved two days on the long, monotonous run through the Ruby valley to the capital of the Mormons. Even so, the trip required some three days of exhausting travel, on the last of which

---

[19] *Hartford Evening Press,* October 19, 1866. Allyn could hardly have guessed that the great discoveries and boom of the 1870s lay just ahead for Virginia City. (See Otis E. Young, *Western Mining,* p. 244ff.)

[20] Ibid. Allyn's reference to "gambling in feet" refers to the practice of selling stock in silver lode veins by the foot.

[21] Ibid.

[22] *Hartford Evening Press,* November 9, 1866.

the party encountered fierce winds, pelting rain, mud, and snow. From the shore of Salt Lake, Allyn caught his first glimpse of the City of the Saints. "It was a pretty sight to look at — those squares of shrubbery sloping up the hill-side as one, chilled and tired, rolled into the churchless city."[23]

Those last words, "chilled and tired," written in his final letter to the *Hartford Evening Press,* were an ominous premonition. The tuberculosis which had plagued his youth and which arrested or "cured" during his Arizona residence had now become reactivated. Had he been able to return home in twentieth-century comfort and speed, he would doubtless have been able to continue an active and promising judicial, political, or journalistic career. But his exhausting journeys in California and Nevada by dust-filled coach and exposed horseback, his spare physique driven to continuous activity by a restless and ever-inquiring mind, were too much for him. And one has no way of estimating the toll of the tension, frustration, and disappointment he had suffered from prolonged heckling by his rivals in the territory. Seriously ill, he yet had to make his way across the remainder of the continent.[24] By coach and train and steamer he returned to Saint Louis and from thence proceeded to his Hartford home, where he was confined for some months of recovery.[25] It was from here that he wrote his letter to President Andrew Johnson resigning his judgeship in Arizona, just four days after his thirty-fourth birthday.[26]

By July 1867 Allyn was sufficiently improved to take passage for Europe in hopes of making, as in his youth, recovery from his affliction.[27] He spent the following winter in Spain, managing, despite his illness, to travel extensively in that warmer clime. He con-

---

[23] Ibid.

[24] *Connecticut Courant,* May 29, 1869. The *Arizona Miner* of November 30, 1866, reported Allyn's arrival in Salt Lake City but did not mention his illness.

[25] Allyn reached home in November. On January 21, 1867, he reported to Attorney General Henry Stanbury and requested an extension of his four-month leave to six months. (Attorneys General Papers, Arizona, 1863–70, Record Group 60, National Archives; Sacks Collection.)

[26] Allyn to Johnson, March 13, 1867. Copy in Connecticut State Library. Allyn's four-year term had actually expired on March 11, 1867. (Sacks Collection.)

[27] *Connecticut Courant,* May 29, 1869. The account of Allyn's last illness which follows is taken from the death notice in this same issue of the paper.

tinued to reside in various Mediterranean countries, including Syria, Algeria, and Egypt. He passed the winter of 1868–69 in Algeria and suffered so from inclement weather there that he went to Cairo for relief in the early spring. Although he experienced a temporary improvement on the Nile, his health soon took a turn for the worse, and his condition became desperate.

In late April he left Egypt, unattended and dying, on his last journey to Paris. He had but one wish now: to be able to cross the Atlantic and reach his home and family. Arriving in the French capital, he was cared for by his physician and, once again by sheer will, seemed to regain strength. He booked passage to America for June 1 on the steamer *Ville de Paris* and cabled his family that he was returning with his old friend and editor, Charles Dudley Warner. But the dreaded hemorrhages were now taking their toll, and it was necessary for the physician to cable again that Allyn could absolutely not leave Paris. His youngest brother sailed for France on May 12 in hopes of reaching the hospital in time. He seems to have arrived just before Joseph died on May 24. The funeral services were held at his father's residence, and he was buried in Hartford's Spring Grove Cemetery "in the presence of his family and many old friends, among them Mr. Secretary [of the Navy] Welles and his family who entertain a warm friendship for Mr. Allyn. . . ."[28]

And what was the reaction in Arizona to the passing of their pioneer judge? After he had left the territory, a vindictive piece had appeared in the *Miner*. It read: "We learn that the report that Judge Allyn has gone to Idaho is incorrect, and that he has gone home to Connecticut. As his term of office expires in March next, we presume we shall not see his lily white hands in Arizona any more."[29] But after word of his death was received, the same paper

[28] *Connecticut Courant,* June 26, 1869. Allyn's will, as reported in this same issue, included gifts of five thousand dollars each to the local orphan asylum, the Hartford Hospital, the Hartford Charitable Society, and the Young Men's Institute. Another five thousand dollars was bequeathed to a fund for the placing of a statue of General Putnam in Bushnell Park. Gideon Welles and William Faxon were each to receive twenty-five hundred dollars "out of regard for their personal friendship." His three surviving brothers received the balance of the estate.

[29] *Arizona Miner,* October 16, 1866. The phrase "lily white hands" is doubtless a sarcastic reference to Allyn's refusal to join the "stampede for gold and graft," and his highly critical attitude toward politicians and "secessionists."

tried to make amends. It carried a story from one of its correspondents which said in part, "Judge Allyn was not without his faults, but he was a genuine, true man."[30] Later the *Miner* printed the text of a resolution offered by the U.S. district attorney and adopted by the members of the bar of Allyn's second judicial district court: "Resolved, that in the death of the Hon. Jos. P. Allyn, we mourn the loss of a brother whose upright, impartial, courteous and dignified bearing on the bench challenged the respect and won the esteem of this bar. . . ."[31] It was decreed that members wear mourning for a period of thirty days.

Whatever the opinions of his friends and enemies in Arizona, there is no doubt of the loyalty and affection of those who knew him in Hartford. To many he was something of a stranger, having spent so much of his life in travel and residence elsewhere; but some had followed his career since his youth. Of these, his closest friend was doubtless his editor, Charles Dudley Warner. At the time of Allyn's death at the age of thirty-six, Warner wrote the following words:[32]

He died on the evening of Monday, May 24th, giving up his breath quietly and without any struggle, and even unexpectedly to those about him. But the fact was, the machinery was all worn out, and stopped of its own accord; the unconquerable will having no longer any material left to work on. . . .

If we dwelt upon what he had really accomplished, by his innate force of character, and in the disheartening company of disease that has clung to him for all the days of his manhood, and upon his capabilities for very considerable achievements if health had been given him, we should easily extend this notice into an eulogy. He was, by the constitution of his mind, never idle. Always an omnivorous devourer of books, he yet knew persons and things quite as well. His memory was something remarkable; it retained everything with the clearness of a photograph. He could recall and command for constant use all that he had read, casual conversations years before, impressions of places and people, details about ten thousand things that people usually forget in a month. Even disease did not dull his keen intellectual activity. He was an excellent observer, and his reports of his travels were always rich with suggestions and comparisons. He had a logical mind of extraordinary clearness, as well as fertility, and he was

---

[30] *Arizona Miner*, July 10, 1869. His death notice appeared in the *Miner* for June 12, 1869.

[31] *Arizona Miner*, October 30, 1869.

[32] *Connecticut Courant*, June 26, 1869. The last paragraph of the following is taken from an earlier sketch of Allyn by Warner which appeared in the *Courant* on May 29, 1869.

especially attracted towards the philosophy of politics and political economy. . . . He had never any reserve about expressing his opinions or avowing his sentiments, and seemed desirous to know and to say the plain truth — whether it should be welcome or not. . . .

He corresponded regularly with the *Evening Press* of this city, and his able and interesting letters over the signature of "Putnam," attracted much attention, and will be remembered by the readers of that paper. He had rare descriptive powers, and his Arizona letters especially were exceedingly interesting and instructive. He had talents which fitted him for great usefulness and his death in the prime of life is-a public as well as a private loss.

Supplementary Information

References

Major Depositories and Libraries

Arizona Historical Foundation, Arizona State University, Tempe
Arizona Historical Society, Tucson
Arizona State Department of Library and Archives, Phoenix
Arizona State Museum, Archaelogical Survey, University of Arizona, Tucson
Bancroft Library, University of California, Berkeley
California Historical Society, San Francisco
Connecticut Historical Society, Hartford
Connecticut State Library, Hartford
Library of Congress, Washington, D.C.
National Archives, Washington, D.C.
New York Public Library
Northern Arizona University, Special Collections, Flagstaff
Sharlot Hall Museum, Prescott
University of Arizona Library, Special Collections, Tucson

Federal and State Records

Published Materials

Arizona Statewide Archival and Records Project. *Arizona State District Courts of the Territory of Arizona 1864–1912.* Phoenix: Historical Records Survey Program, 1941.

———. *Inventory of the County Archives of Arizona.* 3 vols. Phoenix: Historical Records Survey Program, 1937.

Arizona Territory. *Acts, Resolutions and Memorials, First Legislative Assembly.* Prescott: Office of Arizona Miner, 1864.

———. *Acts, Resolutions and Memorials, Second Legislative Assembly.* Prescott: Office of Arizona Miner, 1865.

———. *The Compiled Laws of the Territory of Arizona, Including the Howell Code and the Session Laws from 1864–1871.* Coles Bashford, compiler. Albany, N. Y.: Weed, Parsons and Company, Printers, 1871.

Arizona Territory. *The 1864 Census of the Territory of Arizona.* Records
Survey Division of Professional Projects, Works Projects Administra-
tion. Phoenix, 1938. Mimeographed.
————. *The Howell Code.* Adopted by the First Legislative Assembly of
the Territory of Arizona. Prescott: Office of Arizona Miner, 1866.
————. *Journals of the First Legislative Assembly, 1864.* Prescott: Office
of Arizona Miner, 1864.
————. *Journals of the Second Legislative Assembly, 1865.* Prescott:
Office of Arizona Miner, 1866.
————. *Reports of Cases Argued and Determined in the Supreme Court
of the Territory of Arizona, from January Term, 1866 to January
Term, 1884, Inclusive.* F. P. Dann, reporter. San Francisco: A. L.
Bancroft and Company, 1884.
Tutorow, Norman E., ed. *Preliminary Inventory of the Records of the
Arizona Territorial Court in Los Angeles, Federal Records Center.*
Los Angeles: Federal Records Center, 1970.
United States Department of Interior. *Annual Report.* Washington, D. C.:
U.S. Government Printing Office, 1867.
United States District Court. Arizona Third Judicial District. *Docket No.
22.* Prescott: Office of Arizona Miner, 1864.
United States Senate. *Executive Journal, 1862–1863.* Vol. 13. Washing-
ton, D. C.: U.S. Government Printing Office, 1863.
————. *Federal Census: Territory of New Mexico and Territory of
Arizona.* 89th Congress, 1st Session, 1865. Senate Document No. 13.
United States War Records Office. *War of the Rebellion: Compilation of
Official Records of the Union and Confederate Armies.* 130 vols.
Washington, D. C.: U.S. Government Printing Office, 1880–1901.

Unpublished Materials

"Attorneys General Papers, Arizona, 1863–70." General Records of the
Department of Justice. Record Group 60. National Archives, Wash-
ington, D. C.
"Mortgages." Book 2, December 8, 1874–September 6, 1878. Microfilm
in Pima County Recorder's Office, Tucson, Arizona.
"Old Minute Book of the District Court of the Second Judicial District,
June 28th, 1864, to October 28, 1872." 2 vols. Original in Yuma
County Courthouse, Yuma, Arizona. Copy in Arizona State Library,
Phoenix.
"Returns from U.S. Military Posts 1800–1916." Microfilm in National
Archives, Washington, D. C.:
        Leavenworth, September 1863. Film 1652, Reel #611.
        Fort Union, November 1863. Film 1652, Reel #1305.
        Fort Whipple, January 1864. Film 1652, Reel #1425.
        Tubac, Arizona, December 1864. Film 617, Reel #1297.
"Supreme Court Calendar, Territory of Arizona, 1866–1884, Yavapai
County." Original in Arizona State Library, Phoenix.

Maps

Arizona State Museum Archaeological Survey. Ni-12-4. Site nos. 0:5:11;
0:5:13; 0:5:14; U:6:9; U:6:10. Arizona State Museum, Tucson.
Gird, Richard. Official Map of the Territory Arizona, Oct. 23, 1864.
San Francisco: A. Gensoul, 1864.
Riecker, Paul. Map of Arizona Territory. San Francisco: A. L. Bancroft,
1881. On file in Arizona Historical Society, Tucson.
United States Department of the Interior Geological Survey. California,
Southern Half. Base map, 1970.
————. Congress Quadrangle, Yavapai County, Arizona. N:9, 1948.
————. Fort McDowell Quadrangle, Maricopa County, Arizona.
U:6, 1946.
————. Kingman, Arizona, Nevada, California. Base map, Ni-11-3,
1969.
————. Overton Quadrangle, Clark County, Nevada. 15 series, 1958.
————. Prescott, Arizona. Ni-12-4, 1962.
————. Salton Sea, California, Arizona. Base map, Ni-11-9, 1968.

Newspapers

Alta California (San Francisco), May 7, 1859; June 11, 1859; October
14, 1863; January 1864.
Arizona Daily Star, December 19, 1862.
Arizona Miner (Prescott), March 1864–July 1869.
Arizona Republic (Phoenix), June 30, 1870.
Connecticut Courant (Hartford), May–June 1869.
Hartford Evening Post, September 1, 1863.
Hartford Evening Press, September 1863–November 1866.
Los Angeles Semi-Weekly News, March 27, 1866.
San Francisco Bulletin, March 1864.
Santa Fe Weekly New Mexican, December 29, 1863.
Weekly Arizonian (Tucson), September 1863–February 1866.
Weekly Gazette (Santa Fe), June 1864.

Books, Articles, and Pamphlets

Acuña, Rudolph F. "Ignacio Pesqueira: Sonoran Caudillo." *Arizona and
the West* 12 (Summer 1970): 139–72.
Allyn, Joseph Pratt. *Address: The Fourth of July 1864 at La Paz, Arizona.*
San Francisco: Towne & Bacon, Book and Job Printers, 1864.
————. *Charge of the Hon. Joseph P. Allyn, Associate Justice of the U.S.
Court, to the U.S. and Territorial Grand Juries, September Term,
A.D. 1864 of the District Court of the Third Judicial District of
Arizona.* Prescott: Office of Arizona Miner, 1864.

Almada, Francisco R. *Diccionario de Historia, Geografía y Bibliografía Sonorenses.* Chihuahua, Chih., Mexico: Imp., Ruiz Sandoval, 1952.

Alsberg, Henry G. *The American Guide: A Source Book and Complete Travel Guide for the United States.* New York: Hastings, 1949.

Altshuler, Constance Wynn, ed. *Latest from Arizona! The Hesperian Letters, 1859–1861.* Tucson: Arizona Historical Society, 1969.

Anthony, H. E. *Field Book of North American Mammals.* New York: G. P. Putnam's Sons, 1928.

Arizona Works Progress Administration Writers' Project. *Arizona: A State Guide.* New York: Hastings, 1941.

Arrington, Leonard J. "Inland to Zion: Mormon Trade on the Colorado River, 1864–1867." *Arizona and the West* 7 (Autumn 1966): 239–50.

Avillo, Philip J., Jr. "Fort Mohave: Outpost on the Upper Colorado." *Journal of Arizona History* 11 (Summer 1970): 77–100.

Bailey, Lynn R. *Bosque Redondo: An American Concentration Camp.* Pasadena: Socio-Technical Books, 1970.

Bancroft, Hubert Howe. *History of Arizona and New Mexico 1530–1888.* San Francisco: The History Company, 1889.

―――. *History of California* 6 (1848–59); 7 (1860–90). San Francisco: The History Company, 1890.

―――. History of the North Mexican States and Texas 2 (1801–89). San Francisco: Bancroft, 1889.

Barnes, Will C. *Arizona Place Names.* Tucson: University of Arizona, 1935.

Barney, James A. "Col. King S. Woolsey, Famous Arizona Pioneer." *The Sheriff* 6 (December 1947) & 7 (September 1948).

―――. "Henry Wickenburg — Discoverer of the Vulture Mine." *The Sheriff* 13 (June 1954): 26.

―――. "Riverman of the Colorado." *The Sheriff* 14 (December 1955): 33.

Beale, Edward Fitzgerald. *Wagon Road from Fort Defiance to the Colorado River.* House Executive Document 124, 35th Congress, 1st Session. Washington, D. C.: U.S. Government Printing Office, 1858.

Beebe, Lucius and Charles Clegg. *Virginia and Truckee: A Story of Virginia City and Comstock Times.* Oakland: G. H. Hardy, 1949.

Benson, Lyman. *The Cacti of Arizona.* Tucson: University of Arizona Press, 1950.

Berthrong, Donald J. and Odessa Davenport, eds. *Joseph Reddeford Walker and the Arizona Adventure.* Norman: University of Oklahoma Press, 1956.

Bining, Arthur Cecil and Thomas C. Cochran. *The Rise of American Economic Life.* New York: Charles Scribner's Sons, 1964.

Blum, John M. with Edmund S. Morgan, Willie Lee Rose, Arthur M. Schlesinger, Jr., Kenneth M. Stampp, and Vann C. Woodward. *The National Experience: A History of the United States.* New York: Harcourt Brace Jovanovich, Inc., 1973.

Brandes, Ray. "A Guide to the History of the U.S. Army Installations in Arizona, 1849–1886." *Arizona and the West* I (Spring 1959): 42–65.

———. *Frontier Military Posts of Arizona*. Globe, Arizona: Dale Stuart King, 1960.

Brinckerhoff, Sidney B., ed. Introduction to Richard Cunningham McCormick's *Arizona: Its Resources and Prospects: A Letter to the Editor of the New York Tribune*. Tucson: Arizona Historical Society, 1968.

———. "The Last of Spanish Arizona 1786–1821." *Arizona and the West* 9 (Spring 1967): 5–20.

Brooks, Van Wyck. *The World of Washington Irving*. New York: E. P. Dutton and Co., Inc., 1944.

Browne, John Ross. *A Tour Through Arizona, 1864, or Adventures in the Apache Country*. Tucson: Arizona Silhouettes, 1950.

Carrol, John A., ed. *Pioneering in Arizona; the Reminiscences of Emerson Oliver Stratton and Edith Stratton Kitt*. Tucson: Arizona Historical Society, 1964.

Catton, Bruce. *Never Call Retreat*. New York: Doubleday & Co., 1965.

Caughey, John Walton. *California*. Englewood Cliffs, N. J.: Prentice-Hall, 1964.

Chapman, Hank and Toni. "Midas of New Mexico: the Lucien Bonaparte Maxwell Story." *The American West* 8 (January 1971): 4–9, 62–63.

Colton, Ray C. *The Civil War in the Western Territories, Arizona, Colorado, New Mexico and Utah*. Norman: University of Oklahoma Press, 1959.

Conkling, Roscoe & Margaret B. *The Butterfield Overland Mail, 1857–1869*. 3 vols. Glendale, Calif.: Arthur H. Clark & Co., 1947.

Conrad, David B. "The Whipple Expedition in Arizona 1853–1854." *Arizona and the West* 11 (Summer 1969): 147–78.

Coolidge, E. D. *The Descendants of John and Mary Coolidge of Watertown, Massachusetts*. Boston: Wright & Potter Printing Co., 1930.

Dictionary of American Biography. 22 vols. New York: Charles Scribner's Sons, 1928–58.

Dodge, Natt N. *Poisonous Dwellers of the Desert*. Santa Fe, N. M.: Southwestern Monuments Association, 1953.

Donohue, Augustine J., S. J. "The Unlucky Jesuit Mission of Bac." *Arizona and the West* 2 (Summer 1960): 127–39.

Duffen, William A., ed. "Overland via 'Jackass Mail' in 1858: The Diary of Phocion R. Way." *Arizona and the West* 2 (Autumn 1960): 279–92; (Winter 1960): 353–70.

Dyer, Frederick H. *A Compendium of the War of the Rebellion*. 3 vols. New York: T. Yoseloff, 1959.

Easton, Robert. "Guns of the American West" *in* Jay Monaghan, ed. *The Book of the American West*, pp. 379–426. New York: Messner, 1963.

Elliot, Wallace W., comp. *History of Arizona Territory, Showing Its Resources and Advantages*. San Francisco: Wallace W. Elliott & Co., 1884. Reprint, Flagstaff, Arizona: Northland Press, 1964.

Encyclopedia Americana. 30 vols. International Edition. New York: Americana Corporation, 1972.

Encyclopedia Britannica. 11th ed. 29 vols. Cambridge, England & New York: Cambridge University Press, 1910–11.

Ezell, Paul H. *The Maricopas: An Identification from Documentary Sources*. Anthropological Papers of the University of Arizona, no. 6, Tucson: University of Arizona Press, 1963.

Farish, Thomas E. *A History of Arizona*. 8 vols. Phoenix: Filmer Brothers Electrotype Co., 1915.

Faulk, Odie B. "The Steamboat War that Opened Arizona." *Arizoniana* 5 (Winter 1964): 1–9.

———, ed. *John Baptiste Salpointe, Soldier of the Cross*. Tucson: Diocese of Tucson, 1966.

Favour, Alpheus B. *Old Bill Williams, Mountain Man*. Norman, Okla.: University of Oklahoma Press, 1962.

Favour, Eva. "Journey of Arizona's Territorial Party" *in* Robert C. Stevens, ed., *Echoes of the Past: Tales of Old Yavapai* 2: 41–60. Prescott, Ariz.: The Yavapai Cowbelles, Inc., 1964.

Finch, Boyd. "Sherod·Hunter and the Confederates in Arizona." *Journal of Arizona History* 10 (Autumn 1969): 137–206.

Fireman, Bert M. "What Comprises Treason? Testimony of Proceedings Against Sylvester Mowry." *Arizoniana* 1 (Winter 1960): 5–10.

Fontana, Bernard L. "Biography of a Desert Church: The Story of Mission San Xavier del Bac." *Smoke Signal* 3 (Spring 1961): 1–24.

———. "The Mowry Mine: 1858–1958." *Kiva* 23 (February 1958): 14–16.

Forbes, R. H. *Irrigation and Agricultural Practice in Arizona*. University of Arizona Agricultural Experimental Station Bulletin 63. June 30, 1911.

———. *The Penningtons: Pioneers of Early Arizona, A Historical Sketch*. Tucson: Arizona Archaeological and Historical Society, 1919.

Foreman, Grant. *A Pathfinder in the Southwest: The Itinerary of Lieutenant A. W. Whipple During His Explorations for a Railway Route from Fort Smith to Los Angeles in the Years 1853 and 1854*. Norman: University of Oklahoma Press, 1941.

Galbraith, Frederic W. and Daniel J. Brennan. *Minerals of Arizona*. Tucson: University of Arizona Press, 1959.

Gilluly, James, A. C. Waters, & A. O. Woodford. *Principles of Geology*. 2nd ed. San Francisco: W. H. Freeman, 1959.

Gladwin, Harold Sterling. *A History of the Ancient Southwest*. Portland, Maine: Bond Wheelwright Co., 1957.

Goff, John S. "The Appointment, Tenure and Removal of Territorial Judges: Arizona — A Case Study." *American Journal of Legal History* 12 (1968): 211–31.

––––––. "The Civil War Confiscation Cases in Arizona Territory." *American Journal of Legal History* 14 (1970): 349–54.

––––––. "William T. Howell and the Howell Code of Arizona." *American Journal of Legal History* 11 (1967): 221–33.

Granger, Byrd H., reviser. *Will C. Barnes' Arizona Place Names.* Tucson: University of Arizona Press, 1960.

Gregory, Winifred. *American Newspapers, 1821–1936.* New York: H. W. Wilson, 1937.

––––––, ed. *American Newspapers 1821–1936: A Union List of Files Available in the United States and Canada.* New York: H. W. Wilson, 1937.

Gudde, Erwin G. *California Place Names.* Berkeley: University of California, 1969.

Gustafson, A. M., ed. *John Spring's Arizona.* Tucson: University of Arizona Press, 1966.

Hafen, Le Roy Reuben, ed. *The Mountain Men and the Fur Trade of the Frontier West: Biographical Sketches of the Participants by Scholars of the Subject.* Vols. 5 & 9. Glendale, Calif.: The Arthur H. Clark Co., 1965.

Hall, Martin Hardwick. *Sibley's New Mexico Campaign.* Austin: University of Texas Press, 1960.

––––––. "The Skirmish at Picacho." *Civil War History* 4 (March 1958): 27–36.

Hall, Sharlot M. *First Citizen of Prescott — Pauline Weaver, Trapper and Mountain Man.* Prescott: Arizona Pioneers' Historical Society, 1934.

Halseth, Odd S. *Arizona's 1500 Years of Irrigation History.* Phoenix: Pueblo Grande, n.d.

Hart, Samuel. *Representative Citizens of Connecticut: A Biographical Memorial.* New York: American Historical Society, 1916.

Haury, Emil W. "The Hohokam, First Masters of the American Desert." *National Geographic* 131 (May 1967): 670–95.

Hawkins, Helen B. "A History of Wickenburg to 1875." M. A. Thesis, University of Arizona, Tucson, 1950.

Heitman, Francis B. *Historical Register and Directory of the United States Army, from Its Organization, September 29, 1789, to March 2, 1903.* 2 vols. Washington, D. C.: U.S. Government Printing Office, 1903.

Henson, Pauline. *Founding a Wilderness Capital: Prescott, A. T., 1864.* Flagstaff, Arizona: Northland Press, 1965.

Hinton, Harwood. "Frontier Speculation: A Study of the Walker Mining Districts." *Pacific Historical Review* 29 (August 1960): 245–55.

Hinton, Richard Josiah. *The Hand-Book to Arizona: Its Resources, History, Towns, Mines, Ruins, and Scenery.* Glorieta, New Mexico: Rio Grande Press, 1970.

Hodge, Frederick Webb, ed. *Handbook of American Indians North of Mexico.* Bureau of American Ethnology Bulletin 30. 2 vols. Washington, D. C.: U.S. Government Printing Office, 1910–12.

Hornaday, William T. *Camp-Fires on Desert and Lava.* New York: C. Scribner's Sons, 1921.

Hunt, Aurora. *The Army of the Pacific; Its Operation in California, Texas, Arizona, New Mexico, Utah, Nevada, Oregon, Washington, Plains Region, Mexico, etc., 1860–1866.* Glendale, Calif.: The Arthur H. Clark Co., 1951.

———. *Major General James Henry Carleton, 1814–1873, Western Frontier Dragoon.* Glendale, Calif.: The Arthur H. Clark Co., 1958.

Irving, Washington. *A Biographical and Poetical Remains of the Late Margaret Miller Davidson.* Philadelphia: Lea & Blanchard, 1841.

Ives, Joseph C. *Report upon the Colorado River of the West, Explored in 1857 and 1858 by Lieutenant Joseph C. Ives . . .* 36th Congress, 1st Session, House Executive Doc. no. 90. Washington, D. C., U.S. Government Printing Office, 1861. Reprint, Chicago: Rio Grande Press, 1962.

Jackson, Earl. *Tumacacori's Yesterdays.* Santa Fe: Southwestern Monuments Association, 1951.

Josephy, Alvin M., ed. *The American Heritage Book of Indians.* New York: American Heritage Publishing Company, 1961.

Karolevitz, Robert F. *Newspapering in the Old West: A Pictorial History of Journalism and Printing on the Frontier.* Seattle: Superior Publishing Company, 1965.

Kearney, Thomas H. and Robert H. Peebles. *Arizona Flora.* Berkeley: University of California Press, 1960.

Kelley, George H., comp. *Legislative History of Arizona 1864–1912.* Phoenix: Manufacturing Stationers, Inc., 1926.

Lamar, Howard Roberts, *The Far Southwest, 1846–1912: A Territorial History.* New York: W. W. Norton & Co., 1970.

Lavender, David. *Bent's Fort.* Garden City, N. Y.: Doubleday, 1954.

Lockwood, Frank C. *Life in Old Tucson, 1854–1864.* Los Angeles: The Ward Ritchie Press, 1943.

———. *Pioneer Days in Arizona from the Spanish Occupation to Statehood.* New York: Macmillan Co., 1932.

———. "Tucson — The Old Pueblo." *Arizona Historical Review* 3 (July 1930): 52–53.

Lummis, Charles F. *The King of the Broncos and Other Stories of New Mexico.* New York: C. Scribner's Sons, 1897.

———. *The King of the Broncos.* New York: Scribners, 1897.

Lutrell, Estelle, *Newspapers and Periodicals of Arizona, 1859–1911.* Tucson: University of Arizona, 1950.

Martin, Douglas D. *An Arizona Chronology, The Territorial Years 1846–1912*. Tucson: University of Arizona Press, 1963.

Mattison, Ray H. "Early Spanish and Mexican Settlement in Arizona." *The New Mexico Historical Review* 21 (October 1946): 273–327.

McClintock, James H. *Arizona: Prehistoric, Aboriginal, Pioneer, Modern.* 3 vols. Chicago: The S. J. Clarke Publishing Co., 1916.

McCormick, Richard C. (Sidney Brinckerhoff, ed.) *Arizona: Its Resources and Prospects: A Letter to the Editor of the New York Tribune.* Tucson: Territorial Press, 1968.

———. "There Is No Humbug about the Gold: McCormick Writes From Arizona, 1864." *Arizoniana* 5 (Fall 1964): 61–64.

Miller, Joseph, ed. *Arizona, The Grand Canyon State: A State Guide.* New York: Hastings House, 1956.

Miller, Joseph and Henry G. Alsberg, eds. *New Mexico, A Guide to a Colorful State.* New York: Hastings House, 1962.

Mills, Hazel Emery. "The Arizona Fleet." *The American Neptune* 1 (July 1941): 255–74.

Möllhausen, Baldwin. *Diary of a Journey from the Mississippi to the Coasts of the Pacific, with a United States Government Expedition.* 2 vols. London: Longman, Brown, Green, Longmans, & Roberts, 1858.

Morse, Samuel F. B., ed. *Amir Khan and Other Poems.* Boston, n.p., 1829.

Mott, D. C. "Picacho Pass, A Civil War Key Point." *Arizona Highways* 10 (April 1934): 10–11; 21–22.

Mowry, Sylvester. *Arizona and Sonora: The Geography, History, and Resources of the Silver Region of North America.* New York: Harper & Brother, 1904.

Muligen, Raymond A. "Down the Old Butterfield Trail." *Arizona and the West* 1 (Winter 1959): 358–67.

Murbarger, Nell. *Ghosts of the Adobe Walls.* Los Angeles: Westernlore Press, 1964.

Murphy, James M. *Laws, Courts, and Lawyers: Through the Years in Arizona.* Tucson: University of Arizona Press, 1970.

Myrick, David F. *Railroads of Nevada and Eastern California.* 2 vols. Berkeley: Howell-North Books, 1963.

National Cyclopaedia of American Biography. 66 vols. New York: James T. White & Co., 1907.

Nevins, Allan. *The War for Union.* Vol. 2: *War Becomes Revolution.* New York: Charles Scribner's Sons, 1960.

Nicolson, John. "New England Idealism in the Civil War: The Military Career of Joseph Roswell Hawley." University of Michigan microfilm, 1970.

Niven, John. *Connecticut for the Union.* New Haven: Yale University Press, 1965.

Onions, Charles T., ed. *The Oxford Universal Dictionary on Historical Principles*. Oxford: Clarendon Press, 1955.

Orton, R. H. *Records of California Men in the War of the Rebellion*. San Francisco: Sacramento State Office, J. D. Young, State Printing, 1890.

The Oxford English Dictionary. 13 vols. Oxford: Clarendon Press, 1933.

The Oxford History of the American People. New York: Oxford University Press, 1965.

The Oxford Universal Dictionary. 3rd ed. Oxford: Clarendon Press, 1955.

Pearce, T. M., ed. *New Mexico Place Names: A Geographical Dictionary*. Albuquerque: University of New Mexico Press, 1965.

Pederson, Gilbert J. "The Founding First." *Journal of Arizona History* 7 (Spring/Summer 1966): 45–58.

Pettid, Edward J., S. J. "The Oatman Story." *Arizona Highways* 44 (November 1968): 4–9.

Poston, Charles D. *Building a State in Apache Land*. Tempe,· Arizona: Aztec Press, 1963.

Poston, Lawrence, III, ed. "Poston vs. Goodwin: A Document on the Congressional Election of 1865." *Arizona and the West* 3 (Winter 1961): 351–54.

Prescott, William H. *History of the Conquest of Mexico and History of the Conquest of Peru*. New York: Modern Library, 1936.

Priestly, Herbert Ingham. *The Mexican Nation: A History*. New York: Macmillan, 1935.

Prucha, Francis Paul. *A Guide to the Military Posts of the United States 1789–1895*. Madison, Wisc.: University of Wisconsin Press, 1964.

Pumpelly, Raphael. *Across America and Asia: Notes of a Five Years' Journey Around the World and of Residence in Arizona, Japan and China*. New York: Lepoldt & Holt, 1870.

Quebbeman, Francis E. *Medicine in Territorial Arizona*. Phoenix: Arizona Historical Foundation, 1966.

Riggs, John L. "William H. Hardy: Merchant of Upper Colorado." *Journal of Arizona History* 6 (Winter 1965): 177–87.

Roske, Ralph J. *Everyman's Eden: A History of California*. New York: Macmillan, 1968.

Russell, Frank. *The Pima Indians*. 26th Annual Report of the Bureau of American Ethnology 1904–5. Washington: U.S. Government Printing Office, 1908.

Sacks, Ben. "Arizona's Angry Man, United States Marshall Milton B. Duffield." *Journal of Arizona History* 8 (Spring 1967): 1–29 and (Summer 1967): 91–119.

———. *Be it Enacted: The Creation of the Territory of Arizona*. Phoenix: Arizona Historical Foundation, 1964.

———. "Charles Debrille Poston: Prince of Arizona Pioneers." *Smoke Signal* 7 (Spring 1963): 1–12.

————. "The Origins of Fort Buchanan: Myth and Fact." *Arizona and the West* 7 (August 1965): 207–26.

————. "Proclamation in the Wilderness: The Salary Clause in the Territorial Act, With a Note on Illegal Payments to Gov. Goodwin." *Arizoniana* 5 (Fall 1964): 1–13.

————. "Sylvester Mowry, Artilleryman, Libertine, Entrepreneur." *The American West* 1 (Summer 1964): 14–24.

Savage, Pat. "The Ruby Story." *In* Robert C. Stevens, ed., *Echoes of the Past*. Prescott, Ariz.: The Yavapai Cowbelles Inc., 1964, pp. 139–44.

Shadegg, Stephen C. *Arizona, An Adventure in Irrigation: The Miracle On the Salt River*. Phoenix: n.p. 1949.

Sitgreaves, Lorenzo. *Report of an Expedition Down the Zuni and Colorado Rivers*. U.S. Army Corps of Topographical Engineers Publication. Senate Executive Document No. 59, 33rd Congress, 1st Session. Washington, D. C., U.S. Government Printing Office, 1851.

Spicer, Edward H. *Cycles of Conquest: The Impact of Spain, Mexico and the United States on the Indians of the Southwest, 1533–1960*. Tucson: University of Arizona Press, 1962.

Stiles, Henry R. *History and Genealogies of Ancient Windsor, Connecticut*. Hartford: Case, Lockwood & Brainard Co., 1892.

Stratton, R. B. *Captivity of the Oatman Girls*. 3rd ed. New York: Carlton & Porter, 1858.

Summerhayes, Martha. *Vanished Arizona: Recollections of My Army Life*. Philadelphia: P. Lippincott Co., 1963.

Sykes, Godfrey. *The Colorado Delta*. American Geographical Society Special Publication no. 19, ed. by W. L. G. Joerg. Washington: Carnegie Institution of Washington; New York: American Geographical Society of New York, 1937.

Thompson, Laura. *Culture in Crisis — A Study of the Hopi Indians*. New York: Harper & Bros., 1950.

Thrapp, Dan L. *The Conquest of Apacheria*. Norman, Okla.: University of Oklahoma, 1967.

Turney, Omar A. "Prehistoric Irrigation." *Arizona Historical Review* 2 (April 1929): 12–52; (July 1929): 11–52; (October 1929): 9–45; (January 1930): 33–73.

Tuttle, Henry Edward D. "Arizona Begins Law-Making." *Arizona Historical Review* 1 (April 1928): 50–62.

United States Department of Interior. National Park Service. *Fort Union National Monument, New Mexico*. Washington, D. C.: U.S. Government Printing Office, 1966.

Wagoner, Jay J. *Arizona Territory, 1863–1919: A Political History*. Tucson: University of Arizona Press, 1970.

Wallace, Andrew. *Image of Arizona*. Albuquerque: University of New Mexico Press, 1971.

————. "John W. Swilling." *Arizoniana* 7 (Spring 1961): 16–19.

Wallace, Andrew, ed. *Pumpelly's Arizona: An Excerpt from Across America and Asia by Raphael Pumpelly, comprising Those Chapters which Concern the Southwest.* Tucson: Palo Verde Press, 1965.

Warner, Ezra J. *Generals in Blue, Lives of the Union Commanders.* Baton Rouge: Louisiana State University, 1964.

Welles, Gideon. *The Diary of Gideon Welles.* Boston: Houghton-Mifflin, 1911.

Whalen, Norman M. "The Catholic Church in Arizona, 1820–1870." M.A. Thesis, University of Arizona, Tucson, 1964.

Whipple, Amiel W. *Report of Explorations and Surveys to Ascertain the Most Practical and Economical Route for a Railroad from the Mississippi River to the Ocean, 1853–54.* 2 vols. Washington, D. C., U.S. Government Printing Office, 1856.

Whittelsey, Charles B. *The Ancestry and Descendents of John Pratt of Hartford, Connecticut.* Hartford: Case, Lockwood & Brainard Co., 1900.

Williams, Eugene E. "The Territorial Governors of Arizona: John Noble Goodwin." *Arizona Historical Review* 6 (July 1935): 59–73.

————. "The Territorial Governors of Arizona: Richard Cunningham McCormick." *Arizona Historical Review* 6 (October 1935): 50–60.

Wilson, James Grant and John Fiske, eds. *Appleton's Cyclopaedia of American Biography.* New York: D. Appleton & Co., 1888.

Wood, H. P. "Gold Fields of La Paz, Arizona — The Story of a Former Big Camp." *Los Angeles Mining Review* 9 (March 23, 1901): 22.

Woodward, Arthur. *Feud on the Colorado.* Los Angeles: Westernlore Press, 1955.

Woody, Clara T. "The Woolsey Expeditions of 1864." *Arizona and the West* 4 (Summer 1962): 157–76.

Wormington, H. M. *Prehistoric Indians of the Southwest.* Denver: Colorado Museum of Natural History, 1961.

Wyllys, Rufus Kay. *Arizona: The History of a Frontier State.* Phoenix: Hobson & Herr, 1950.

Young, Otis E. *How They Dug the Gold: An Informal History of Frontier Prospecting, Lode-Mining, and Milling in Arizona and the Southwest.* Tucson: Arizona Historical Society, 1967.

————. *Western Mining, an Informal Account of Precious Metals Prospecting, Placering, Lode Mining, and Milling on the American Frontier from Spanish Times to 1893.* Norman: University of Oklahoma Press, 1970.

Index